INTERNATIONAL JOURNAL OF PSYCHOLOGY, 2006, 41 (5), 321–323

Preface

Neuropsychological functions across the world—common and different features: From digit span to moral judgment

Feggy Ostrosky-Solís

Universidad Nacional Autónoma de México, Lomas de Reforma, Mexico

Gunilla Oberg

Danish Neuropsychological Society, Copenhagen, Denmark

Experience influences the development of the nervous system; and the brains, minds, and actions of people from different cultures are both similar and different. The description and understanding of such similarities and differences is a major theme of the emerging field of transcultural neuropsychology. In clinical practice as well as research and theory, the neuropsychologist in a "globalized" world will increasingly be expected to take cultural influences into account, not as interfering variables of nuisance, but as factors of basic neurobiological importance and far-ranging behavioural effects.

Little is known about the cross-cultural aspects of even the most commonly used neuropsychological tests and methods of rehabilitation. Which cultural variables (i.e., formal and informal characteristics of education) affect the performance of a particular task? To what extent can test norms be transferred from one country to another? Does a given test reflect brain activity in the same way in different cultures? What do we currently know about the biologic bases and the processes that lie behind the emotions and their alterations? How should rehabilitation programs be composed in different cultural settings, and in what way should outcome best be evaluated?

This Special Issue is a first step towards the analysis of the similarities and differences of several neuropsychological measures, from digit span to moral emotions, across different languages and different cultures. With regard to neuropsychological rehabilitation, given the interaction of cognitive, behavioural, psychological, and physical factors, clinical data has shown that patients are best served by a comprehensive, multidisciplinary, and neuropsychologically oriented rehabilitation. The principles of the holistic approach and its application to different countries are presented.

The article by Ardila, Ostrosky-Solís, and Bernal: *Cognitive testing toward the future: The example of semantic verbal fluency (ANIMALS)*, outlines four criteria that psychological and neuropsychological testing should fulfil. They point out that, ideally, a neuropsychological test should be contained in an international database, with normative test results obtained from subjects of different ages and with different levels of education (including illiteracy). The effects of brain damage on different aspects of performance of the task should be known, as well as the pattern of brain activation that occurs during the performance. Finally, it is valuable to know how the test of choice correlates with other tests. The four criteria are applied in an analysis of semantic verbal fluency.

Digit span forward and backward is the most commonly used measure of immediate verbal recall, attention capacity, and working memory, and the test is commonly regarded as relatively culture-free. In the article *Digit span: Effects of education and culture*, Ostrosky-Solís and Lozano studied digit span performance in 2574 Spanish-speaking individuals and compared the findings with data collected in 14 other countries on five

Correspondence should be addressed to Feggy Ostrosky-Solís, PhD, Universidad Nacional Autónoma de México, Rivera de Cupia 110-71, Lomas de Reforma, México, DF 11930 (E-mail: feggy@servidor.unam.mx).

DOI: 10.1080/00207590500345450

continents. It was found that, contrary to the common belief that this task is a culture-free test, variables such as age, education, and country all made a difference. The reasons for this variability are not clear; however, the authors discussed the possibility that learning to read and write might affect the development or usage of the abilities measured by the digit span task, and that cultural variables such as language and quality of education might also contribute to the differences found between countries.

In contrast to digit span, other neuropsychological measures could be relatively culture-fair tests; this is the case for phonological verbal fluency. Phonological fluency is an economical, easily administered, and expedient test, which appears to be sensitive to many forms and different levels of brain dysfunction. Hence, it is a useful tool for following improvement or deterioration in a patient's neuropsychological status. Although it is a frequently used test, cross-cultural studies comparing phonological verbal fluency in different languages are scarce. In the article *Cross-linguistic meta-analysis of phonological fluency: Normal performance across cultures*, Oberg and Ramírez analyse the influence of education, culture, and primary language the phonological verbal fluency of 926 neurologically intact subjects from five different countries: Mexico, Argentina, Denmark, USA, and Israel. Results suggest that level of education has an influence on the number of words produced, and higher-frequency letters produced a higher number of words in all languages. The authors point out that as long as years of education and letter frequency within each language were considered, the number of words generated were remarkably similar across languages and across countries.

Emotions are a crucial aspect for neuropsychological function in normal and pathological conditions. Emotions are central to the solution of basic problems and to interpersonal relationships. Patients with orbito-frontal damage, in spite of maintaining a high intellectual coefficient, behave irrationally and do not consider the consequences of their actions. Neurobiological and neuropsychological research has started to study the neural correlates of basic and complex or secondary emotions like moral behaviour. The study of moral emotions and its disorders is reviewed by Vélez García and Ostrosky-Solís in the article *From morality to moral emotions*. They emphasize that moral emotions differ from basic emotions (sadness, joy, anger, fear, surprise, disgust) in that they are intrinsically linked to the welfare interests of each society in terms of the welfare of individuals. In this way, moral emotions spring from the interaction between individuals or when moral violations are perceived. It has also been suggested that, unlike complex deductive reasoning, they appear rapidly, and automatically, and that there is a cognitive assessment that is unconscious of interpersonal events. Moral emotions are critical for promoting cohesion in groups. Guilt, gratitude, and compassion are examples of prosocial moral emotions. However, moral emotions can also act to promote social dissolution and reorganization. Such emotions include contempt, indignation, and xenophobia. The article includes a review of the latest findings on the biological and evolutionist bases of emotion, and presents data regarding the neural correlates of moral emotions.

Diagnosis must be linked to rehabilitation. Rehabilitation is a process whereby people who are disabled by injury or disease work together with professional staff, relatives, and members of the wider community to achieve their optimum physical, psychological, social, and vocational well-being. Holistic neuropsychological rehabilitation was developed by Ben-Yishay and his associates, and it has now been implemented in more than 20 different countries. In the article *Ego-identity: Can it be reconstituted after a brain injury?* Biderman, Daniels-Zide, Reyes, and Marks, collaborators of Ben-Yishay, discuss how ego-identity can be reconstituted after brain injury. It is argued that intervention must start with building awareness and understanding of functional deficits. As such insight is established, and the patient accepts intervention from others, intense cognitive training and psychotherapy lead to the final stage of treatment, where identity is reconstituted and the patient finds a new meaning in life.

The clinical application of this program is presented in the article *Holistic neuropsychological rehabilitation in Finland. The INSURE program: A transcultural outgrowth of perspectives from Israel to Europe via the USA*. The authors Sarajuuri and Koskinen applied the holistic model to Finnish patients with traumatic brain injury (TBI). The INSURE is a post-acute, interdisciplinary, 6-week rehabilitation program for selected groups of TBI patients. The core of the program is neuropsychological rehabilitation and psychotherapy with vocational interventions, and follow-up support. The authors discuss their personal experiences and ideas for the future in the field of holistic neurospychological rehabilitation in terms of ongoing research work, computer-administered cognitive remediation, and quality of life assessment.

INTERNATIONAL JOURNAL OF PSYCHOLOGY

Aims and Scope

The ***International Journal of Psychology*** is the journal of the International Union of Psychological Science (IUPsyS) and is published under the auspices of the IUPsyS. Its purpose is to circulate, in an international framework, scientific information within and among subdisciplines of psychology and to foster the development of psychological science around the world. The journal emphasizes empirical research and theory in basic and applied psychology, especially with an international focus. It does not publish technical articles, validations of questionnaires and tests, or clinical case studies. Regular issues include two types of articles: empirical articles and review articles. Empirical articles report data from single or multiple studies in one of the major fields of scientific psychology. Review articles provide overviews of the international literature on a particular topic; authors are especially encouraged to include in their review relevant publications from regions of the world not typically cited and/or in languages other than English. Special topical issues or sections are also published two or three times a year.

The International Platform for Psychologists

Associate Editors: M. Bullock (USA); P.L.-J. Ritchie (Canada)
Many of *IJP*'s issues include a second section, the *International Platform for Psychologists*, which provides an opportunity to exchange news and opinions on psychology as an academic and applied profession. This section also contains information about the IUPsyS, about major international meetings, and about the activities of the National Psychological Societies. Finally it offers an opportunity to express opinions and to discuss internationally significant psychological issues. There is also a United Nations section with the *International Platform for Psychologists*.

First published 2006 by Psychology Press

Published in 2021 by Routledge
2 Park Square, Milton Park, Abingdon, Oxon OX14 4RN
605 Third Avenue, New York, NY 10017

Routledge is an imprint of the Taylor & Francis Group, an informa business

The ***International Journal of Psychology*** is covered by the following abstracting, indexing, and citation services: Assia; Biosis; Bell & Howell Learning (formerly University Microfilms); Current Contents – Social/Behavioural Sciences (ISI); Ergonomics Abstracts; Linguistic and Language Behavior Abstracts; NISC/Family Studies Database; Psychological Abstracts/PsychINFO; Research Alerts (ISI); Social SciSearch (ISI); Social Science Citation Index (ISI); Social Services Abstracts (formerly SOPODA); Sociological Abstracts; and UnCover.

Typeset by Charlesworth, Wakefield, UK

ISBN 13: 978-1-84169-807-6 (pbk)
Online ISSN: 1464-066X

For Product Safety Concerns and Information please contact our EU representative: GPSR@taylorandfrancis.com.
Taylor & Francis Verlag GmbH, Kaufingerstraße 24, 80331 München, Germany.

We hope that this issue will contribute to a broader awareness of transcultural issues in neuropsychology, and stimulate development of both basic knowledge and clinical skills for work with clients whose cultural backgrounds may be different from that of the neuropsychologist.

In the longer perspective, an interdisciplinary understanding of culture–brain–behaviour relationships is bound to emerge.

INTERNATIONAL JOURNAL OF PSYCHOLOGY, 2006, 41 (5), 324–332

Cognitive testing toward the future: The example of Semantic Verbal Fluency (ANIMALS)

Alfredo Ardila
Florida International University, Miami, FL, USA

Feggy Ostrosky-Solís
Universidad Nacional Autónoma de México, Lomas de Reforma, Mexico

Byron Bernal
Miami Children's Hospital, FL, USA

We are proposing that, in the future, tests included in psychological and neuropsychological batteries should fulfil the following criteria. (1) Have a large enough normative database ("normative criterion"). Performance of subjects of different ages and different educational levels, including illiterates, should be well established. Normative data from different countries and cultural contexts should be available. (2) Know the effects of brain damage on different characteristics on the test ("clinical criterion"). (3) Know how the brain is activated when the test is performed ("experimental criterion"). (4) Know how this test correlates with other cognitive tests ("psychometric criterion"). Few contemporary tests fulfil all these criteria. A notable exception is Semantic Verbal Fluency test using the category ANIMALS. This test requires the generation of words corresponding to a specific semantic category, such as animals, fruits, vegetables, etc. Typically, the number of correct words produced in 1 minute is counted. Semantic verbal fluency taps lexical knowledge and semantic memory organization. Using regional cerebral blood flow measures, it has been reported that both frontal and temporal activation are observed while performing this test. Optimal fluency performance involves generating words within a subcategory and, when a subcategory is exhausted, switching to a new subcategory. Although different semantic categories have been used in this test, ANIMALS is the most frequent due to some significant advantages: (1) it is a clear enough semantic category across languages and cultures; (2) it is a relatively easy semantic category with only minor differences among people living in different countries, different educational systems, or belonging to different generations; and (3) it is an easy-to-administer, short, and common test included in different neuropsychological test batteries. It is concluded that obtaining similar information for other cognitive tests represents a huge research endeavour for psychology and neuropsychology during the 21st century.

Nous proposons, qu'à l'avenir, les tests inclus dans le testing psychologique et neurologique doivent remplir les critères suivants: (1) avoir une base de données normatives assez grande («critère normatif»). La performance des sujets d'âge et de niveaux d'éducation différents, incluant les illétrés, doit être bien établie. Les données normatives provenant de pays et de contextes culturels différents doivent être disponibles; (2) connaître les effets du dommage cérébral sur les différentes caractéristiques sur ce test («critère clinique»); (3) savoir comment le cerveau est activé quand le test est exécuté («critère expérimental»); et (4) savoir comment ce test est corrélé avec d'autres tests cognitifs («critère psychométrique»). Peu de tests contemporains remplissent tous ces critères. Une exception remarquable est la Fluence Verbale Sémantique utilisant la catégorie ANIMAUX. Ce test requiert la génération de mots correspondant à une catégorie sémantique spécifique, tel que les animaux, les fruits, les végétaux, etc. Typiquement, la quantité de mots produits en une minute est comptée. La fluence verbale sémantique capte la connaissance lexicale et l'organisation de la mémoire sémantique. En utilisant des mesures régionales de débit sanguin cérébral, il a été rapporté qu'une activation frontale et temporale est observée en exécutant ce test. La performance optimale au test de fluence implique la génération de mots à l'intérieur d'une sous-catégorie et, lorsqu'une sous-catégorie est épuisée, le passage à une nouvelle sous-catégorie. Même si

Correspondence should be addressed to Alfredo Ardila, PhD, ABPN, Florida International University, Department of Communication Sciences and Disorders, HLS144, Miami, Florida 33199, USA (E-mail: ardilaa@fiu.edu).

 DOI: 10.1080/00207590500345542

différentes catégories sémantiques ont été utilisées dans ce test, les ANIMAUX est celle la plus utilisée à cause des avantages significatifs suivants: (1) il s'agit d'une catégorie sémantique assez claire à travers les langues et les cultures, (2) c'est une catégorie sémantique relativement facile, avec seulement des différences mineures entre les gens vivant dans des pays différents, des systèmes éducatifs différents ou appartenant à des générations différentes, et (3) il s'agit d'un test qui est facile à administrer, bref et commun, inclus dans différentes batteries de tests neuropsychologiques. Nous concluons que l'obtention d'informations similaires pour d'autres tests cognitifs représente un défi de taille pour la recherche en psychologie et en neuropsychologie durant le 21ème siècle.

Se propone que en el futuro, las pruebas utilizadas en la evaluación psicológica y neuropsicológica deberían cubrir los siguientes criterios: (1) Contar con un base de datos normativa lo suficientemente grande. Establecer claramente el desempeño de sujetos de diferentes edades y niveles educativos. Contar con datos normativos de diferentes países y contextos culturales ("criterio normativo"); (2) conocer los efectos del daño cerebral en diferentes aspectos de la prueba ("criterio clínico"); (3) conocer la activación cerebral ante la ejecución de la prueba ("criterio experimental"); y (4) conocer cómo se correlaciona la prueba con otras pruebas cognitivas ("criterio psicométrico"). Pocas pruebas contemporáneas cubren estos criterios. Una excepción es la prueba de fluidez verbal semántica con la categoría ANIMALES. Esta prueba requiere la generación de palabras correspondientes a una categoría semántica como animales, frutas, vegetales, etc. Generalmente la cantidad de palabras correctas generadas en un minuto es contabilizada. Usando medidas del flujo sanguíneo cerebral se ha reportado una activación frontal y temporal mientras se ejecuta esta tarea. El desempeño óptimo en esta prueba implica la generación de palabras dentro de una subcategoría y cuando ésta se agota, cambiar a una nueva. Aunque diferentes categorías semánticas han sido utilizadas en esta prueba, la categoría ANIMALES es la más frecuente debido a algunas ventajas significativas: (1) es una categoría clara entre idiomas y culturas, (2) es una categoría relativamente sencilla con pequeñas diferencias entre personas de diferentes países, sistemas educativos o entre personas pertenecientes a distintas generaciones, y (3) es una prueba sencilla de administrar, corta e incluida en varias baterías neuropsicológicas. Se concluye que el obtener información semejante para otras pruebas cognitivas representa un enorme reto para la psicología y neuropsicología durante el siglo XXI.

During the last decades, psychology and neuropsychology have been significantly interested in developing reliable and valid enough cognitive testing procedures (e.g., Lezak, 2004; Mitrushina, Boone, & D'Elia, 1999; Spreen & Strauss, 1998; Wechsler, 1997). Important controversies, however, have been frequent (e.g., Ardila, 1999). We are proposing that in the future, in addition to the fundamental psychometric test properties (e.g., reliability), cognitive tests should fulfil at least the following four criteria.

1. *Normative criterion.* That is, to have a large enough normative database *to understand the variables impacting test performance.* Performance in subjects with different ages and educational levels, including illiterates (about one fifth of the world population; www.portal.unesco.org), should be well established. As a matter of fact, norms in illiterates are crucial in order to understand cognition without education as a confounding variable. Developmental data and performance in elderly populations are also necessary. Normative data from different countries and cultural contexts should also be available. This information will be most important to identify variables affecting the test performance. For some tests (e.g., language tests), educational level plays a major role; for others (e.g., memory tests), age may be most significant; in other tests (e.g., spelling), language may be crucial, etc.
2. *Clinical criterion.* That is, to know reasonably well the effects of different types of brain pathology on this test: right, left, anterior, posterior, cortical, and subcortical. In addition, information regarding test performance in major pathological conditions (dementia, traumatic brain injury, Parkinson's disease, etc.) is highly desirable.
3. *Experimental criterion.* That is, to know reasonably well how the brain is activated in normal individuals when this particular test is performed. fMRI and/or PET studies are required to know how different brain areas participate when performing the test.
4. *Psychometric criterion.* To know how this specific test correlates with other cognitive measures; i.e., the communality existing with other assessment procedures.

Few contemporary tests fulfil these optimal criteria. A notorious exception, however, is Semantic Verbal Fluency for ANIMALS. This paper analyses the three last criteria in the Semantic Verbal Fluency test when the category ANIMALS is used. The analysis of the first criterion was presented elsewhere (Ardila, Ostrosky-Solís, & Bernal, 2005).

SEMANTIC VERBAL FLUENCY (ANIMALS)

Controlled oral word association or word or verbal fluency has become one of the most popular tests in neuropsychology (Lezak, 2004; Spreen & Strauss, 1998). Two different conditions can be used: (1) phonemic fluency (words beginning with a particular letter, usually in English F, A, and S); and (2) category or semantic verbal fluency (words corresponding to a specific semantic category, such as animals, fruits, vegetables, etc.). Typically, the number of correct words produced in 1 minute is counted. A normal person can produce about 12 words beginning with a specific letter, and about 16 words corresponding to a semantic category, within 1 minute (Spreen & Strauss, 1998). The level of productivity, however, depends upon the letter or the semantic category. A very strong educational effect has been demonstrated in both conditions, especially in the phonemic condition (Ostrosky-Solís, Ardila, & Rosselli, 1999; Ostrosky-Solís, Ardila, Rosselli, López, & Mendoza, 1998; Ostrosky-Solís, Ramírez, Lozano, Picasso, & Vélez, 2004; Rosselli, Ardila, & Rosas, 1990). Ardila, Ostrosky-Solís, Rosselli, and Gomez (2000) found that the educational level accounted for 38.5% of the variance in the phonemic condition and for 23.6% of the variance in the semantic condition. A moderate to middle correlation (around .30–.60) between scores in both conditions has also been reported (Ardila, Rosselli, & Bateman, 1994; Ardila, Galeano, & Rosselli, 1998; Matute, Rosselli, & Ardila, 2004; Ostrosky et al., 1999).

Verbal fluency tests have often been interpreted as executive functioning tests (Bruyer & Tuyumbu, 1980; Parks et al., 1988; Perret, 1974; Ramier & Hecaen, 1970; Ruff, Allen, Farrow, Niemann, & Wylie, 1994). Difficulties in performing this test are found in cases of frontal lobe damage, usually left and bilateral frontal lesions. In general, it is assumed that phonemic verbal fluency is superior to semantic fluency as an executive functioning test. Semantic verbal fluency is rather tapping lexical knowledge and semantic memory organization. Using regional cerebral blood flow measures, it has been reported that frontal and temporal activation are both observed while performing this test. PET studies have demonstrated that the frontal lobe is activated in phonemic generation while the temporal lobe is more active in semantic generation of words (Warburton et al., 1996). Several investigators have observed that words tend to be produced in semantic clusters on the semantic fluency task and in phonemic clusters on the phonemic fluency task. The clusters are defined by bursts of words over time, which are semantically or phonemically related. Optimal fluency performance involves generating words within a subcategory and, when a subcategory is exhausted, switching to a new subcategory. Troyer, Moscovitch, and Winocur (1998a) devised a method to quantify these processes as switches and average cluster size. These components are differentially affected by various neurological disorders. Clustering is related to temporal lobe functioning, while switching is related to frontal functions (Testa, Tröster, Fields, Gleason, Salmon, & Beatty, 1998; Troyer, Moscovitch, Winocur, Alexander, & Stuss, 1998b).

Although different semantic categories have been used in this test, ANIMALS is the most frequent. Using ANIMALS has some significant advantages. (1) It is a clear enough semantic category across languages and cultures. The semantic field of other categories can vary across different languages. For example, the semantic field of the English word "vegetables" is only partially coincidental with the semantic field of the Spanish word *vegetales*. Furthermore, in Spanish, *vegetales* may be a confusing semantic category, whereas "vegetables" is a clear one in English. In Spanish, trees or grass can be considered as vegetables. Interestingly, many English-speaking people include some fruits as vegetables (e.g., tomatoes are indeed fruits, but many people consider them to be vegetables). Furniture, clothes, and other categories can be different in different countries and different languages. ANIMALS do not present these ambiguities. (2) ANIMALS is a relatively easy semantic category with only minor differences among people living in different countries, exposed to different educational systems, or belonging to different generations (for example, a generation effect can be conjectured for the category "tool"). The brain activity, therefore, is not expected to vary as much as it could with a task based on phonological clues when used in different languages (Chinese and Spanish, for example). Nell (2000) has suggested that Semantic Verbal Fluency using ANIMALS represents a reliable test for adults with low education. Lopera (n.d.), using 16 different semantic categories in a 3000-participant sample, found that the easiest semantic categories were BODY-PARTS, THINGS TO EAT, and ANIMALS (Table 1). That is, there is a hierarchy of difficulty when finding elements corresponding to a particular semantic category. (3) ANIMALS Verbal Fluency is an easy to administer, short, and common test included in different neuropsychological test batteries (e.g., Boston Diagnostic

TABLE 1
Average number of words generated by Spanish speakers in 1 minute in different semantic categories (n=3000) (Lopera, n.d.)

Category	*Words in 1 minute*
Body-parts	18
Things to eat	17
Animals	16
Kitchen elements	14
Fruits	13
Colours	13
Places or sites	12
Adjectives	12
Parts of the house	12
Transportation means	11
School elements	11
Verbs	11
Tools	10
Personal care elements	10
Furniture	10
Flowers	8

Aphasia Examination, Goodglass & Kaplan, 1972; CERAD neuropsychological test battery, Morris et al., 1989; Neuropsi, Ostrosky Solís et al., 1999). Instructions are simple, and no special instruments (except a stopwatch, a pencil, and paper) are required. It is also a cheap test, accessible anywhere.

CLINICAL CRITERION

A number of brain conditions can affect the performance in verbal fluency tests: focal brain damage, especially frontal lobe pathology (Herrmann, Ehlis, & Fallgatter, 2003; Ravnkilde, Videbech, Rosenberg, Gjedde, & Gade, 2002), Parkinson's disease (Donovan, Siegert, & McDowall, 1999; Troyer et al., 1998a), schizophrenia (Chen, Chen, Chan, Lam, & Lie-Mak, 2000; Curtis et al., 1998), subcortical dementia (Testa et al., 1998; Troster et al., 1998), traumatic brain injury (Bradley, Torner, Fisher, & Aharon Peretz, 2001), Huntington's disease (Ho et al., 2002; Suhr & Jones, 1998), depression (Crowe, 1992; Okada, Okamoto, Morionobu, Yamawaki, & Yokota, 2003; Ravdin, Katzen, Agraval, & Relkin, 2003), vascular and degenerative dementias (Cooper et al., 2001; Troyer et al., 1998a), and amyotrophic lateral sclerosis (Abrahams et al., 2000).

Two major conclusions can be drawn: (1) in general, Semantic Verbal Fluency is a task that is quite sensitive to diverse types of brain abnormalities, particularly those involving the left hemisphere; (2) in addition to quantitative scores, a diversity of pathological phenomena may be observed: intrusions, perseverations, difficulties in maintaining instructions, etc. Qualitative analysis should complement the quantitative scoring.

EXPERIMENTAL CRITERION

Diverse studies have been published, analysing the brain areas involved in semantic verbal fluency (Abrahams et al., 2003; Fama et al., 2000; Gaillard et al., 2003; Hugdahl et al., 1999; Lurito, Kareken, Lowe, Chen, & Mathews, 2000; Pihlajamaki et al., 2000; Schlosser et al., 1998; Tucha, Smely, & Lange, 1999; Vingerhoets et al., 2003; Weiss et al., 2003). There is converging evidence that verbal fluency activates the left posterior aspect of the middle temporal gyrus, and other brain areas can additionally participate, such as the left dorsolateral prefrontal convexity and the hippocampus. Pihlajamaki et al. (2000) observed that the medial temporal lobe is required for the process of retrieval by category.

Semantic fluency tasks differ somewhat in their application from the regular manner in which they are applied in the clinical neuropsychology context. The tasks are applied with some changes, which are summarized in Table 2. Vascular responses of the brain coupled to the task have to be switched *on* and *off* several times to obtain enough statistical power to demonstrate activation. The duration of the free retrieval is shortened, as the generation decays considerably in the second half of the minute. Since a second attempt to generate nouns within the same category would add some difficulty, as the subject may run out of salient nouns, the generation of animals is usually followed by other categories. Usually an fMRI

TABLE 2
Task differences between regular and fMR laboratories

Test type	*Duration*	*Off period*	*Several items*	*Motion restriction*	*Speech*	*Controlled*
Regular laboratory	1 min	None	Not necessarily	No	Overt	Yes
FMR laboratory	20–40 s (usually 30 s)	20–40 s	Yes	Yes	Covert	No

consists of three or four *on* epochs, preceded, ended, and separated by *off* epochs of the same duration. Thus, generating only animals during three different periods would require division of this category; for example, asking for the retrieval of wild animals in the first attempt, then insects in the second, and birds for the third.

Semantic fluency, phonological fluency, and verb generation activate left lateral frontal areas. Left Brodmann's 44, 45, 46, 9, 7, and 8 are activated most frequently, with other areas varying among different subjects. These ancillary areas are the supplementary motor area (SMA), posterior temporal areas, cingulate gyrus, contralateral frontopolar area, and visual areas. Figures 1 and 2 show activation obtained with a semantic fluency task and a verb generation task in the same subject. The similarities are limited to the activation of areas directly related to fluency (Brodmann's 44, 9, and SMA). However, some differences appear: Verb generation also elicited activation in Wernicke's area, left caudate nucleus, and contralateral Broca's area. Not all subjects show the same differences, but there are cases in which the activation is almost identical.

No differences according to language or gender have been reported in this task. Vingerhoets et al. (2003) analysed activation patterns in 12 multilingual right-handed men performing a word fluency task, a picture naming task, a comprehension reading task, and their respective control tasks in three languages (Dutch, French, and English) while whole-head fMRI was applied. In general, all language tasks revealed predominantly overlapping regions of activation for the different languages. Weiss et al. (2003) observed that men and women who did not differ significantly in

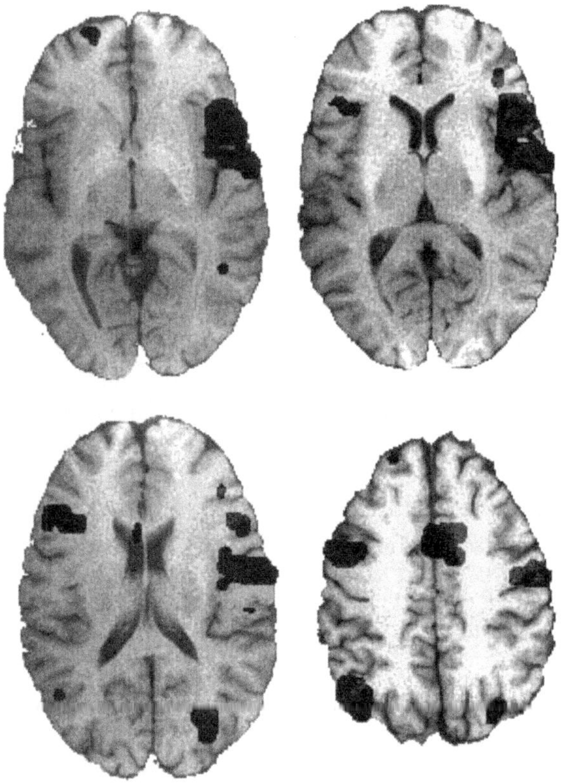

Figure 1. Brain activation of semantic fluency. These clusters were obtained from a paradigm consisting of 3 *on* epochs alternating with 3 *off* epochs. During *on* the subject was silently generating names of animals, vegetables, and fruits (respectively). The volunteer was asked to think of a blue sky during the *off* periods. The largest clusters of activation are located in left Broca, left mouth premotor area, and SMA. Some activation also appears in the left interparietal sulcus, right Brodmann's 7, and contralateral Broca's area (from the Miami Children's Hospital, department of radiology; www.mch.com/clinical/radiology/fmri).

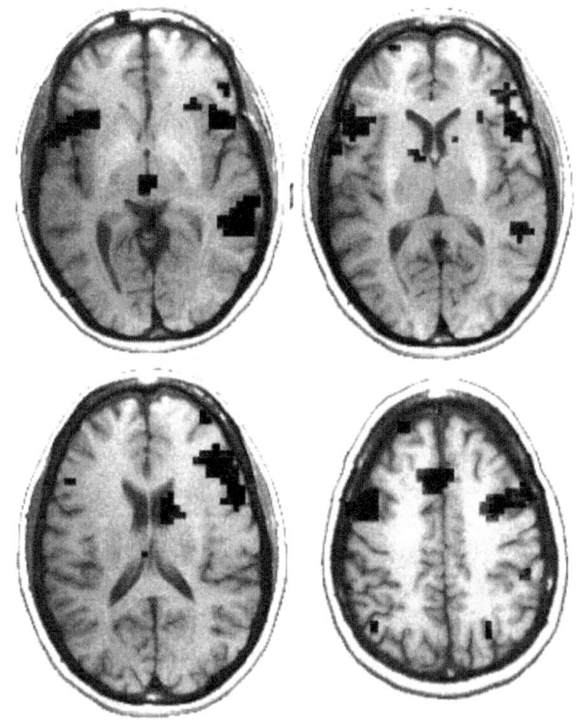

Figure 2. Brain activation of verb generation. This image was obtained with the same techniques utilized for the Semantic Fluency Task. The skull was not removed in the post-processing. During the *on* blocks, the subject was asked to think of verbs related to a list of nouns aurally presented at 0.2 Hz. In addition to the areas activated in the Semantic Fluency Task shown in Figure 1, there is activation the left caudate nucleus and stronger participation of contralateral Broca. Wernicke's area is expected to activate because of the stimulus delivery mode. Notice the small activation in the right frontopolar area (Brodmann's 10), which, strikingly is common to both tasks, and probably related to working memory or retrieving (from the Miami Children's Hospital, department of radiology; www.mch.com/clinical/radiology/fmri).

Verbal Fluency Task performance showed a very similar pattern of brain activation.

PSYCHOMETRIC CRITERION

Three studies were selected to analyse the Semantic Verbal Fluency pattern of correlations with other tests (Ardila et al., 1994, 1998; Ostrosky-Solís et al., 1999) (Tables 3, 4, and 5). It is observed that Semantic Verbal Fluency correlates with phonologic verbal fluency, verbal memory (immediate and delayed), backwards digits, and language comprehension. Correlation with naming is lower than correlation with language understanding. Interestingly, phonemic verbal fluency, but not Semantic Verbal Fluency, significantly correlates with the Finger Tapping Test (Ardila et al., 1994, 1998). Some correlation with arithmetic and, in general, with conceptual functions is also observed. These data suggest that attention, working memory, and immediate and delayed verbal memory are cognitive functions that contribute to semantic verbal fluency.

TABLE 3
Statistically significant correlations over .15 ($p < .01$), Semantic Verbal Fluency and other cognitive tests (Ardila et al., 1998)

Test	*r*
Phonologic Verbal Fluency	.31
WAIS: Arithmetic	.27
Information	.22
Digits	.19
Perceptual speed: Similarities	.18
Verbal IQ	.18
Full Scale IQ	.19

TABLE 4
Correlations between Semantic Verbal Fluency (ANIMALS) and other neuropsychological tests in the NEUROPSI neuropsychological test battery (adapted from Ostrosky et al., 1999)

Subtest	*r*
Orientation: Time	.29
Place	.16
Person	.12
Attention: Digits backwards	.40
Visual detection	.38
20 minus 3	.37
Encoding: Verbal memory	.34
Copy of a semi-complex figure	.43
Language: Naming	.25
Repetition	.14
Comprehension	.45
Verbal fluency: Phonologic	.61
Reading	.30
Writing: Dictation	.14
Copy	.18
Conceptual functions: Similarities	.38
Calculation abilities	.33
Sequences	.41
Motor functions: Changing left-hand position	.22
Changing right-hand position	.21
Alternating movements	.39
Opposite reactions	.12
Memory: Words	.35
Cueing	.21
Recognition	.10
Semi-complex figure	.42

CONCLUSIONS

Recent decades have seen an exponentially growing interest in developing valid and reliable neuropsychological testing instruments that can be used in different clinical settings. An enormous diversity of tests has been developed (see, for example, Lezak, 2004). Simultaneously, the need to adapt these instruments to cultural and

TABLE 5
Correlations between semantic verbal fluency and other neuropsychological tests in 98 subjects aged 11–12 years (Ardila et al., 1994)

Subtest	*r*
Phonologic verbal fluency	.50
Wechsler Memory Scale:	
Information	.07
Orientation	−.17
Mental control	.01
Logical memory	.25
Digits	.22
Visual reproduction	.22
Associative learning	.05
Logical memory: delayed	.19
Associative learning: delayed	.05
Visual reproduction: delayed	−.10
Verbal memory	
Maximum	44
Delayed recall	.46
Praxis	
Left hand	.05
Right hand	−.17
Tapping test	
Right hand	.04
Left hand	−.19
Figure recognition	−.03
Token test	.11
WCST	
Correct responses	.25
Categories	.01
Boston Naming test	.13
Rey-Osterrieth Complex Figure	
Copy	.13
Immediate recall	.03

linguistic contexts other than the context for which they were originally developed has become evident. This effort has been observed in many different countries worldwide.

Until recently, test ability to detect brain pathology was enough. Today, sophisticated neuroimaging techniques are available, which could potentially contribute to extending our understanding of cognitive testing procedures. Furthermore, today we have extended databases for many neuropsychological instruments, which can be used to have a better understanding of the variables affecting test performance and the score dispersions that can be found.

We are proposing that neuropsychological tests should fulfil four different criteria: to have a large enough normative database; to know the effects of different types of brain damage on this test; to know how the brain is activated when the test is performed; and to know how this test correlates with other cognitive tests). This means that the test:

1. Has been administered to a diversity of populations, and diverse normative data are available. The test has been demonstrated to be appropriate to evaluate different populations ("normative criterion"). Simpler tests with simple instructions have a better chance of becoming widely used tests.
2. Has been demonstrated to be clinically useful ("clinical criterion"). This means that specific patterns of performance and error types on the test are known to be associated with specific brain pathologies.
3. Has been used experimentally in normal populations, and the pattern of brain activation correlated with the performance in this test is well known ("experimental criterion").
4. Correlates with other assessment tests ("psychometric criterion"). Validity of the test would be established not only based on the intercorrelation with other tests, but also from the specific pattern of performance in the test found in individuals with different types of pathologies.

We have taken the example of Semantic Verbal Fluency using the category ANIMALS. But, potentially, the same type of analysis could be carried out with other basic neuropsychological tests; for example, the Token Test, the Wisconsin Card Sorting Test (using a simpler version), or the naming tests (assuming that it is possible to develop a good cross-cultural and cross-linguistic naming test). This type of analysis may advance our understanding of current neuropsychological instruments.

It can be anticipated that, in the future, some instruments may become relatively universal tests in neuropsychology. It can be also anticipated that some instruments may be usable only within certain cultural and/or linguistic contexts. This is an open question, and much more research is required.

REFERENCES

Abrahams, S., Goldstein, L. H., Simmons, A., Brammer, M. J., Williams, S. C., Giampietro, V. P., Andrew, C. M., & Leigh, P. N. (2003). Functional magnetic resonance imaging of verbal fluency and confrontation naming using compressed image acquisition to permit overt responses. *Human Brain Mapping*, *20*, 29–40.

Abrahams, S., Leigh, P. N., Harvey, A., Vythelgum, G. N., Grisé, D., & Goldstein, L. H. (2000). Verbal Fluency and executive dysfunction in amyotrophic lateral sclerosis (ALS). *Neuropsychologia*, *38*, 734–747.

Ardila, A. (1999). A neuropsychological approach to intelligence. *Neuropsychology Review*, *9*, 117–136.

Ardila, A., Galeano, L. M., & Rosselli, M. (1998). Toward a model of neuropsychological activity. *Neuropsychology Review*, *8*, 171–190.

Ardila, A., Ostrosky-Solis, F., & Bernal, B. (2005). The effect of culture, language and education on Semantic Verbal Fluency (ANIMALS). *Archives of Clinical Neuropsychology*. Manuscript submitted for publication.

Ardila, A., Ostrosky-Solis, F., Rosselli, M., & Gomez, C. (2000). Age related cognitive decline during normal aging: The complex effect of education. *Archives of Clinical Neuropsychology*, *15*, 495–514.

Ardila, A., Rosselli, M., & Bateman, J. R. (1994). Factorial structure of cognitive activity. *Behavioural Neurology*, *7*, 49–58.

Bradley, N. A., Torner, R., Fisher, T., & Aharon-Peretz, J. (2001). Preliminary analyses of Hebrew verbal fluency measures. *Applied Neuropsychology*, *8*, 248–250.

Bruyer, R., & Tuyumbu, B. (1980). Fluence verbale et lesions du cortex cerebrale: performances et types d'erreurs. *Encephale*, *6*, 287–197.

Chen, R. Y. L., Chen, E. Y. H., Chan, C. K. Y., Lam, L. C. W., & Lie-Mak, F. (2000). Verbal Fluency in schizophrenia: Reduction in semantic store. *Australian and New Zealand Journal of Psychiatry*, *34*, 43–48.

Crowe, S. F. (1992). Dissociation of two frontal lobe syndromes by a test of verbal fluency. *Journal of Clinical and Experimental* Neuropsychology, *14*, 327–339.

Cooper, D. B., Epker, M., Lacritz, L., Weine, M., Rosenberg, R. N., Honig, L., & Cullum, C. M. (2001). Effects of practice on category fluency in Alzheimer's disease. *The Clinical Neuropsychologist*, *15*, 125–128.

Curtis, V. A., Bullmore, E. T., Bramer, M. J., Wright, I. C., Williams, S. C., Morris, R. G., Sharma, T. S., Murray, R., & McGuire, P. K. (1998). Attenuated frontal activation during a verbal fluency task in patients with schizophrenia. *The American Journal of Psychiatry, 155*, 1056–1063.

Donovan, K., Siegert, R., & McDowall, J. (1999). Clustering and switching in verbal fluency in Parkinson's disease. *New Zealand Journal of Psychology, 28*, 61–66.

Fama, R., Sullivan, E. V., Shear, P. K., Cahn-Weiner, D. A., Marsh, L., Lim, K. O., Yesavage, J. A., Tinklenberg, J. R., & Pfefferbaum, A. (2000). Structural brain correlates of verbal and nonverbal fluency measures in Alzheimer's disease. *Neuropsychology, 14*, 29–40.

Gaillard, W. D., Sachs, B. C., Whitnah, J. R., Ahmad, Z., Balsamo, L. M., Petrella, J. R., Braniecki, S. H., McKinney, C. M., Hunter, K., Xu, B., & Grandin, C. B. (2003). Developmental aspects of language processing: fMRI of verbal fluency in children and adults. *Human Brain Mapping, 18*, 176–185.

Goodglass, H., & Kaplan, E. (1972). *The assessment of aphasia and related disorders*. Philadelphia: Lea & Febiger.

Herrmann, M. J., Ehlis, A. C., & Fallgatter, A. J. (2003). Frontal activation during a Verbal Fluency task as measured by near-infrared spectroscopy. *Brain Research Bulletin, 61*, 51–56.

Ho, A. K., Sahakian, B. J., Robbins, T. W., Barker, R. A., Rosser, A. E., & Hodges, J. R. (2002). Verbal fluency in Huntington's disease: A longitudinal analysis of phonemic and semantic clustering and switching. *Neuropsychologia, 40*, 1277–1284.

Hugdahl, K., Lundervold, A., Ersland, L., Smievoll, A. I., Sundberg, H., Barndon, R., & Roscher, B. E. (1999). Left frontal activation during a semantic categorization task: An fMRI-study. *International Journal Neuroscience, 99*, 49–58.

Goodglass, H., & Kaplan, E. (1972). *The assessment of aphasia and related disorders*. Philadelphia: Lea & Febiger.

Lezak, M. D. (2004) *Neuropsychological assessment* (4th ed.). New York: Oxford University Press.

Lopera, F. (n.d.). *Fluidez verbal en diferentes categorías semánticas* [Verbal fluency in different semantic categories]. Unpublished data.

Lurito, J. T., Kareken, D. A., Lowe, M. J., Chen, S. H., & Mathews, V. P. (2000). Comparison of rhyming and word generation with fMRI. *Human Brain Mapping, 10*, 99–106.

Matute, E., Rosselli, M., & Ardila, A. (2004). Verbal and nonverbal fluency in 6- to 15-year-old Spanish-speaking children. *Developmental Neuropsychology, 26*, 647–660.

Mitrushina, M. N., Boone, K. B., & D'Elia, L. F. (1999). *Handbook of normative data for neuropsychological assessment*. New York: Oxford University Press.

Morris, J. C., Heyman, A., Mohs, R. C., Hughes, J. P., Van Belle, G., Fillenbaum, G., Mellits, E. D., Clark, C., the CERAD investigators, (1989). The Consortium to Establish a Registry for Alzheimer's Disease (CERAD). Part I. Clinical and neuropsychological assessment of Alzheimer's disease. *Neurology, 39*, 1159–1165.

Nell, V. (2000). *Cross-cultural neuropsychological assessment: Theory and practice*. Hillsdale, NJ: Lawrence Erlbaum Associates Inc.

Okada, G., Okamoto, Y., Morinobu, S., Yamawaki, S., & Yokota, N. (2003). Attenuated left prefrontal activation during a Verbal Fluency Task in patients with depression. *Neuropsychobiology, 47*, 21–26.

Ostrosky-Solis, F., Ardila, A., & Rosselli, M. (1999). "Neuropsi": A brief neuropsychological test battery in Spanish with norms by age and educational level. *Journal of the International Neuropsychological Society, 5*, 413–433.

Ostrosky-Solís, F., Ardila, A., Rosselli, M., López, G., & Mendoza, V. (1998). Neuropsychological test performance in illiterates. *Archives of Clinical Neuropsychology, 13*, 645–660.

Ostrosky-Solís, F., Ramirez, M., Lozano, A., Picasso, H., & Velez, A. (2004). Culture or education: A study with indigenous Maya population. *International Journal of Psychology, 39*, 36–46.

Parks, R. W., Loewenstein, D. A., Dodrill, K. L., Barker, W. M., Yoshii, F., Chang, J. Y., Emran, A., Apicella, A., Sheramata, W. A., & Duara, R. (1988). Cerebral metabolic effects of verbal fluency tests: A PET scan study. *Journal of Clinical and Experimental Neuropsychology, 10*, 565–575.

Perret, E. (1974). The left frontal lobe of man and the suppression of habitual responses in verbal categorical behavior. *Neuropsychologia, 12*, 323–330.

Pihlajamaki, M., Tanila, H., Hanninen, T., Kononen, M., Laakso, M., Partanen, K., Soininen, H., & Aronen, H. J. (2000). Verbal fluency activates the left medial temporal lobe: A functional magnetic resonance imaging study. *Annals of Neurology, 47*, 470–476.

Radvin, L. D., Katzen, H. L., Agraval, P., & Relkin, N. R. (2003). Letter and semantic fluency in older adults: Effects of mild depressive symptoms and age stratified normative data. *The Clinical Neuropsychologist, 17*, 195–202.

Ramier, A. M., & Hecaen, H. (1970). Role respectif des attaintes frontales et la lateralisation lesionelle dans le deficits de la "fluence verbale". *Revue Neurologique, 123*, 17–22.

Ravnkilde, B., Videbech, P., Rosenberg, R., Gjedde, A., & Gade, A. (2002). Putative test of frontal lobe function: A PET-study of brain activation during a Stroop's test and Verbal Fluency. *Journal of Clinical and Experimental Neuropsychology, 24*, 534–547.

Rosselli, M., Ardila, A., & Rosas, P. (1990). Neuropsychological assessment in illiterates II: Language and praxic abilities. *Brain and Cognition, 12*, 281–296.

Ruff, R. M., Allen, C. C., Farrow, C. E., Niemann, H., & Wylie, T. (1994). Figural fluency: Differential impairment in patients with left versus right frontal lobe lesions. *Archives of Clinical Neuropsychology, 9*, 41–55.

Schlosser, R., Hutchinson, M., Joseffer, S., Rusinek, H., Saarimaki, A., Stevenson, J., Dewey, S. L., & Brodie, J. D. (1998). Functional magnetic resonance imaging of human brain activity in a verbal fluency task. *Journal of Neurology, Neurosurgery and Psychiatry, 64*, 492–498.

Spreen, O., & Strauss, E. (1998). *A compendium of neuropsychological tests* (2nd ed.). New York: Oxford University Press.

Suhr, J. A., & Jones, R. D. (1998). Letter and semantic fluency in Alzheimer, Huntington and Parkinson's disease. *Archives of Clinical Neuropsychology*, *13*, 447–454.

Testa, J. A., Tröster, A. I., Fields, J. A., Gleason, A. C., Salmon, D., & Beatty, W. W. (1998). Semantic fluency performance of patients with cortical and subcortical neurodegenerative diseases. *Aging, Neuropsychology and Cognition*, *5*, 203–214.

Troster, A. I., Fields, J. A., Testa, J. A., Paul, R. H., Blanco, C. R., Hames, K. A., Salmon, D. P., & Beatty, W. W. (1998). Cortical and subcortical influences on clustering and switching in the performance of verbal fluency tasks. *Neuropsychologia*, *36*, 295–304.

Troyer, A. K., Moscovitch, M., & Winocur, G. (1998a). Clustering and switching on verbal fluency tests in Alzheimer's and Parkinson's disease. *Journal of the International Neuropsychological Society*, *4*, 137–143.

Troyer, A. K., Moscovitch, M., Winocur, G., Alexander, M. P., & Stuss, D. (1998b). Clustering and switching on verbal fluency: The effects of focal frontal- and temporal-lobe lesions. *Neuropsychologia*, *25*, 388–493.

Tucha, O. W., Smely, C. W., & Lange, K. W. (1999). Verbal and figural fluency in patients with mass lesions of the left or right frontal lobes. *Journal of Clinical and Experimental Neuropsychology*, *21*, 229–236.

Vingerhoets, G., Van Borsel, J., Tesink, C., Van den Noort, M., Deblaere, K., Seurinck, R., Vandemaele, P., & Achten, E. (2003). Multilingualism: An fMRI study. *Neuroimage*, *20*, 2181–2196.

Warburton, E., Wise, R. J. S., Price, C. J., Weiller, C., Harad, U., Ramsay, S., & Frackowiak, R. S. J. (1996). Noun and verb retrieval in normal subjects studies with PET. *Brain*, *119*, 159–179.

Wechsler, D. (1997). *WAIS-III: Administration and scoring manual.* San Antonio, TX: The Psychological Corporation.

Weiss, E. M., Siedentopf, C., Hofer, A., Deisenhammer, E. A., Hoptman, M. J., Kremser, C., Golaszewski, S., Felber, S., Fleischhacker, W. W., & Delazer, M. (2003). Brain activation pattern during a verbal fluency test in healthy male and female volunteers: A functional magnetic resonance imaging study. *Neuroscience Letters* 1–4.

INTERNATIONAL JOURNAL OF PSYCHOLOGY, 2006, 41 (5), 333–341

Digit Span: Effect of education and culture

Feggy Ostrosky-Solís and Asucena Lozano

Universidad Nacional Autónoma de México, Lomas de Reforma, Mexico

The Digit Span test is one of the most commonly used measures of immediate verbal recall, attentional capacity, and working memory in neuropsychological research and clinical evaluations. This test comprises two modalities, digits forward and digits backward. It has been established that age, education, and culture are important variables that affect performance on this test. The purposes of this study were as follows. First, performance on digit span in a Spanish-speaking sample was analysed to establish appropriate age and educational ranges in which data from the Digit Span test can be best analysed, and to determine the contribution of age and education to performance on the digit span forward and backward. Second, different studies on digit span were compared and reviewed in order to identify differences in terms of the variables of age, education, and culture. This study evaluated 2574 Spanish-speaking subjects and three studies were included in the cross-cultural analysis. Scores from the Spanish-speaking sample were matched with the data presented by the other studies according to age and level of education. Results showed that the stronger predicting variable in the Spanish-speaking sample was the level of education, both for digits forward and backward. Regarding culture, differences were found among the studies on digit span for both the forward and backward conditions. It can be argued that learning to read and write affects the development or usage of the abilities measured by the Digit Span task, and that cultural variables such as language and quality of education might also contribute to the differences found between countries.

L'épreuve de «*Digit Span*» est une des mesures de rappel verbal immédiat, de capacité attentionnelle et de mémoire de travail les plus fréquemment utilisées dans la recherche neuropsychologique et dans les évaluations cliniques. Ce test comporte deux modalités: les digits en avant (forward) et ceux en arrière (backward). Il a été établi que l'âge, l'éducation et la culture sont des variables importantes qui affectent la performance à ce test. Les objectifs de cette étude étaient les suivants: Premièrement, analyser la performance à l'épreuve de la digit span dans un échantillon d'hispanophones, ceci dans le but d'établir l'écart d'âge et d'éducation dans lequel les données du test du digit span peuvent être analysées et de déterminer la contribution de l'âge et de l'éducation à la performance au digit span en avant et en arrière; Deuxièmement, réviser une comparaison entre différentes études sur le digit span afin de déterminer s'il existe des différences quant aux variables d'âge, d'éducation et de culture. L'échantillon se compose de 2574 participants hispanophones qui ont été évalués dans le cadre de cette étude et 3 études ont été incluses dans l'analyse trans-culturelle. Les scores de l'échantillon hispanophones ont été appariés avec les données présentées par les autres études par rapport à l'âge et à l'éducation. Les résultats ont indiqué que, dans l'échantillon hispanophone, le prédicteur le plus important était le niveau d'éducation à la fois pour les digits en avant et pour ceux en arrière. En ce qui concerne la culture, des différences ont été observées entre les études sur le digit span tant pour les conditions en avant que pour celles en arrière. Il est possible d'argumenter que l'apprentissage de la lecture et de l'écriture affecte le développement ou l'usage des habiletés mesurées par la tâche du digit span. De plus, les variables culturelles comme le langage et la qualité de l'éducation peuvent aussi contribuer aux différences entre les pays.

La prueba de retención de dígitos es una de las más utilizadas para medir memoria verbal inmediata, capacidad atencional y memoria de trabajo en evaluaciones neuropsicológicas tanto en el ambiente experimental como clínico. Esta prueba incluye dos modalidades, retención de dígitos en progresión y en regresión. Se ha establecido que la educación y la cultura son variables importantes que afectan el desempeño en esta prueba. Los objetivos de este estudio fueron: primero, analizar en una muestra de sujetos hispanohablantes la prueba de retención de dígitos para establecer los rangos de edad y escolaridad más apropiados para analizar el desempeño y determinar la contribución de la edad y escolaridad al puntaje de dígitos en progresión y regresión;

Correspondence should be addressed to Feggy Ostrosky-Solís, PhD, Universidad Nacional Autónoma de México, Rivera de Cupia 110-71, Lomas de Reforma, México, DF 11930 (E-mail: feggy@servidor.unam.mx).

 DOI: 10.1080/00207590500345724

segundo, comparar diferentes estudios que utilizaron la prueba de retención de dígitos para determinar si existe alguna diferencia en el desempeño en términos de las variables de edad, educación o cultura. Se evaluaron 2574 sujetos hispanohablantes y se incluyeron 3 estudios para el análisis transcultural. La muestra de hispanohablantes fue pareada por edad y escolaridad con las muestras utilizadas por los otros estudios para hacer las comparaciones en el desempeño en esta prueba en diferentes países. Los resultados muestran que la variable predictora más importante en la muestra de sujetos hispanohablantes es la escolaridad para dígitos en progresión y dígitos en regresión. En relación a la cultura, se encontraron diferencias en el desempeño entre los diferentes estudios revisados tanto en dígitos en progresión como en regresión. Se concluye que el aprendizaje de la lectoescritura afecta el desarrollo y uso de aquellas habilidades que implica la prueba de retención de dígitos y que variables culturales como el idioma y la calidad de la educación contribuyen a las diferencias encontradas entre diferentes estudios.

The Digit Span test included in the Wechsler batteries (intelligence and memory) is one of the most commonly used measures of immediate verbal recall and attentional capacity in neuropsychological research and clinical evaluations. In this test subjects are exposed to larger amounts of information, with instruction to indicate how much of the given information they remembered by immediately repeating what they heard. This test comprises two modalities, Digits Forward and Digits Backward. A series of strings of digits are read to subjects who are then asked to repeat them orally in the correct sequence (either forward or backward). The number of digits in each string increases from 3 to 9 forward and 2 to 8 backward. The test is discontinued if the subject fails two consecutive trials. Total score corresponds to the maximum number of digits the subject is able to repeat correctly.

These modalities of digit span require an adequate auditory attention and both depend on a short-term retention capacity. Recently, it has been argued that the Digit Span tests implicate verbal working memory (Baddeley, 2000). Baddeley and Hitch (1974) proposed a model in which working memory is comprised of a supervisory controlling system (the central executive) aided by two peripheral "slave" systems: the phonological (or articulatory) loop, involved in the temporary storage and maintenance of speech-based material; and the visuospatial sketchpad for visual and spatial information. The central executive is conceptualized as an attention control system responsible for strategy selection, control, and coordination of cognitive processes. Within this framework, forward digit span would be managed primarily by the phonological loop, while more extensive involvement of the central executive is expected to occur when the digits are repeated in the reversed order, as the number strings have to be remembered and then reversed in order to give the correct answer.

In clinical populations this test has shown to be more vulnerable to left-hemisphere damage than to right or diffuse damage (Lezak, 1995). Other studies have found impaired backward span performance in clinical samples, such as TBI (Curtiss, Vanderploeg, Spencer, & Salazar, 2001) and chronic fatigue syndrome (Dobbs, Dobbs, & Kiss, 2001).

Some studies have shown conflicting results regarding the influence of education and age on digit span performance. Ardila, Ostrosky-Solís, Rosselli, and Gómez (2000a) evaluated a sample of 883 subjects ranging from 16 to 85 years of age; with 0 to 24 years of education. They found that subjects with little or no education tend to maintain the same level of performance for digits backward across different age ranges, whereas older subjects with 10 and more years of education show a decrement in performance. The authors concluded that performance on specific cognitive domains will be affected differentially by the interaction of both education and age. Other studies have pointed out that age is a stronger predictive variable than education on the Digit Span test. This result was obtained from data taken from the normative sample of the Wechsler Memory Scale (Hester, Kinsella, & Ong, 2004). Age-related decrease has also been described for the forward and backward conditions of the Digit Span task. In a metanalysis of 14 studies by Babcock and Salthouse (1990), decreases for the backward digit span performance were greater than in performance of the forward condition (14% and 8% respectively). These results are in accordance with clinical reports that the greater the age, the greater the deficits shown in the backward span task (Lezak, 1995). However, other studies have not found such an effect, and report the same rate of decline for both digits forward and backward (Myerson, Emery, White, & Hale, 2003; Wilde, Strauss, & Tulsky, 2004).

Recently, another variable that affects performance in neuropsychological testing has been the subject of much attention. Cross-cultural research has focused on comparisons between different neuropsychological tests in different cultures. Culture can be defined as the way of life of a self-regulating human group, and includes values, attitudes, and beliefs that are made manifest in speech, behaviours, laws, and customary practices (Harris, 1983; Shweder, 1999). Clinical neuropsychology has looked to develop suitable measures for testing in different cultural contexts; the first attempts considered the nonverbal test to be more appropriate due to the "supposed" culture-free characteristics of nonverbal abilities. However, it has been demonstrated that such abilities are equally, if not more greatly, affected by culture than verbal skills (Rosselli & Ardila, 2003).

On digit span, there are few articles regarding this issue. Reynolds, Willson, and Ramsey (1999) evaluated white American, Mexican American, and Native American (Papagos) children from 6 to 16 years and from grade 1 to 9 with the WISC-R. Differences were found on digit span only between the white American and Papagos children. Authors relate this finding to the development of specific abilities that depend upon what certain cultures determine to be important. Another possible explanation is unfamiliarity with testing procedures in the Papagos children.

Another comparison among different countries on the Digit Span test was made by Nell (2000). He shows data from 12 countries (in Europe, North America, Australasia, South America, and South Africa) for the forward and backward conditions according to some age and educational ranges. Overall, it appears that the average of the number of digits correctly repeated across countries is very similar if the above-mentioned variables are held constant, especially among European countries, whereas there seem to be differences if a wide range of schooling is considered. Furthermore, the Digit Span test has been included in a core test battery for adults with fewer than 12 years of education that is designed to be applicable in different countries, cultures, and languages (Nell, 2000).

However, it has been shown that the effect of education on neuropsychological test performance is not a linear one. Instead, it represents a negatively accelerated curve tending to a plateau (Ardila, 2000; Ostrosky-Solís, Ardila, Rosselli, López-Arango, & Uriel-Mendoza, 1998). The differences between subjects with 0, 1, 2, 3, or 4 years of education are greater than those expected between subjects with 5 to 9 years of education, and even fewer differences are expected between subjects with more than 10 years of education. Thus, important characteristics in the digit span performance among subjects might be lost due to the use of a wide educational range.

Therefore, the purpose of this study was twofold. First, performance on digit span in a Spanish-speaking sample was analysed in order to establish appropriate age and educational ranges in which data from the Digit Span test can be best analysed. Second, a comparison among different studies on digit span will be reviewed in order to identify if any differences exist in terms of the variables of age, education and culture.

METHOD

Participants (Mexican sample)

For this study, 2574 subjects agreed to be evaluated (male = 967 and female = 1607). Sample age ranged from 16 to 96 years (mean age = 42.09, *SD* = 24.12) and level of education ranged from 0–24 years (mean level of education = 6.42 years, *SD* = 5.55). Illiterate subjects included in this study did not attend school due to lack of opportunity (lack of schools or socioeconomic reasons). Some of them could write either their initials or their name, but were unable to recognize or write other letters of the alphabet or to read single words. All participants were functionally independent, and those with any psychiatric or neurological impairment were discarded by taking a brief clinical history.

Procedure

Total scores for digits backward were taken from the NEUROPSI neuropsychological test battery (Ostrosky-Solís, Ardila, & Rosselli, 1999) and the NEUROPSI Attention & Memory battery (Ostrosky-Solís et al., 2003). Total scores for digits forward were obtained from the NEUROPSI Attention & Memory battery. Testing procedure for the Digit Span task was done according to the standard administration, that is, strings of digits are read to subjects at a rate of 1 per second and the subject is asked to repeat them orally in the correct sequence (either forward or backwards). The number of digits in each string increases from 3 to 9 forward and from 2 to 8 backward. The test is discontinued if the subject fails two consecutive trials. Total score corresponds to the maximum number of digits the subject is able to repeat correctly.

In order to make comparisons between countries, a search of articles was conducted in several computerized databases: PsycINFO, Science direct, EBSCO, and Swetwise. The following keywords were used: digit span, attention span, digits forward, digits backward, and normative data. Only those studies published in peer-reviewed journals were considered. The selected studies were either normative or studies in which a control group of normal participants was used. Although a great number of studies have been published regarding normative or experimental data for the Digit Span test, only those containing the number of subjects, mean, and standard deviation on performance for digits forward and digits backward in each age range and educational level were considered in order to compare the means.

Statistical analyses

Two sets of analyses were done for this study. First, data from the Mexican sample on the Digit Span test was used to establish which age and educational ranges were the most appropriate to use according to subject's performance on this test. A stepwise regression analysis was performed to obtain the contribution of both education and age to the Digit Span score (forward and backward).

The second analysis was carried out comparing the means on digits forward and backward from the published studies in different countries to establish whether any difference exists between subjects' performance. The Mexican sample was paired according to the age and educational level used in each of the studies. The means of digits forward and backward were analysed for each of the studies with a *t*-test using the Computerized Program for Metanalysis (Schwarzer, 1994).

RESULTS

Mexican data on Digit Span tests

Digits forward

Table 1 presents the demographic characteristics of the sample. A total of 485 participants were evaluated (173 men and 312 women). Mean age was 42.98 (SD = 20.16) and mean years of education was 9.51 (SD = 5.6). The mean number of digits correctly repeated was 5.35 (SD = 1.15).

In order to make a finer analysis of the sample's performance on the Digits Forward test, age and years of education were grouped into ranges of 5 years. An analysis of variance and post hoc tests were used to identify age and educational ranges in which there were differences in the performance on the Digits Forward test. Results showed that the sample could be divided into three educational ranges: 0 to 2 years of education, 3 to 7 years, and >8 years. Age ranges were established as follows: 16 to 30 years, 31 to 74 years, and >75 years. Means and standard deviation of digits forward in each of these ranges are shown in Table 2.

As can be observed, in the educational range of 0 to 2 years, performance is stable across different age ranges, whereas in the 3 to 7 and > 8 years of education groups, performance decreases in the older age range.

A stepwise regression analysis was performed to obtain the contribution of age and education to performance on the digit forward test. These

TABLE 1
Digits forward: Characteristics of the sample (n=485)

	Sex		*Age*		*Education*		*Digits forward*	
n	*Male*	*Female*	*X*	*SD*	*X*	*SD*	*X*	*SD*
485	173	312	42.98	(20.16)	9.51	(5.6)	5.35	(1.15)

TABLE 2
Means and standard deviations of digits forward according to educational and age ranges: Mexico (n=485)

	Age					
Years of education	*16–30*		*31–74*		*75–90*	
	X	*SD*	*X*	*SD*	*X*	*SD*
0–2	4.36	(1.46)	4.20	(0.99)	4.50	(0.81)
3–7	5.50	(1.00)	5.00	(1.00)	4.63	(0.95)
8–22	5.94	(0.97)	5.58	(0.97)	4.57	(1.13)

variables were entered as the independent variables, and the score for digits forward was the dependent variable. The percentage of variance explained by education was 25% and it was 14% for age. The equation obtained was:

$$\text{Digits forward} = 4.785 + \text{education}(0.092) + \text{age}(0.007)$$

Digits backward

Table 3 presents the demographic characteristics of the sample. A total of 2089 participants were evaluated (794 men and 1295 women). Mean age was 49.32 (*SD* = 20.68) and mean years of education was 6.79 (*SD* = 5.97). The mean number of digits correctly repeated was 3.23 (*SD* = 1.24).

As in the digits forward sample, age and years of education were grouped into ranges of 5 years and an analysis of variance and post hoc tests were used to identify age and educational ranges in which there were differences in performance on the Digits Backward test. Results showed that the sample could be grouped into the following educational ranges: illiterates, 1 to 6 years of education, and >7 years. Age can also be grouped into three ranges: 16–30 years, 31–74 years, and >75 years. Means and standard deviation of digits forward for each of these ranges are shown in Table 4. Results show that illiterates and the 1 to 6 years educational ranges maintain a stable performance across the three age ranges, whereas subjects with more than 7 years of education tend to show a decrease in the mean score as age increases.

A stepwise regression analysis was also performed to obtain the contribution of age and education to the digit backward score. These variables were entered as the independent variables, and the score for digits backward was the dependent variable. Education was the only variable left in the model; it explained 31% of the variance for the total score. The equation obtained was:

$$\text{Digits backward} = 2.440 + \text{education } (0.117)$$

Cross-cultural comparisons on digit span

A total of three studies were considered for comparison purposes: a study from the USA (Powell & Hiatt, 1996), one from Denmark (Öberg, personal communication), and a table reported by Nell (2000). In Nell's table, data from 12 countries (in Europe, North America, Australasia, South America, and South Africa) for the forward and backward conditions, for some age and educational ranges, is presented, but only those studies that included means of age and education were considered. Table 5 shows mean age and educational levels of the samples used in each study. The Mexican sample was paired according to these data, and the mean score for digits forward and backward was obtained.

Table 6 shows means and standard deviations of digits forward for each country and for the Mexican sample. As can be seen, there were differences between the Mexican sample and Poland, Venezuela, South Africa 1, South Africa 4, and South Africa 6.

Table 7 shows means and standard deviations of digits backward for each country and for the Mexican sample. All countries showed significant

TABLE 3
Digits backward: Characteristics of the sample (n=2089)

	Sex		*Age*		*Education*		*Digits backward*	
n	*Male*	*Female*	*X*	*SD*	*X*	*SD*	*X*	*SD*
2089	794	1295	49.32	(20.68)	6.79	(5.97)	3.23	(1.24)

TABLE 4
Digits backward (n=2089): Means and standard deviations by age and level of education

	Age					
Years of	*16–30*		*31–74*		*75–90*	
education	*X*	*SD*	*X*	*SD*	*X*	*SD*
Illiterates	2.34	(1.23)	2.38	(1.16)	2.22	(0.84)
1–6	2.78	(1.24)	2.93	(1.03)	2.74	(0.92)
7–22	4.14	(1.00)	3.96	(1.00)	3.58	(0.95)

TABLE 5
Characteristics of the samples used in each study considered for comparison with the Mexican sample: Means and standard deviations of age and education are presented

Country	*n*	*Age years*	*Education years*
Austria[a]	19	26–35	8–10
France[a]	24	26–35	8–10
Hungary[a]	18	26–35	8–10
Italy[a]	112	26–35	8–10
Netherlands[a]	35	26–35	8–10
Poland[a]	28	26–35	8–10
China[a]	23	35.4 (8.4)	6.2 (2.7)
Venezuela[a]	47	35 (11)	8 (3)
South Africa 1[a]	100	24 (4.2)	13–14
South Africa 2[a]	140	25 (3.3)	9–12
South Africa 2[a]	63	25 (3.3)	13–15
South Africa 3[a]	247	36 (10)	5 (2.9)
South Africa 4[a]	54	46 (9)	6 (3.5)
South Africa 5[a]	15	35–50	6 (1.7)
South Africa 6[a]	20	41 (8.2)	5 (8.2)
Denmark	49	70.68 (6.08)	9.3 (1.7)
USA	80	24.3 (8.8)	14.2 (2.4)

[a]Taken from Nell (2000).

differences in the mean scores compared to the Mexican sample, except studies 4, 5, and 6 from South Africa.

DISCUSSION

The first objective of this study was to establish age and educational ranges through which the effect of these variables on Digit Span test performance could best be analysed. As can be seen from the tables and the results from the regression analysis, these variables do not affect performance equally. In the digits forward, no differences are found between illiterates and subjects with 1 and 2 years of education, whereas in the backward condition, no merging can be done because there are significant differences among illiterates and subjects with 1 to 6 years of education. Furthermore, many studies have pointed out that age is the main variable that explains an adequate performance on the Digit Span task in either the forward or backward conditions. However, in this study the stronger variable is education, followed by a small contribution from age in the forward condition; this variable was excluded from the regression model in the digits backward condition. This effect may be due to the educational ranges included in the studies, most of which merge subjects with little or no education and subjects with up to 8 years of formal schooling (Groeger, Field, & Hammond, 1999; Hester et al., 2004; Myerson et al., 2003; Wilde et al., 2004), or only include subjects with a high level of education (Powell & Hiatt, 1996; Wilde & Strauss, 2002).

In the higher level of education (8 to 22 years) it is observed that performance decreases in the older adults; this tendency has been seen in most studies on digit span (Groeger et al., 1999; Hester et al., 2004; Myerson et al., 2003; Wilde et al., 2004). It has been proposed that this effect is in accordance with research indicating that working memory

TABLE 6
Comparisons with *t*-test of total scores on digits forward among samples of other countries and Mexico: The Mexican sample was paired according to age and level of education to the sample of the different countries (X=mean, SD=standard deviation)

	Digits forward			*Digits forward: Mexico*			
Country	*X*	*SD*	*n*	*X*	*SD*	*n*	*t*
Austria	7.7	(1.9)	19	5.3	(0.93)	20	4.969**
France	6.6	(2.0)	24	5.3	(0.93)	20	2.837**
Hungary	6.1	(0.9)	18	5.3	(0.93)	20	2.693**
Italy	6.7	(1.9)	112	5.3	(0.93)	20	5.095**
Netherlands	6.1	(1.7)	35	5.3	(0.93)	20	2.255**
Poland	5.4	(1.1)	28	5.3	(0.93)	20	0.340
China	6.8	(3.5)	23	5.4	(1.01)	27	1.853**
Venezuela	5.2	(2.0)	47	5.3	(0.83)	45	−0.315
South Africa 1	6.2	(0.9)	100	6.0	(1.16)	18	0.694
South Africa 2	7.4	(2.3)	140	5.5	(0.91)	25	7.135**
South Africa 2	7.9	(2.0)	63	5.6	(1.03)	25	7.066**
South Africa 3	4.8	(1.0)	247	5.4	(0.82)	11	2.350**
South Africa 4	5.2	(1.0)	54	5.1	(0.96)	37	0.438
South Africa 5	4.3	(1.7)	15	5.1	(0.90)	31	1.710**
South Africa 6	4.5	(0.9)	20	4.8	(0.98)	41	1.186
Denmark	6,02	(0.85)	49	5.19	(1.10)	27	3.401**
USA	7.3	(1.14)	80	5.8	(0.89)	25	6.851**

$^{**}p>.05$.

TABLE 7

Comparisons with *t*-test of total scores on digits backward among samples of other countries and Mexico: The Mexican sample was paired according to age and level of education to the sample of the different countries (*X*=mean, *SD*=standard deviation)

	Digits backward			*Digits backward: Mexico*			
Country	*X*	*SD*	*n*	*X*	*SD*	*n*	*t*
Austria	6.7	(1.3)	19	3.7	(0.91)	27	8.674**
France	5.8	(2.3)	24	3.7	(0.91)	27	4.190**
Hungary	4.5	(0.9)	18	3.7	(0.91)	27	2.908**
Italy	4.5	(2.1)	112	3.7	(0.91)	27	3.022**
Netherlands	6.4	(1.9)	35	3.7	(0.91)	27	7.381**
Poland	5.0	(0.9)	28	3.7	(0.91)	27	5.325**
China	4.6	(1.6)	23	3.4	(0.88)	35	3.285**
Venezuela	4.3	(2.0)	47	3.5	(0.97)	107	2.610**
South Africa 1	5.0	(0.9)	100	4.0	(0.82)	23	5.175**
South Africa 2	5.6	(2.2)	140	3.9	(0.88)	44	7.442**
South Africa 2	6.3	(2.0)	63	4.1	(0.85)	38	7.659**
South Africa 3	3.3	(1.1)	247	3.1	(1.12)	81	1.400**
South Africa 4	3.3	(1.0)	54	3.1	(0.90)	113	1.247
South Africa 5	2.7	(1.1)	15	3.3	(0.98)	56	1.918
South Africa 6	2.8	(1.4)	20	2.7	(1.13)	272	0.312
USA	5.6	(1.27)	80	4.2	(0.98)	151	8.596**

**p>.05.

declines with increasing age (Baeckman, Small, Wahlin, & Larsson, 2000; Salthouse, Fristoe, Lineweaver, & Coon, 1995). Hester et al. (2004) suggest that the efficiency of the central executive might be reduced due to an age-related limiting capacity of the amount of information that can be processed by the slave systems at one time, therefore affecting performance in the elderly.

Several studies have pointed out that illiterates underperform in neuropsychological tasks that require working memory and immediate verbal attention (Ostrosky-Solís et al., 1998, 1999), which are processes required by the Digit Span task. A possible explanation relates to the fact that illiterates and subjects with little formal schooling find the usual testing situation very unfamiliar (Reis & Castro-Caldas, 1997; Rosselli, Ardila, & Rosas, 1990). Poor performance might be accounted for by this unusual testing situation as well as by the effect of the acquisition or development of some cognitive strategies.

In accordance with previous data (Ardila, Rosselli, & Rosas, 1989; Reis, Guerreiro, García, & Castro-Caldas, 1995), there was a significant literacy effect on the Digit Span task. That is, the literates performed significantly better than the illiterate subjects. This task was sensitive not only to literacy but also to years of formal education, thus indicating that the latter is an important factor in influencing the cognitive processes required to perform the task. The literacy effect on digit span has also been investigated in terms of the influence of the magnitude component of digit representations. Reis et al. (1995) compared the performance of illiterates and literate subjects on a Digit Span task with digits smaller or larger than 5. Illiterates performed significantly worse on digits larger than 5 as compared to numbers smaller than 5, while this was not the case for the literate group.

It has been proposed that lack of schooling has an impact on the development of cognition; that is, formal education promotes an alternative way in which information can be conceptually processed, thus enhancing the acquisition of specific abilities essential to the development of a number of cognitive strategies. It may be argued that learning to read and write promotes the practice and reinforces the usage of these abilities and strategies, Ardila, Ostrosky-Solís, and Uriel-Mendoza (2000b) showed that illiterates who are taught to read and write improve their neuropsychological test performance, including the Digit Span task.

Petersson, Reis, and Ingvar (2001) applied a network analysis approach based on structural equation modelling (SEM) to study patterns of interactions between functionally specialized brain regions. They analysed the observed covariance structure in a PET data set from an auditory verbal repetition paradigm in literate and illiterate subjects. The results indicate that illiterate subjects show differences in attentional modulation of the language network and executive aspects of verbal working memory compared to literate subjects. This suggests that the language system would then be differently developed in the illiterates; the abilities implicated by the Digit Span task may not be fully developed in this group, so that they obtain lower scores than literate subjects and maintain the same level of performance across different age ranges. As Baddeley (1996, 2001) has pointed out, the Digit Span task would imply relatively little complex processing, determined more by storage than by executive functioning, but as the number of digits to be recalled increases, so does the recruitment of the phonological loop and the central executive. This would also explain poor performance among illiterates in the Digit Span task and the fact that, in the digits backward condition, no merging can be done between illiterates and subjects with 1 year of formal schooling. This condition would involve more attentional and executive resources, which illiterates do not possess, and even 1 year of schooling might provide enough training in these abilities to make a difference in performance of the test.

The second objective was to compare different studies of digit span to identify if there are any differences in terms of the variables of age, education, and culture. Recently, researchers have focused on the impact of culture on neuropsychological test performance. Few studies have addressed this issue regarding the Digit Span task. The results obtained in this study, comparing the total scores on digits forward and backward between different countries and a Mexican sample, show a difference that cannot be fully explained in terms of differences in age or years of schooling.

Some studies have suggested that differences in performance on the Digit Span task in different countries could be accounted for by the language spoken by the subjects. A cross-linguistic study by Naveh-Benjamin and Ayres (1986) found that digit span was larger for languages in which speech rate (estimated by reading speed) was faster. For instance, the mean of digit span for English was 7.2 and for Arabic it was 5.77. Studies of bilinguals have also shown that larger digit spans are obtained in the language in which speech rate is fastest (Chincotta & Hoosain, 1995; Chincotta & Underwood, 1996). Chincotta and Underwood (1997) examined the effect of articulatory suppression in order to clarify its influence on the discrepancies observed between different languages in this test. They visually presented series of digits that subjects had to repeat verbally after presentation. In the articulatory suppression condition, the legend *la-la* appeared on the screen 2 seconds prior to the sequences of digits, and subjects had to commence by articulating the suppression phrase. They found that when the articulatory suppression task is present during the Digit Span task, performance is equivalent among different languages. It is argued that under the articulatory suppression condition, the translation of visual stimuli into phonological codes is prevented by the disablement of the articulatory control process, reducing the contribution of the phonological loop.

The differences found in our comparisons might partially be accounted for by this effect of speech rate. However, this effect has only been shown in the digits forward condition and with bilingual subjects, thus the possible effect on monolingual subjects and in the backward condition remains unclear.

Another possible factor that may explain the differences observed in digit span performance across countries is that education can be considered as an element that includes both literacy and schooling. Viewed in this way, school is a subculture that dictates which abilities and attitudes the educational system should develop and reinforce and at what age (Ardila, 2000; Ardila et al., 2000b; Rosselli & Ardila, 2003). Although school promotes the acquisition of certain values and abilities regardless of the location, differences in the education system in terms of structure and quality might impact upon the development of certain cognitive abilities like verbal attention and working memory, thus affecting performance on a test that measures these abilities, such as Digit Span.

In conclusion, learning to read and write during childhood influences brain functional organization and behaviour, so the study of illiterates creates an opportunity to acquire knowledge regarding the interactions between neurobiological and cultural factors on cognitive development. Recently, there has been an enormous interest in the development of valid norms for illiterate populations for clinical purposes, cognitive research, and cross-cultural comparisons.Thus, the data obtained in this study suggest that in order to obtain meaningful norms for interpreting performance on the Digit Span task both in clinical and experimental settings, it is necessary to use narrower educational ranges when assessing subjects with wide educational attainment. On the other hand, with the available data it cannot be assumed that measures of verbal attention and working memory as assessed by the Digit Span task are equally developed in different contexts (i.e., cultures). This makes it necessary to generate and valid norms for each group to which this test is applied, and to consider the confounding effects of the relevant variables when assessing patients from a different cultural background to that of the examiner, in order to avoid a wrong diagnosis.

REFERENCES

Ardila, A. (2000). Evaluación cognoscitiva en analfabetas. *Revista de Neurología, 30*, 465–468.

Ardila, A., Ostrosky-Solís, F., Rosselli, M., & Gómez, C. (2000a). Age-related cognotive decline during normal aging: The complex effect of education. *Archives of Clinical Neuropsychology, 15*, 495–513.

Ardila, A., Ostrosky- Solís, F., & Uriel-Mendoza, V. (2000b). Learning to read is much more than learning to read: A neuropsychologically-based learning to read method. *Journal of the International Neuropsychological Society, 6*, 789–801.

Ardila, A., Rosselli, M., & Rosas, P. (1989). Neuropsychological assessment in illiterates: Visuospatial and memory abilities. *Brain and Cognition, 11*, 147–166.

Babcock, R. L., & Salthouse, T. A. (1990). Effects of increased processing demands on age differences in working memory. *Psychology and Aging, 5*, 421–428.

Baddeley, A. (1996). Exploring the central executive. *Quarterly Journal of Experimental Psychology: Human Experimental Psychology, 49A*, 5–28.

Baddeley, A. (2000). The episodic buffer: A new component of working memory? *Trends in Cognitive Sciences, 4*, 417–423.

Baddeley, A. (2001). Is working memory still working? *American Psychologist, 56*, 851–864.

Baddeley, A., & Hitch, G. (1974). Working memory. In G. H. Bower (Ed.), *The psychology of learning and motivation.* San Diego: Academic Press.

Baeckman, L., Small, B. J., Wahlin, A., & Larsson, M. (2000). Cognitive function in very old age. In F. I. M. Craik (Ed.), *Handbook of aging and cognition.* Mahwah, NJ: Lawrence Erlbaum Associates Inc.

Chincotta, D., & Hoosain, R. (1995). Reading rate articulatory suppression and bilingual digit span. *European Journal of Cognitive Psychology, 36*, 233–252.

Chincotta, D., & Underwood, G. (1996). Mother tongue, language of schooling and bilingual digit span. *British Journal of Psychology, 87*, 193–208.

Chincotta, D., & Underwood, G. (1997). Digit span and articulatory suppression: A cross-linguistic comparison. *European Journal of Cognitive Psychology, 9*, 89–96.

Curtiss, G., Vanderploeg, R. D., Spencer, J., & Salazar, A. M. (2001). Patterns of verbal learning and memory in traumatic brain injury. *Journal of the International Neuropsychological Society, 7*, 574–585.

Dobbs, B. M., Dobbs, A. R., & Kiss, I. (2001). Working memory deficits associated with chronic fatigue syndrome. *Journal of the International Neuropsychological Society, 7*, 285–293.

Groeger, J. A., Field, D., & Hammond, S. A. (1999). Measuring memory span. *International Journal of Psychology, 34*, 359–363.

Harris, M. (1983). *Culture, people, nature: An introduction to general anthropology* (3rd ed.). New York: Harper & Row.

Hester, R. L., Kinsella, G. J., & Ong, B. (2004). Effect of age on forward and backward span tasks. *Journal of the International Neuropsychological Society, 10*, 475–481.

Lezak, M. (1995). *Neuropsychological assessement* (3rd ed.). New York: Oxford University Press.

Myerson, J., Emery, L., White, D. A., & Hale, S. (2003). Effects of age, domain, and processing demands on memory span: Evidence for differential decline. *Aging Neuropsychology and Cognition, 10*, 20–27.

Naveh-Benjamin, M., & Ayres, T. J. (1986). Digit span, reading rate, and linguistic relativity. *Quarterly Journal of Experimental Psychology, 38A*, 739–751.

Nell, V. (2000). *Cross-cultural neuropsychological assessment. Theory and practice.* Mahwah, NJ: Lawrence Erlbaum Associates, Inc.

Ostrosky-Solís, F., Ardila, A., & Roselli, M. (1999). NEUROPSI: A brief neuropsychological test battery in Spanish with norms by age and educational level. *Journal of the International Neuropsychological Society, 5*, 413–433.

Ostrosky-Solís, F., Ardila, A., Roselli, M., Lopez-Arango, G., & Uriel-Mendoza, V. (1998). Neuropsychological test performance in illiterates. *Archives of Clinical Neuropsychology, 13*, 645–660.

Ostrosky-Solís, F., Gómez, M. E., Matute, E., Rosselli, M., Ardila, A., & Pineda, D. (2003). *NEUROPSI Atención y Memoria 6 a 85 años [NEUROPSI Attention and Memory 6 to 85 years].* Mexico: American Book Store.

Petersson, K. M., Reis, A., & Ingvar, M. (2001). Cognitive processing in literate and illiterate subjects: A review of some recent behavioural and functional neuroimaging data. *Scandinavian Journal of Psychology, 42*, 251–267.

Powell, D. H., & Hiatt, M. D. (1996). Auditory and visual recall of forward and backward digit spans. *Perceptual and Motor Skills, 82*, 1099–1103.

Reis, A., & Castro-Caldas, A. (1997). Illiteracy: A bias for cognitive development. *Journal of the International Neuropsychological Society, 3*, 444–450.

Reis, A., Guerreiro, M., García, C., & Castro-Caldas, A. (1995). How does an illiterate subject process the lexical component of arithmetics. *Journal of the International Neuropsychological Society, 1*, 206.

Reynolds, C. R., Willson, V. L., & Ramsey, M. (1999). Intellectual differences among Mexican Americans, Papagos and Whites, independent of g. *Personality and Individual Differences, 27*, 1181–1187.

Rosselli, M., & Ardila, A. (2003). The impact of culture and education on non-verbal neuropsychological measurements: A critical review. *Brain and Cognition, 52*, 326–333.

Rosselli, M., Ardila, A., & Rosas, P. (1990). Neuropsychological assessment in illiterates II. Language and praxic abilities. *Brain and Cognition, 12*, 281–296.

Salthouse, T. A., Fristoe, N. M., Lineweaver, T. T., & Coon, V. E. (1995). Aging of attention: Does the ability to divide decline? *Memory and Cognition, 23*, 59–71.

Schwarzer, R. (1994). *Meta-analysis programs* (Version 5.3.1) [Computer software]. Berlin: Author.

Shweder, R. A. (1999). Why cultural psychology? *Ethos, 27*, 62–73.

Wilde, N., & Strauss, E. (2002). Functional equivalence of WAIS-III/WSM-III digit and spatial span under forward and backward recall conditions. *The Clinical Neuropsychologist, 16*, 322–330.

Wilde, N. J., Strauss, E., & Tulsky, D. S. (2004). Memory span on the Wechsler scale. *Journal of Clinical and Experimental Neuropsychology, 26*, 539–549.

INTERNATIONAL JOURNAL OF PSYCHOLOGY, 2006, 41 (5), 342–347

Cross-linguistic meta-analysis of phonological fluency: Normal performance across cultures

Gunilla Oberg

Committee for Cross-cultural Neuropsychology, Danish Neuropsychological Society, Copenhagen, Denmark

Maura Ramírez

National University of Mexico, Mexico City, Mexico

The Verbal Fluency test is used extensively in clinical neuropsychological assessment as well as in research protocols. The phonological fluency task can be administered to individuals of various ages and different levels of education. Diverse investigations suggest that phonological fluency can be influenced by age and education. Up to now, cross-cultural studies comparing phonological verbal fluency in different languages are scarce, and those studies that exist do not report subjects' execution comparing the level of education and age ranges. The purpose of the present study was to analyse the influence of education, culture, and primary language on the performance of phonological verbal fluency in neurologically intact subjects from different countries. The performance of phonological fluency in high- and lower-frequency letters of a sample of 926 healthy subjects living in five different countries and speaking diverse languages (Danish, English, Spanish, Hebrew), with a higher level of education (more than 10 years), was analysed. Results of the meta-analysis suggest that level of education influenced the number of words generated, and higher-frequency letters produced a higher number of words in all languages. As long as years of education and letter frequency within each language were considered, the number of words generated was remarkably similar across languages and across countries. However, level of education and letter frequency within each language are relevant variables, therefore norms for one type and/or set of letters may be inappropriate for another group. In summary, regardless of the primary language and the ethnic background of the examinee, phonological verbal fluency could be a useful diagnostic tool if the level of education of the subjects being evaluated is considered. More extensive investigations that analyse the influence of culture on neuropsychological tests will clarify its effects on cognitive processes.

Le test de la fluence verbale est substantiellement utilisé à la fois dans l'évaluation neuropsychologique clinique et dans les protocoles de recherche. La fluence phonologique peut être administrée à des individus d'âges variés et de niveaux d'éducation différents. De diverses études suggèrent que la fluence phonologique peut être influencée par l'âge et par l'éducation. Jusqu'à présent, les études trans-culturelles qui comparent la fluence verbale phonologique dans différentes langues sont rares. Il en est ainsi pour les études qui ne rapportent pas l'exécution des participants en comparant leur niveau d'éducation et l'étendue de leur âge. Le but de la présente étude était d'analyser l'influence de l'éducation, de la culture et de la langue primaire sur la performance au test de la fluence verbale phonologique chez des participants neurologiquement intacts provenant de pays différents. Nous avons analysé la performance à l'épreuve de la fluence phonologique dans les lettres de haute et basse fréquence d'un échantillon de 926 participants en santé qui vivent dans cinq pays différents et parlent diverses langues (danois, anglais, espagnol, hébreu) et qui possèdent un niveau d'éducation plus élevé (plus de 10 ans). Les résultats de la méta-analyse suggèrent que le niveau d'éducation a une influence sur le nombre des mots générés et une fréquence plus élevée de lettres produit un nombre plus élevé dans toutes les langues. Tant que les années d'éducation et la fréquence des lettres dans chacune des langues sont considérées, le nombre des mots générés est remarquablement similaire à travers les langues et les pays aussi. Cependant, le niveau d'éducation et la fréquence des lettres dans chacune des langues sont des variables appropriées. Ainsi, les normes pour un type et/ou un ensemble de lettres pourraient être inappropriées pour un autre groupe. En somme, indépendamment de la langue primaire et de l'origine ethnique de l'examiné(e), la fluence verbale phonologique peut être un instrument diagnostique utile, lorsque le niveau d'éducation des participants évalués est considéré. Des recherches plus substantielles qui analysent l'influence de la culture sur les tests neuropsychologiques clarifieront ses effets sur les processus cognitifs.

Correspondence should be addressed to Gunilla Oberg, Sortedam Dossering 65, 2100 Copenhagen, Denmark (E-mail: gunilla@oeberg.edu).

DOI: 10.1080/00207590500345872

La prueba de fluidez verbal se ha utilizado extensamente en evaluaciones neuropsicológicas así como en protocolos de investigación. La fluidez fonológica puede administrarse a individuos de varias edades y diferentes niveles de educación. Diversas investigaciones sugieren que la fluidez fonológica puede estar influenciada por la edad y el nivel educativo. Actualmente son escasos los estudios que comparan la fluidez verbal fonológica en diferentes lenguas. En general, los estudios realizados no informan sobre la ejecución del sujeto por rango de edad y nivel de escolaridad. El propósito del presente estudio fue analizar la influencia de la educación, de la cultura y de la lengua materna en el desempeño en la fluidez verbal fonológica en sujetos neurológicamente intactos de diferentes países. Se analizó la ejecución en la fluidez fonológica de letras de alta y baja frecuencia de 926 sujetos sanos provenientes de cinco países que hablan diversos idiomas (danés, inglés, español, hebreo) y con un alto nivel de educación (más de 10 años). Los resultados del meta-análisis sugieren que el nivel de educación influye en el número de palabras generadas y una letra de alta frecuencia produce un alto número de palabras en todas las lenguas. Teniendo en cuenta los años de educación y la frecuencia de la letra en cada idioma, el número de palabras que los sujetos neurológicamente intactos generaron fue similar entre los diversos idiomas y los distintos países. En resumen, la fluidez fonológica es un instrumento diagnóstico útil con validez transcultural, siempre y cuando se ajuste la ejecución de acuerdo al nivel educativo de la persona evaluada y la frecuencia de la letra. El análisis detallado del cómo influye la cultura en las pruebas neuropsicológicas, ayudará a esclarecer su acción sobre el desempeño en procesos cognoscitivos.

Due to economic and cultural issues, health care professionals are now faced with a growing number of patients from different ethnic groups and different socioeconomic backgrounds. In the field of neuropsychology there is a growing need for reliable and culturally-fair assessment measures. The Verbal Fluency test is used extensively in clinical neuropsychological assessment as well as in research protocols. It can be administered to individuals of various ages and different levels of education. The task consists of generating as many words as possible with a phonological and/or semantic restriction. In the semantic task the participant is asked to name as many words as possible belonging to a particular semantic group (e.g., animals, vegetables, fruits, tools), while in the phonetically cued task subjects must say as many words as possible that begin with a given letter in a fixed time period, usually 1 minute (Bryan & Luszcz, 2000; Lezak, 1995). Variations exist with respect to which letters are given. In English, popular forms of the test include giving the letters "F," "A," and "S" (Benton, 1968; Miller, 1984) "C," "F," and "L" (Rosen, 1980), or "P," "R," and "W" (Benton & Hamsher, 1978), when an average of the three conditions is reported. In the short form only one letter is used (Harrison, Bouxton, Husain, & Wise, 2000).

It has been suggested that Verbal Fluency (semantic and phonological) measures the speed and facility of verbal production and the ability to initiate a behaviour in response to a novel task (Lezak, 1995; Parker & Crawford, 1992), as well as a language's functions (denomination, size of vocabulary), speed of answer, mental organization, search strategies, and short- and long-term memory (Ruff, Ligth, Parker, & Levin, 1997).

Semantic and phonological verbal fluency deficits have been reported in patients with focal cortical brain lesions, particularly frontal lobe damage (Herrmann, Ehlis, & Fallgatter, 2003; Ravnkilde, Videbech, Rosenberg, Gjedde, & Gade, 2002), multiple sclerosis (Rao, Leo, Bernandin, & Unversagt, 1991; Rovaris et al., 2002; Zivadinov et al., 2001), Parkinson's disease (Donovan, Siegert, & McDowall, 1999; Troyer, Moscovitch, & Winocur, 1998a), schizophrenia (Chen, Chen, Chan, Lam, & Lie-Mak, 2000; Curtis et al., 1998), subcortical dementia (Testa, Tröster, Fields, Gleason, Salmon, & Beatty, 1998), traumatic brain injury (Axelrod, Tomer, Fisher, & Aharon-Peretz, 2001), Huntington's disease (Suhr & Jones, 1998), depression (Okada, Okamoto, Morinobu, Yamawaki, & Yokota, 2003; Radvin, Katzen, Agraval, & Relkin, 2003), vascular and Alzheimer dementia (Troyer et al., 1998a), and amyotrophic lateral sclerosis (Abrahmas, Leigh, Harvey, Vythelgum, Grisé, & Goldstein, 2000). It has been reported that verbal fluency measures discriminate better than other measures of cognitive function between patients with early Alzheimer's disease and normal controls, and better predict which healthy elders, individuals with age-associated memory impairment, and those with Parkinson's, are most likely to develop dementia (Hänninen et al., 1995). Semantic category fluency is known to be more impaired than letter fluency in dementia (Barr & Brandt, 1996; Crossley, D'Arcy, & Rawson, 1997; Pasquier, Lebert, Grymonprez, & Petit, 1995). This same effect was also observed with normal ageing (Crossley et al., 1997; Kozora & Cullum, 1995; Tomer & Levin, 1993). Functional neuroimaging experiments point to left frontal areas as the anatomofunctional substrate of phonological word fluency, whereas semantically cued fluency would be associated with activation of the temporal or retrosplenial areas of the left hemisphere (Mummery, Patterson, Hodges, & Wise, 1996; Paulesu et al, 1997).

Factors that influence the performance of phonological fluency are age (Phillips, 1999), sex (Capitani, Laiacona, & Basso, 1998; Mathuranath, George, Cherian, Alexander, Sarma, & Sarma, 2003; Weiss et al., 2003), and level of education (Ardila, Ostrosky-Solís, Rosselli, & Gómez, 2000; Ostrosky-Solís, Ardila, & Rosselli, 1999; Ostrosky-Solís, Ardila, Rosselli, López, & Mendoza, 1998). Norms for several languages have been developed, yielding varying results. It has been pointed out that normative data could vary according to letter frequency even within the same language. To date, cross-cultural studies comparing phonological verbal fluency in different languages have been scarce.

The purpose of the present study was to analyse the influence of education, culture, and primary language on the performance of phonological verbal fluency in neurologically-intact subjects.

METHOD

A comprehensive search of the computerized databases MEDLINE, PsycINFO, EBSCO, and the Internet was conducted to identify articles of normative data in phonological fluency in healthy adult subjects with the following criteria of inclusion.

1. Date of publication 1985–2004.
2. Healthy subjects without neurological or psychiatric disease.
3. Journal and/or International Meeting publication.
4. Reported mean and standard deviation.
5. Providing the *n* of each range of age and education.
6. Providing the instructions given.

RESULTS

The selected studies were either normative or were studies in which a control group of normal participants was used. Although a great number of studies have been published regarding normative or experimental data for phonological fluency (Auriacombe et al., 2001; Bolla, Gray, Resnick, Galante, & Kawas, 1998; Capitani et al., 1998; Harrison et al., 2000; Johnson-Selfridge, Zalewski, & Aboudarham, 1998; Kosmidis, Vlahou, Panagiotaki, & Kiosseoglou, 2004; Mathuranath et al., 2003; Phillips, 1999; Ratcliff et al., 1998; Tombaugh, Kozak, & Rees, 1999), only those studies reporting single letter production, which gave the number of subjects and the mean and standard deviation of performance according to age and educational level, were considered. A very strong educational effect has been demonstrated in the phonemic condition (Ostrosky-Solís et al., 1998, 1999; Ostrosky-Solís, Ramírez, Lozano, Picasso, & Velez, 2004; Rosselli, Ardila, & Rosas, 1990). Ostrosky-Solís et al. (1998) and Ardila et al. (2000) found that educational level accounted for 38.5% of the variance in the phonemic condition and for 23.6% of the variance in the semantic condition, and that education had a larger effect than age. Therefore, in order to determine the effects of culture and language background, only subjects with more than 9 years of education were included.

Data from 926 neurologically-intact subjects from five different countries with four different languages were analysed. The sample included studies from Denmark (Nielsen, Knudsen, & Daugbjerg, 1989), Mexico (Ostrosky-Solís et al., 2003, 1999), Israel (Axelrod et al., 2001), USA (Radvin et al., 2003), and Argentina (Butman, Allegri, Harris, & Drake, 2000). The demographic characteristics of the total sample are shown in Table 1.

According to the authors, in most of the studies participants were given the fluency tasks as part of a larger battery. Subjects were asked to generate as many different words as possible beginning with a given letter in 1 minute. They were instructed to begin generating words as soon as the researcher announced the letter, avoiding repetitions, variations of the same word (e.g., eat-eats-eating) and proper nouns. Three of the studies used several letters that, according to the authors, were selected based on the frequency of each language. For example in English the letters selected were "C," "F," "L." In Spanish the letters were "F" and "P," in Danish "S," "N," "F," and in Hebrew they were "S" (shin), "Y" (yud), "M" (mem).

In scoring test performance, identical variations of a previously given word (e.g., run, running), or words beginning with another letter were considered as errors and did not count in the total number of words generated.

The means and standard deviations of the number of words reported by each group is presented in Table 2.

The mean number of words produced by the sample with more than 9 years of education was 13.86. However, the number of words varied according to the selected letter. In all languages, the mean number of words for the highest-frequency letter was 15.89 whereas for the low-frequency letters the mean number of words was 11.78. It is important to point out that in each language the low- and high-frequency letters differ.

DISCUSSION

Phonological fluency appears to be a useful tool for detecting functional deficits and specific, local, brain function. Many studies reported the average of three letters: "F," "A," and "S," or "C," "F," and "L"; short forms including only one letter are often used, but there is a lack of data regarding normal performance.

Spreen and Stauss (1998) suggested that normal subjects are able to generate an average of 12 words per minute for different letters including "B," "F," "L," "M," "R," "S," and "T." However, they do not distinguish factors such as age, educational level, linguistic background, or orthographic idiosyncrasics of thc writing systcm.

Other studies had reported that education is a strong predictor of performance, with increasing educational attainment being associated with higher fluency scores (Ardila et al., 2000; Ostrosky-Solís et al., 1999). In the present study only subjects with more than 9 years of education were included. Another consistent factor was the influence of the frequency of the letter selected. Thus higher-frequency letters produced a greater number of words; howcvcr, linguistic factors of each language should be considered. The letter "F" is not as frequent in Spanish as it is in the English language.

As long as years of education and letter frequency within each language were considered, the number of words generated were remarkably similar across the languages Spanish, English, Danish, and Hebrew and across the countries Mexico, Argentina, Denmark, USA, and Israel. Due to the nature of the publications included, it was not possible to analyse the effects of other significant demographic variables such as age, sex, and IQ. Other neuropsychological data such as

TABLE 1
Demographic characteristics of the samples with more than 9 years of education

			Age		*Educational level*	
Author	*Country*	*n*	*X*	*(SD)*	*X*	*(SD)*
Nielsen et al. (1989)	Denmark	54	30–39		9–20	
Ostrosky-Solís et al.	Mexico	250	33.39	(15.93)	14.02	(2.61)
(2003; 1999)		399	49.22	(19.44)	14.75	(3.27)
Ravdin et al. (2003)	USA	149	74.8	(6.6)	15.57	(2.67)
Butman et al. (2000)	Argentina	40	56–65		13+	
Axelrod et al. (2001)	Israel	34	31.0	(11.9)	14.6	(2.3)

TABLE 2
Mean and standard deviation of letter fluency for each country in subjects with more than 9 years of education

		Letter fluency		
Author	*Country*	*Letter*	*X*	*(SD)*
Nielse et al. (1989)	Denmark	S	14.07	(4.39)
		N	8.70	(3.43)
		F	12.15	(9.64)
Ostrosky-Solís et al.	Mexico	P	16.06	(2.61)
		F	13.38	(4.33)
Ravdin et al. (2003)	USA	C	16.64	(4.10)
		L	15.50	(4.27)
		F	14.74	(4.10)
Butman et al. (2000)	Argentina	P	16.6	(3.2)
Axelrod et al. (2001)	Israel	Shin	14.4	(4.20)
		Yud	10.3	(3.05)
		Mem	16.1	(4.90)

clustering, switching strategies, and type and frequency of errors could improve the diagnostic proprieties of this simple test.

Correlation between performance between the long (i.e. "F," "A," "S") and short forms (a single letter) could be important for clinical diagnosis.

In summary, results show that, regardless of the primary language and the ethnic background of the examinee, phonological verbal fluency could be a useful diagnostic tool. However, level of education and letter frequency within each language are relevant variables, so norms for one type or set of letters may be inappropriate for another group. Transcultural neuropsychology needs to use instruments that take into account the interrelationships between affecting variables such as age, sex, race, culture, formal schooling, and quality of education. If these variables are not considered, health care professionals might perform inadequate diagnoses.

REFERENCES

Abrahmas, S., Leigh, P. N., Harvey, A., Vythelgum, G. N., Grisé, D., & Goldstein, L. H. (2000). Verbal fluency and executive dysfunction in amyotrophic lateral sclerosis (ALS). *Neuropsychologia, 38*, 734–747.

Ardila, A., Ostrosky-Solis, F., Rosselli, M., & Gomez, C. (2000). Age-related cognitive decline during normal aging: The complex effect of education. *Archives of Clinical Neuropsychology, 15*, 495–514.

Auriacombe, S., Fabrigoule, C., Lafont, S., Amieva, H., Jacqmin-Gadda, H., & Dartigues, J. (2001). Letter and category fluency in normal elderly participants: A population-based study. *Aging Neuropsychology and Cognition, 8*, 98–101.

Axelrod, B. N., Tomer, R., Fisher, T., & Aharon-Peretz, J. (2001). Preliminary analyses of Hebrew verbal fluency measures. *Applied Neuropsychology, 8*, 248–250.

Barr, A., & Brandt, J. (1996). Word-list generation deficits in dementia. *Journal of Clinical and Experimental Neuropsychology, 18*, 810–812.

Benton, A. L. (1968). Differential behavioral effects in frontal lobe disease. *Neuropsychologia, 6*, 53–60.

Benton, A. L., & Hamsher, K. (1978). *Multilingual aphasia examination manual.* Iowa City, IA: University of Iowa.

Bolla, K. I., Gray, S., Resnick, S., Galante, R., & Kawas, C. (1998). Category and letter fluency in highly educated older adults. *The Clinical Neuropsychologist, 12*, 330–338.

Bryan, J., & Luszcz, M. (2000). Measurement of executive function: Considerations for detecting adult age differences. *Journal of Clinical and Experimental Neuropsychology, 22*, 40–55.

Butman, J., Allegri, R., Harris, P., & Drake, M. (2000). Fluencia Verbal en Español, datos normativos en Argentina. *Medicina (Buenos Aires), 60*, 561–564.

Capitani, E., Laiacona, M., & Basso, A. (1998). Phonetically cued word-fluency, gender differences and aging: A reappraisal. *Cortex, 34*, 779–783.

Chen, R. Y. L., Chen, E. Y. H., Chan, C. K. Y., Lam, L. C. W., & Lie-Mak, F. (2000). Verbal fluency in schizophrenia: Reduction in semantic store. *Australian and New Zealand Journal of Psychiatry, 34*, 43–48.

Crossley, M., D'Arcy, C., & Rawson, N. S. B. (1997). Letter and category fluency in community-dwelling Canadian seniors: A comparison of normal participants to those with dementia of the Alzheimer or vascular type. *Journal of Clinical and Experimental Neuropsychology, 19*, 52–62.

Curtis, V. A., Bullmore, E. T., Bramer, M. J., Wright, I. C., Williams, S. C., Morris, R. G., Sharma, T. S., Murray, R., & McGuire, P. K. (1998). Attenuated frontal activation during a verbal fluency task in patients with schizophrenia. *American Journal of Psychiatry, 155*, 1056–1063.

Donovan, K., Siegert, R., & McDowall, J. (1999). Clustering and switching in verbal fluency in Parkinson's Disease. *New Zealand Journal of Psychology, 28*, 61–66.

Hanninen, T., Hallikainen, M., Koivisto, K., Helkala, E. L., Reinikainen, K. J., Soininen, H., Mykkanen, L., Laakso, M., Pyorala, K., & Riekkinen, P. J., Sr. (1995). A follow-up study of age-associated memory impairment: Neuropsychological predictors of dementia. *Journal of American Geriatric Society, 43*, 1007–1015.

Harrison, J. E., Bouxton, P., Husain, M., & Wise, R. (2000). Short test of semantic and phonological fluency: Normal performance, validity and test–retest reliability. *British Journal of Clinical Psychology, 39*, 181–191.

Herrmann, M. J., Ehlis, A. C., & Fallgatter, A. J. (2003). Frontal activation during a Verbal Fluency task as measured by near-infrared spectroscopy. *Brain Research Bulletin, 61*, 51–56.

Johnson-Selfridge, M. T., Zalewski, C., & Aboudarham, J. (1998). The relationship between ethnicity and word fluency. *Archives of Clinical Neuropsychology, 13*, 319–325.

Kosmidis, M., Vlahou, C. H., Panagiotaki, P., & Kiosseoglou, G. (2004). The verbal fluency task in the Greek population: Normative data and clustering and switching. *Journal of the International Neuropsychological Society, 10*, 164–172.

Kozora, E., & Cullum, C. M. (1995). Generative naming in normal aging: Total output and qualitative changes using phonemic and semantic constraints. *The Clinical Neuropsychologist, 9*, 313–320.

Lezak, M. D. (1995). *Neuropsychological assessment* (3rd ed.). New York: Oxford University Press.

Mathuranath, P. S., George, A., Cherian, P. J., Alexander, A., Sarma, S. G., & Sarma, P. S. (2003). Effects of age, education and gender on verbal fluency. *Journal of Clinical Experimental Neuropsychology, 25*, 1057–1064.

Miller, E. (1984). Verbal fluency as a function of a measure of verbal intelligence and in relation to different types of cerebral pathology. *British Journal of Clinical Psychology, 25*, 53–57.

Mummery, C. J., Patterson, K., Hodges, J. R., & Wise, R. J. (1996). Generating 'tiger' as an animal name or a word beginning with T: Differences in brain activation. *Proceedings of the Royal Society of London – Series B: Biological Sciences*, *263*, 989–995.

Nielsen, H., Knudsen, L., & Daugbjerg, O. (1989). Normative data for eight neuropsychological tests based on a Danish sample. *Scandinavian Journal of Psychology*, *39*, 37–45.

Okada, G., Okamoto, Y., Morinobu, S., Yamawaki, S., & Yokota, N. (2003). Attenuated left prefrontal activation during a Verbal Fluency task in patients with depression. *Neuropsychobiology*, *47*, 21–26.

Ostrosky-Solís, F., Ardila, A., & Rosselli, M. (1999). "Neuropsi": A brief neuropsychological test battery in Spanish with norms by age and educational level. *Journal of the International Neuropsychological Society*, *5*, 413–433.

Ostrosky-Solís, F., Ardila, A., Rosselli, M., López, G., & Mendoza, V. (1998). Neuropsychological test performance in illiterates. *Archives of Clinical Neuropsychology*, *13*, 645–660.

Ostrosky-Solís, F., Gómez, M. E., Matute, E., Rosselli, M., Ardila, A., & Pineda, D. (2003). *Neuropsi Atención y Memoria 6 a 85 años*. Mexico City: American Book Store.

Ostrosky-Solís, F., Ramírez, M., Lozano, A., Picasso, H., & Velez, A. (2004). Culture or education: A study with indigenous Maya population. *International Journal of Psychology*, *39*, 36–46.

Parker, D. M., & Crawford, J. R. (1992). Assessment of frontal lobe function. In J. R. Crawford, D. M. Parker, & W. W. McKinlay (Eds.), *A handbook of neuropsychological assessment* (pp. 267–291). London: Lawrence Erlbaum Associates Ltd.

Pasquier, F., Lebert, F., Grymonprez, L., & Petit, H. (1995). Verbal fluency in dementia of frontal lobe type and dementia of Alzheimer type. *Journal of Neurology, Neurosurgery, and Psychiatry*, *58*, 81–84.

Paulesu, E., Goldacre, B., Scifo, P., Cappa, S. F., Gilardi, M. C., Castiglioni, I., Perani, D., & Fazio, F. (1997). Functional heterogeneity of left inferior frontal cortex as revealed by fMRI. *Neuroreport*, *8*, 2011–2017.

Phillips, L. (1999). Age and individual differences in letter fluency. *Developmental Neuropsychology*, *15*, 249–267.

Radvin, L. D., Katzen, H. L., Agraval, P., & Relkin, N. R. (2003). Letter and semantic fluency in older adults: Effects of mild depressive symptoms and age stratified normative data. *Clinical Neuropsychology*, *17*, 195–202.

Rao, S. M., Leo, G. J., Bernandin, L., & Unversagt, F. (1991). Cognitive dysfunction in multiple sclerosis. I. Frequency, patterns, and prediction. *Neurology*, *41*, 685–691.

Ratcliff, R. G., Ganguli, M., Chandra, V., Sharma, S., Belle, S., Seaberg, E., & Pandav, R. (1998). Effects of literacy and education on measures of word fluency. *Brain and Language*, *61*, 115–122.

Ravnkilde, B., Videbech, P., Rosenberg, R., Gjedde, A., & Gade, A. (2002). Putative test of frontal lobe function: A PET-study of brain activation during a Stroop's test and Verbal Fluency. *Journal of Clininical and Experimental Neuropsychology*, *24*, 534–547.

Rosen, W. G. (1980). Verbal fluency in aging and dementia. *Journal of Clinical Neuropsychology*, *2*, 135–146.

Rosselli, M., Ardila, A., & Rosas, P. (1990). Neuropsychological assessment in illiterates II: Language and praxic abilities. *Brain and Cognition*, *12*, 281–296.

Rovaris, M., Iannucci, G., Falautano, M., Possa, F., Martinelli, V., Comi, G., & Filippi, M. (2002). Cognitive dysfunction in patients with mildly disabling relapsing-remitting multiple sclerosis: An exploratory study with diffusion tensor MR imaging. *Journal of Neurological Sciences*, *195*, 103–109.

Ruff, R. M., Ligth, R. H., Parker, S. B., & Levin, H. S. (1997). The psychological construct of word fluency. *Brain and Language*, *57*, 349–405.

Spreen, O., & Strauss, E. (1998). *A compendium of neuropsychological tests* (2nd ed.). New York: Oxford University Press.

Suhr, J. A., & Jones, R. D. (1998). Letter and semantic fluency in Alzheimer, Huntington and Parkinson's disease. *Archives of Clinical Neurospychology*, *13*, 447–454.

Testa, J. A., Tröster, A. I., Fields, J. A., Gleason, A. C., Salmon, D., & Beatty, W. W. (1998). Semantic fluency performance of patients with cortical and subcortical neurodegenerative diseases. *Aging Neuropsychology and Cognition*, *5*, 203–214.

Tombaugh, T. M., Kozak, J., & Rees, L. (1999). Normative data stratified by age and education for two measures of verbal fluency: FAS and animal naming. *Archives of Clinical Neuropsychology*, *14*, 167–177.

Tomer, R., & Levin, B. E. (1993). Differential effects of aging on two verbal fluency tasks. *Perceptual and Motor Skills*, *76*, 465–466.

Troyer, A. K., Moscovitch, M., & Winocur, G. (1998a). Clustering and switching on verbal fluency tests in Alzheimer's and Parkinson's disease. *Journal of the International Neuropsychological Society*, *4*, 137–143.

Troyer, A. K., Moscovitch, M., Winocur, G., Alexander, M. P., & Stuss, D. (1998b). Clustering and switching on verbal fluency: The effects of focal frontal- and temporal-lobe lesions. *Neuropsychologia*, *25*, 388–493.

Weiss, E. M., Siedentopf, C., Hofer, A., Deisenhammer, E. A., Hoptman, M. J., Kremser, C., Golaszewski, S., Felber, S., Fleischhacker, W. W., & Delazer, M. (2003). Brain activation pattern during a verbal fluency test in healthy male and female volunteers: A functional magnetic resonance imaging study. *Neuroscience Letter*, *352*, 191–194.

Zivadinov, R., Sepcic, J., Nasuelli, D., De Masi, R., Bragadin, L. M., Tommasi, M. A., Zambito Marsalla, S., Moretti, R., Bratina, A., Ukmar, M., Pozzi-Mucelli, R. S., Grop, A., Cazzato, G., & Zorzon, M. (2001). A longitudinal study of brain atrophy and cognitive disturbances in the early phase of relapsing-remitting multiple sclerosis. *Journal of Neurology, Neurosurgery and Psychiatry*, *70*, 773–780.

INTERNATIONAL JOURNAL OF PSYCHOLOGY, 2006, 41 (5), 348–354

From morality to moral emotions

Alicia E. Vélez García and Feggy Ostrosky-Solís

Universidad Nacional Autónoma de México, Lomas de Reforma, Mexico

Morals (defined in terms of justice, well-being, and rights) can be distinguished from social conventionalities, which are standards for particular behaviours that are determined consensually by a certain social group. In all cultures, the notions of psychological damage, injustice, and violation of rights have been determinants for the concept of morals. The study of moral behaviour has been dominated for decades by theories that emphasize the role of reasoning in the moral judgment of adults. Debates about morality have occupied the centre of discussion among theoreticians. Morality-driven behaviours have traditionally been attributed to logically and verbally mediated processes, commonly referred to as moral reasoning and judgment. However, certain aptitudes, such as social sensitivity and cognition, have been considered to lie at the heart of the evolution of humankind. The assimilation of rules based on punishment or reward, and the attribution of intentions, beliefs, feelings, and desires to other people are some examples of these aptitudes, which are now considered or interpreted as forerunners of human morality. The study of emotions—moral emotions in particular—has increased significantly in the last few decades. Recent proposals have emphasized the role of emotional and intuitive processes in human decision making and that *emotions* are central to the solution of basic problems and to interpersonal relationships. This change in perspective is the result of recent work in the fields of philosophy, cognitive psychology, affective neurosciences, and neurobiology. The field of affective neurosciences has begun to explore different types of moral emotions with different techniques, in particular neuroimaging techniques. In the field of neurobiology, investigators have started to study neural correlates of moral emotions, and have encountered interesting findings, which indicate that the human brain shows a network specialized in moral processing.

La moralité (définie en termes de justice, de bien-être et de droits) peut se distinguer des conventions sociales qui, quant à elles, sont standard pour des comportements particuliers déterminés de manière consensuelle par un certain group social. Dans toutes les cultures, les notions de dommage psychologiques, d'injustice et de violation des droits ont été des déterminants pour le concept de la moralité. L'étude du comportement moral a été dominée pendant décennies par les théories qui mettent l'emphase sur le rôle du raisonnement dans le jugement moral des adultes. Les débats autour de la moralité sont au centre de la discussion des théoriciens. Les comportements dictés par la moralité ont été traditionnellement attribués à des processus conduits par la logique et le verbal, communément appelés raisonnement moral et jugement. Cependant, certaines aptitudes comme la sensibilité sociale et la cognition ont été considérées au cœur de l'évolution humaine. L'assimilation des règles sur la base de la punition ou de la récompense ainsi que l'attribution des intentions, des croyances, des sentiments et des désirs à d'autres personnes sont quelques exemples de ces aptitudes. Ces aptitudes sont maintenant considérées ou interprétées comme étant les précurseurs de la moralité humaine. L'étude des émotions, particulièrement les émotions morales, dans les dernières décennies a augmenté significativement. Les projets récents mettent l'emphase sur le rôle des processus émotionnels et intuitifs dans la prise de décision humaine et ont souligné que *les émotions* sont centrales à la solution des problèmes de base et aux relations interpersonnelles. Ce changement de perspective est le résultat des travaux récents dans le domaine de la philosophie, de la psychologie cognitive, des neurosciences affectives et de la neurobiologie. Le domaine des neurosciences affectives a commencé à explorer différents types d'émotions morales avec différentes techniques, plus particulièrement les techniques de neuroimagerie. Dans le domaine de la neurobiologie, les chercheurs ont commencé à étudier les corrélats neuraux des émotions morales et ont rencontré des résultats intéressants qui indiquent que le cerveau humain montre un réseau spécialisé dans le traitement de l'information morale.

Correspondence should be addressed to Feggy Ostrosky-Solís, Laboratory of Neuropsychology and Psychophysiology, National Autonomous University of Mexico, Rivera de Cupia 110-71, Lomas de Reforma, México, DF, 11930, MEXICO (E-mail: feggy@servidor.unam.mx).

 DOI: 10.1080/00207590500345898

La moralidad (definida en términos de justicia, bienestar y derechos) puede distinguirse de otras convenciones sociales, las cuales son estándares de conductas particulares determinadas en consenso por ciertos grupos sociales. En todas las culturas, las nociones de daño psicológico, injusticia y violación de los derechos han sido determinantes para el concepto de moral. El estudio de la conducta moral durante décadas ha estado dominado por teorías que enfatizan el rol del razonamiento en el juicio moral en adultos. El debate alrededor de la moralidad a ocupado el centro de discusiones entre los teóricos. Las conductas dirigidas moralmente han sido atribuidas tradicionalmente a procesos mediados lógica y verbalmente, comúnmente referidos como razonamiento y juicio moral. Sin embargo ciertas aptitudes tales como la sensibilidad social y la cognición se han considerado parte muy importante de la evolución de la humanidad. La asimilación de reglas basadas en el castigo y la recompensa, y la atribución de intenciones, creencias sentimientos y deseos hacia otras personas, son algunos ejemplos de esas aptitudes. Actualmente estas habilidades son consideradas o interpretadas como precursores de la moralidad humana. El estudio de las emociones, particularmente de las emociones morales, ha incrementando significativamente en la ultima década. Recientes propuestas enfatizan el rol de los procesos intuitivos y emocionales en la toma de decisión en los seres humanos y han enfatizado que las emociones son centrales para la solución de problemas básicos y de relaciones interpersonales. Este cambio de perspectiva es el resultado de trabajos recientes en el campo de la filosofía, psicología cognitiva, neurociencia afectiva y neurobiología. El campo de la neurociencia afectiva ha comenzado a explorar diferentes tipos de emociones morales con diferentes técnicas, en particular con técnicas de neuroimagen. En el campo de la neurobiología se ha iniciado el estudio de los correlatos neurales de las emociones morales, se ha postulado que existe una red especializada en el procesamiento moral.

In the theoretical sense, moral psychology has been dominated for decades by theories that emphasize the role of reasoning in the moral judgment of adults (Eisenberg, 2000; Haidt, 2003; Kohlberg, 1982). Nevertheless, recent proposals emphasize the role of emotional and intuitive processes in human decision making. This change in perspective is the result of recent work in the fields of philosophy, cognitive psychology, and neurobiology (Damasio, 1994; Haidt, 2001; Rozin, Loewry, Imada, & Haidt, 1999).

Every day humans judge other people's behaviours. These judgments are based on moral beliefs, and can only be the interpretation of the actor and the possible results of these intentions.

In daily discourse, morality simply refers to standards: right and wrong behaviours. The controversy, however, is about what are considered "correct or incorrect morals," and which criteria should be used to judge the adequacy of some actions.

Debates about morality have occupied the centre of discussion among theoreticians. Morality-driven behaviours have traditionally been attributed to logically and verbally mediated processes, commonly referred to as moral reasoning and judgment. However, certain aptitudes, such as social sensitivity and cognition, have been considered to lie at the heart of the evolution of humankind. The assimilation of rules based on punishment or reward, and the attribution of intentions, beliefs, feelings, and desires to other people are some examples of these aptitudes, which are now considered or interpreted as forerunners of human morality (Baron-Cohen, 1995; Schulkin, 2000).

On an individual basis, concepts of correct or incorrect social behaviour are organized within conceptual and developmental frameworks. Recent research in the fields of social psychology and cognitive psychology has stated that when determining social standards, some forms of social behaviour are based on universal morals; other forms remain matters of personal subjective choice. More specifically, these conceptual differences come up when formal criteria regarding morality are used. Within this concept, moral standards, such as interpersonal behaviour that is considered correct or incorrect, are defined regardless of rules governing society that are considered to be universal. The conditions included in these criteria are those regarding the impact of the behaviour on others, as in beating, hurting, stealing, or slandering. Thus, morals can be defined as concepts, reasoning, and actions related to well-being, rights, and the fair treatment of other people. Morals (defined in terms of justice, well-being, and rights) can be distinguished from social conventionalities, which are standards for particular behaviours that are determined consensually by a certain social group (Nucci, 1997).

In all cultures, the notions of psychological damage, injustice, and violation of rights have been determinants of the concept of morals. Investigators of the cognitive development tradition have argued that particular rules may vary between cultures; however, moral problems in all cultures involve matters of damage, rights, or justice, for example stealing, cheating, etc. (Kohlberg, 1969; Piaget, 1932; Turiel, Killen, & Helwig, 1987). An opposite standpoint has been adopted by cultural psychologists, who argue that the concept of morality is variable and goes beyond damage, rights, and justice in many cultures, such as certain customs regarding clothes, food, religion, etc. (Miller, Bersoff, & Harwood, 1990; Shweder, Mahapatra, & Millar, 1987; Shweder & Sullivan, 1993).

In terms of how morals are developed, the theories of cognitive development or morality put forward initially by Piaget (1932) and Kohlberg (1969) have limited the concept of morality to the actions affecting the material and psychological welfare of other people. For Kohlberg, "the center of moral choice and feelings are based on the outcome of personal well being" (p.393). The theory put forward by Kohlberg has been considered to be the most successful and thorough attempt to understand moral development from a sociocognitive approach. Although it has been identified as a "*moral development theory*," its emphasis was on the description of the "moral judgment" development. Its main contribution was the application of moral development to the concept of development in the stages Piaget described for cognitive development; thus, for Kohlberg, moral judgment is a cognitive process, which is developed naturally (Kitwood, 1996).

Unlike Piaget and Kohlberg, who discuss logical and moral reasoning, Rest (1984) provides a framework within which to understand moral behaviour. He puts forth a model with four components: moral sensitivity, moral judgment, moral decision making, and moral action. Moral sensitivity is the acknowledgement of an existing situation in which morals are necessary and the action of which has consequences on others. Moral judgment is a judgment about what one has to do, while moral decision making entails considering alternatives and assessing the pros and cons of their possible consequences for the self and for others. Finally, moral action includes the will and the ability to implement such decision. It is indicated in this model that for a moral behaviour, the proper performance of each of the four components is necessary.

For theoreticians of cognitive development such as Turiel (1983) and Nucci (1981), morality is "prescriptive judgments of justice, rights and wellbeing relevant to the way people should relate among them" (Turiel, 1983, p. 3). Turiel points out that moral prescriptions do not depend on the social context, nor are they defined by it. Correspondingly, the moral judgments of children do not stem directly from institutional social systems, but from traces inherent in social relationships, including experiences that entail damage to others, the violation of some rights, and conflicts between opposed claims. They point out that moral matters are intrinsically interpersonal matters, and that actions are judged by their material and psychological consequences, as these affect others. Moral prescriptions of the individual (i.e., regarding murder and value of life) are determined by factors inherent to social relationships, and not by a particular form of social organization. They put forward that moral development evolves as children distinguish social events based on three knowledge fields: personal, moral, and conventional. It is said that the consequences of actions that fall mainly on the actor are part of the *personal* scope. In contrast, acts that have "intrinsically harmful" consequences for others, such as violence and theft, are part of the *moral* field. Turiel (1983) points out that intrinsic damage is perceived directly, that is to say, it is inferred from direct perceptions. For example, children know that some actions such as beating or stealing contain features that are intrinsically harmful or that have psychological consequences for others. Since the damage is intrinsic to the act, children reason that these acts are universally wrong, even in other countries.

Finally, events that have interpersonal consequences that are not intrinsically harmful are part of the *conventional knowledge* field. For example, it is not intrinsically harmful, according to a child, to wear denim pants; nevertheless, within the school scope, where the children are required to wear a uniform, the child is violating a social convention. Children might say that the action of this child is wrong, but not universally wrong; that is to say, the situation can be correct in a different school, with a different set of rules.

Turiel et al. (1987; Turiel, Hildebrandt, & Wainryb, 1991) have shown that Americans distinguish "prototypical" examples among these three domains, based on how harmful these consequences are perceived to be. However, recent studies have suggested that the distinctions made by their American subjects are not universal, and point out that the domain of morality varies among cultures. Miller et al. (1990) found out that, for Americans, the decision to help friends and strangers is perceived as a personal choice, while in India all subjects consider helping or offering help to others to be a moral duty.

In contrast, Shweder (1990) argues that there are three codes of thought and moral speech that each culture develops to different extents. In the *ethics of autonomy*, which prevails in Western secular societies, the self is conceptualized as a structure of individual choice, and the point of moral regulation is to increase choice, autonomy, and control. This code, set forth by Shweder, has a close correspondence to the moral domain proposed by Turiel, where moral discourse is centred on harm, rights, and justice, and is highly elaborated in legal systems and in the moral philosophy of Western societies. Nevertheless, Shweder outlines the fact that anthropologic literature suggests two additional ways in which people think and speak about morals. One of them is the *ethics of community*, where the ego is conceptualized as performing a duty or a role as part of an interdependent group. This code requires duty, respect, obedience to the authorities, and actions consistent with gender, caste, age, and other components of social networks. The family, the guide, the clan, the community, the corporation, or the nation—they have priority over individual interest, and moral values protect such entities. That is to say, duty, honour, chastity, respect, modesty, and self-control are valued. In this world, individual choices such as whom to marry, how to address others, and how to dress have a moral significance and acquire ethic significance. To pursue individual goals can be a cause of shame. In the third moral code, *ethics of divinity*, the ego is conceptualized as a spiritual entity, where subjects strive to avoid pollution and achieve purification and sanctity. Although they do not entail damage for others, acts that threaten this purity are condemned. In this code, people and animals are part of God, and central moral values are those which protect and dignify the divinity inherent in people. The body is thought of as a temple, so matters related to personal choice such as diet, sexual preference, or personal hygiene become moral and spiritual problems related to values such as purification, pollution, and sanctification. This moral code, which emphasizes corporal practices, is considered bizarre by members of Western societies. However, the ethics of divinity are highly elaborated in Hindu purity and pollution rules (Fuller, 1992). Shweder (1990) concludes that the domain of morality has been restricted to the ethics of autonomy (damage, rights, and justice) in the West, but that it is wider in other cultures.

Cognitivist theories have tried to identify the particular blend of intellectual styles and interpersonal experiences that enable people to learn or deduce a moral truth (Kohlberg, 1969; Piaget, 1932, 1969; Turiel, 1983). However, other approaches have put forth the so-called intuitionist cognitivism (i.e., Kagan, 1984; Lazarus, 1991a). These theories postulate that moral appraisals are generated rapidly and automatically, without deliberate or deductive reflection or deductive reasoning. It is assumed that verbal judgments of actions and goals (whether they are correct or good), and emotional, morally relevant appraisals (pride, displeasure, empathy, shame, guilt, anger, fear) are generated based on a group of self-evident truths that are neither deducible nor inducible.

A model derived from this theory is the social intuitionist model. Intuitionism in philosophy means the vision of moral truths, and that when people reach those truths it is not through a rationalizing and reflection process, but through a process similar to perception (Harrison, 1967). Intuitionist approaches in moral psychology put forth the idea that moral intuitions (including moral emotions) arise first and directly cause a moral judgment (Haidt, 2003; Haidt, Koller, & Dias, 1993; Kagan, 1984; Shweder & Haidt, 1993; Wilson, 1993). Moral intuition is a type of cognition, but not a type of reasoning (Haidt, 2001).

As has been pointed out, theories on the development of morality disagree on whether moral knowledge and moral judgment are the result of emotional and nonrational processes (Haidt, 2001; Haidt et al., 1993; Shweder & Haidt, 1993), or of reasoning and complex cognitive processes (Kohlberg, 1969; Piaget, 1932; Turiel, 1983). However, recent approaches have emphasized that *emotions* are central to the solution of basic problems and to interpersonal relationships. Damasio (1994) reports patients who, after suffering frontal damage, despite maintaining a high intellectual coefficient, behave irrationally and do not measure the consequences of their actions. He concludes that emotion is a key element for learning, decision making, and moral behaviour.

In the study of emotions there are also several positions; for example, for the evolutionist theoreticians emotions are universal, affective programs that solve former and current traits of survival (Ekman, 1992; Haidt & Kelter, 1999; Lazarus, 1991b; Plutchik, 1980; Tooby & Cosmides, 1990). But for social constructivists, emotions are socially learned answers, built on processes of social discourse according to specific cultures concerning identity, morality, and social structure (Lutz & White, 1986).

During the last decade, research on biologic and evolutionist bases of emotion has increased significantly. As a matter of fact, a new term has been coined to refer to a new discipline: *affective neuroscience* (Davidson & Sutton, 1995), the objective of which is to investigate the biologic bases and the processes that lie behind the emotions and their changes. Based on the findings from the areas of affective neuroscience and evaluative neuroscience, it has been suggested that automatic emotional processes are determinant in moral behaviour, and the concept of moral emotions has been introduced (Greene & Haidt, 2002).

According to Haidt (2003), moral emotions differ from basic emotions (sadness, joy, anger, fear, surprise, disgust) in that they are intrinsically linked to the welfare interests of a society in terms of the welfare of individuals. In this way, moral emotions appear when individuals interact or when moral violations are perceived. It has been suggested that, unlike effortful deductive reasoning, they appear rapidly and automatically, and that there is cognitive assessment unconscious of interpersonal events. Haidt mentions that while basic emotions stem from ideas, imagination, recollection, or perception with immediate personal relevance, moral emotions are complex, and are linked to the interests or the welfare of societies as well as individuals. Additionally, moral emotions are evoked in circumstances that go beyond the sphere of the self. They are critical for promoting cohesion in groups. Guilt, gratitude, and compassion are examples of prosocial moral emotions. However, moral emotions like contempt, indignation, and xenophobia can also act to promote social dissolution and reorganization.

Haidt (2003) and Moll, Oliveira-Souza, and Eslinger (2003) propose that moral behaviour is instantiated by spontaneous implicit dispositions, and that moral emotions operate automatically and unconsciously. They point out that moral behaviour comes from a delicate balance between prosocial and altruistic behaviour on one hand, and antisocial behaviour on the other.

Moll et al. (2003) suggest that moral behaviour is the result of the evaluative pressure that makes up neurobehavioural processes related to the selective perception of social signals, the experience of moral emotions, and the adaptation of behavioural responses to the social environment. Thus, sensitivity, and social and moral cognition have been determinant in human evolution. Certain aptitudes, such as the assimilation of rules based on reward and punishment and the attribution of intentions, beliefs, feelings, and desires to other people, were developed in our primate and hominid ancestors (Kagan, 1984; Moll et al., 2003).

To date, moral emotions have not been clearly described; however, some authors (Eisenberg, 2000; Haidt, 2003) mention guilt, shame, empathy, compassion, and indignation as examples of this concept. Haidt (2003) mentions four subtypes of moral emotions:

1. *Emotions concerning others*: i.e., contempt, rage, displeasure.
2. *Self-conscious emotions*: i.e., shame, embarrassment, guilt.
3. *Emotions related to the suffering of others*: i.e., empathy.
4. *Emotions related to praising others*: i.e., gratitude, fear, elevation.

In the psychobiological aspect, many studies (Aguado, 2002; Berridge, 2003; Damasio, 1998; Hagemann, Waldstein, & Thayer, 2003; LeDoux, 1998; Panksepp, 2003) have been focused on determining which brain structures are involved in processing basic emotions. However, the biologic bases of social cognition and moral emotion are complex, and although the debate on the nature of morality in humans has gone on for many years, it is only recently that the neural organization of moral behaviour has been explored. These findings are mainly the result of the analysis and study of patients with changes in their social and moral behaviour as a consequence of acquired brain injuries, as well as the study of normal and pathologic behaviours with structural and functional neuroimaging (Dolan, 1999). In the case of patients with acquired brain damage, they seem to develop a condition called acquired sociopathy, which results from injury to specific brain sites, particularly the orbitomedial and frontopolar cortex, the anterior temporal lobe, the superomedial frontal lobe, and certain subcortical nuclei, particularly related to the amygdala, the hypothalamus, dorsomedial thalamus, and head of the caudate nucleus. Sociopathic behaviour has also been related to the polar frontal and orbitofrontal cortex (Damasio, 1994; Eslinger & Damasio, 1985; Goldberg, 2001; Moll et al., 2003).

Moreover, a dysfunction in the frontal lobe has been observed in some patients with sociomoral deterioration in emotions and behaviour; these patients show dissociation between social cognition and moral knowledge, that is to say, there is a lack of coherence between the understanding or moral rules and the behaviours they show (Anderson, Bechara, Damasio, Tranel, & Damasio, 1999; Eslinger & Damasio, 1985).

Exploration of the role of the regions of the prefrontal cortex to connect lymbic areas to the frontal regions is difficult; nevertheless, studies in humans with focal brain damage, and experimental injuries in monkeys have shown the relationship between the prefrontal cortex (PFC) and planning, decision making, emotions, attentions, spatiotemporal memory and acknowledgement. Damage to the ventral and medial prefrontal cortex is linked to the deterioration of moral type decision making. Patients with focal ventromedial injuries show flat (abnormal) responses when they see emotional pictures and perform poorly in tasks where feelings are required to make complex self-directed choices (Casebeer, 2003).

The above studies stress that a great part of human behaviour is moral and is the result of multiple processes, both psychological and neurobiological. Currently, these investigations aim to describe specific brain areas that participate in moral processing, in particular moral emotions.

Investigations carried out recently are intended to describe the participation of neural structures involved in stimuli processing (pictures, auditive phrases, etc.) with emotional load (pleasant, unpleasant, with no moral content, unpleasant with moral content, personal moral and interpersonal moral as well as neutrals) through the Functional Magnetic Resonance technique. The outcomes of these investigations (Greene & Haidt, 2002; Greene, Sommerville, Nystrom, Darley, & Cohen, 2001; Moll, Eslinger, & Oliveira-Souza, 2001; Moll, Oliveira-Souza, Bramati, & Grafman, 2002a; Moll, Oliveira-Souza, & Eslinger, 2002b) have shown that processing of stimuli with emotional load, in particular unpleasant and with or without moral content, triggers a common network of brain areas that include the amygdala, insula, thalamus, and midbrain. Nevertheless, the medial and posterior orbitofrontal cortex and the frontopolar and the posterior superior temporal sulcus (STS) are also involved in the processing of stimuli with moral-emotional load. These findings suggest the existence of a brain network specialized in the generation of moral emotions.

In conclusion, the study of emotions in the last decades has increased significantly—particularly the study of moral emotions, which had been previously dominated by rationalist or cognositivist theories—and has now drawn the attention of investigators in the field of affective neurosciences, thus starting to explore different types of moral emotions with different techniques, in particular neuroimaging techniques. However, to date it is not clear how the causative processes of moral emotions appear, since each of the theories tackled by their study finds explanations limited to each discipline; however, they agree that both moral behaviour and moral emotions are the result of the interaction of several factors. In the field of neurobiology, investigators have started to study neural correlates of moral emotions, and have encountered interesting findings indicating that the human brain shows a network specialized in moral processing. Nevertheless, there is still much left to explore. The use of techniques that allow the measurement and assessment at different processing levels (behavioural, psychophysiologic and cognoscitive processes) of how the appearance, processing and execution of moral emotions are carried out, will provide better conditions to explain them, both in normal and pathologic conditions, and will enable the development and implementation of rehabilitation programs adequate for patients who show problems in their moral behaviour as a consequence of brain damage.

REFERENCES

Aguado, L. (2002). Procesos cognitivos y sistemas cerebrales de la emoción. *Revista de Neurolgía, 34*, 1161–1170.

Anderson, S. W., Bechara, A., Damasio, H., Tranel, D., & Damasio, A. R. (1999). Impairment of social and moral behavior related to early damage in human prefrontal cortex. *Nature Neuroscience, 2*, 1032–1037.

Baron-Cohen, S. (1995). *Mindblindness. An essay on autism and theory of mind.* Cambridge, MA: MIT Press.

Berridge, K. C. (2003). Pleasures of the brain. *Brain and Cognition, 52*, 106–128.

Casebeer, W. D. (2003). Moral cognition and its neural constituents. *Nature Reviews Neuroscience, 4*, October.

Damasio, A. R. (1994). *El error de Descartes*. Barcelona: Andrés Bello.

Damasio, A. R. (1998). Emotion in the perspective of an integrated nervous system. *Brain Research, 26*, 83 86.

Davidson, R. J., & Sutton, S. D. (1995). Affective neuroscience: The emergence of a discipline. *Current Opinion in Neurobiology, 5*, 217–224.

Dolan, R. (1999). On the neurology of morals. *Nature Neuroscience, 2*, 927–929.

Eisenberg, N. (2000). Emotion, regulation, and moral development. *Annual Review of Psychology, 51*, 665–697.

Ekman, P. (1992). A set of basic emotions. *Psychological Review, 99*, 550–553.

Eslinger, P. J., & Damasio, A. R. (1985). Severe disturbance of higher cognition after bilateral frontal lobe ablation: Patient EVR. *Neurology, 35*, 1731–1741.

Fuller, C. J. (1992). *The camphor flame: Popular Hinduism and society in India.* Princeton, NJ: Princeton University Press.

Goldberg, E. (2001). *The executive brain. Frontal lobes and the civilized mind.* New York: Oxford University Press.
Greene, J., & Haidt, J. (2002). How (and where) does moral judgment work? *Trends in Cognitive Neuroscience, 6*, 517–523.
Greene, J., Sommerville, R. B., Nystrom, L. E., Darley, J. M., & Cohen, J. (2001). An fMRI investigation of emotional engagement in moral judgment. *Science, 293*, 2105–2108.
Hagemann, D., Waldstein, S., & Thayer, J. (2003). Central and autonomic nervous system integration in emotion. *Brain and Cognition, 52*, 79–87.
Haidt, J. (2001). The emotional dog and its rational tail: A social intuitionist approach to moral judgment. *Psychological Review, 108*, 804–834.
Haidt, J. (2003). The moral emotions. In R. J. Davidson, K. R. Scherer & H. H. Goldsmith (Eds.), *Handbook of affective sciences.* Oxford: Oxford University Press.
Haidt, J., & Kelter, D. (1999). Culture and facial expression: Open-ended methods fund more expressions and a gradient of recognition. *Cognition and Emotion, 13*, 225–266.
Haidt, J., Koller, S. H., & Dias, M. G. (1993). Affect, culture and morality, or is it wrong to eat your dog? *Journal of Personality and Social Psychology, 65*, 613–628.
Harrison, J. (1967). Ethical objectivism. In P. Edwards (Ed.), *The encyclopedia of philosophy, Vol. 3 & 4.* New York: Macmillan.
Kagan, J. (1984). *The nature of the child.* New York: Basic Books.
Kitwood, T. (1996). *La preocupación por los demás* (pp. 121–151). Bilbao, Spain: Descleé De Brouwer.
Kohlberg, L. (1969). Stage and sequence: The cognitive-developmental approach to socialization. In D. A. Goslin (Ed.), *Handbook of socialization theory and research* (pp. 347–480). Chicago: Rand McNally.
Kohlberg, L. (1982). *Psicologia del desarrollo moral.* Bilbao, Spain: Descleé de Brouwer.
Lazarus, R. S. (1991a). Ethical intuitionism II. *Philosofy, 46*, 1–11.
Lazarus, R. S. (1991b). *Emotion and adaptation.* New York: Oxford University Press.
LeDoux, J. (1998). Fear and the brain: Where have we been, and where are we going? *Biological Psychiatry, 44*, 1229–1238.
Lutz, C., & White, G. (1986). The anthropology of emotions. *Annual Review of Anthropology, 15*, 405–436.
Miller, J., Bersoff, D. M., & Harwood, R. L. (1990). Perceptions of social responsibilities in India and the United States: Moral imperatives or personal decisions? *Journal of Personality and Social Psychology, 58*, 33–47.
Moll, J., Eslinger, P., & Oliveira-Souza, R. (2001). Frontopolar and anterior temporal cortex activation in a moral judgment task. *Arquivos Neuropsiquiatria, 59*, 657–664.
Moll, J., Oliveira-Souza, R., Bramati, I. E., & Grafman, J. (2002a). Functional networks in emotional moral and nonmoral social judgment. *Neuroimage, 16*, 696–703.
Moll, J., Oliveira-Souza, R., & Eslinger, P. (2002b). The neural correlates of moral sentivity: A functional magnetic resonance imaging investigation of basic and moral emotions. *The Journal of Neuroscience, 22*, 2730–2736.
Moll, J., Oliveira-Souza, R., & Eslinger, P. (2003). Morals and the human brain: A working model. *NeuroReport, 14*, 299–305.
Nucci, L. (1981). Conceptions of personal issues: A domain distinct from moral or societal concepts. *Child Development, 52*, 114–121.
Nucci, L. (1997). Moral development and character formation. In H. J. Walberg & G. D. Haertel (Eds.), *Psychology and educational practice.* Berkeley, CA: MacCarchan.
Panksepp, J. (2003). At the interface of the affective, behavioral and cognitive neuroscience: Decoding the emotional feelings of the brain. *Brain and Cognition, 52*, 4–14.
Piaget, J. (1932). *The moral judgment of the child.* London: Routledge & Kegan Paul.
Piaget, J. (1969). *The psychology of the child.* London: Routledge & Kegan Paul.
Plutchik, R. (1980). *Emotion: A psychoevolutionary synthesis.* New York: Harper & Row.
Rest, J. (1984). The major components of morality. In W. Kurtinez & J. Gewirtz (Eds.), *Morality, moral behavior and moral development.* Miami, FL: Florida International University. A Wiley Interscience Publication.
Rozin, P., Loewry, D., Imada, S., & Haidt, J. (1999). The CAD triad hypothesis: A mapping between three moral emotions (contempt, anger, disgust) and three moral codes (community, autonomy, divinity). *Journal of Personality and Social Psychology, 76*, 574–586.
Schulkin, J. (2000). *Roots of social sensivity and neural function.* Cambridge, MA: MIT Press.
Shweder, R. A. (1990). In defense of moral realism: Reply to Gabennesch. *Child Development, 61*, 2060–2067.
Shweder, R., & Haidt, J. (1993). The future of moral psychology. *Psychological Science, 4*, 360–365.
Shweder, R. A., Mahapatra, M., & Millar, J. (1987). Culture and moral development. In J. Kagan & S. Lamb (Eds.), *The emergence of morality in young children.* Chicago: University of Chicago Press.
Shweder, R. A., & Sullivan, M. A. (1993). Cultural psychology: Who needs it? *Annual Review of Psychology, 44*, 497–523.
Tooby, J., & Cosmides, L. (1990). On the universality of human nature and the uniqueness of the individual: The role of genetics and adaptation. *Journal Personality, 58*, 17–67.
Turiel, E. (1983). *The development of social knowledge: Morality and convention.* Cambridge: Cambridge University Press.
Turiel, E., Hidebrandt, C., & Wainryb, C. (1991). Judging social issues: Difficulties, inconsistencies, and consistencies. *Monographs of the Society for Research in Child Development, 56*, 1–103.
Turiel, E., Killen, M., & Helwig, C. C. (1987). Morality: Its structure, function, and vagaries. In J. Kagan & S. Lamb (Eds.), *The emergence of morality in young children* (pp. 155–243). Chicago: University of Chicago Press.
Wilson, J. (1993). *The moral sense.* New York: Free Press.

INTERNATIONAL JOURNAL OF PSYCHOLOGY, 2006, 41 (5), 355–361

Ego-identity: Can it be reconstituted after a brain injury?

D. Biderman, E. Daniels-Zide, A. Reyes, and B. Marks

New York University, New York, USA

Cognitive alterations are frequently observed and studied in persons who present with psychiatric and neurological disorders. Recently an increased number of investigations on the self and attendant processes have interested psychologists, psychiatrists, and neuropsychologists, particularly when a person has suffered brain damage that upsets their daily function in economic, social, personal, behavioural, and emotional ways. At the same time, many theories have been developed to explain the observable changes in ego-identity of persons with brain injury as well as diverse rehabilitation programs centred on the re-establishment of the ego-identity changes. The present article focuses on: (1) the elucidation of the construct of self in current personality theoretical formulations; (2) the major negative effects of brain impairments on the cognitive, neurobehavioural, emotional, and personality functions of persons with brain injuries; (3) the conceptual underpinnings of Kurt Goldstein's views on the neuropsychological rehabilitation endeavour; (4) the illustration, using several clinical examples, that it is possible, following intensive neuropsychological rehabilitative interventions, to restore the shattered self of some brain-injured persons; and (5) the growing number of holistic programs of rehabilitation for brain-injured persons all over the world. In conclusion, the sequelae of brain injury not only imply alterations in neurological or cognitive process, but also involve changes in personality aspects. Nevertheless the number of holistic programs has increased, and a particular model of the holistic approach to the neuropsychological rehabilitation of persons with brain injury has been implemented in diverse countries such as Australia, Belgium, Denmark, England, Finland, France, Germany, Holland, Israel, Italy, South Africa, and the United States. Although each one of these programs has been modified to resolve the particular necessities and resources of the different countries, all of them implement Kurt Goldstein's ideas concerning the rehabilitation of persons with brain injuries.

Les altérations cognitives sont fréquemment observées et étudiées chez les personnes qui présentent des troubles psychiatriques et neurologiques. Récemment, un nombre croissant de recherches sur le moi et sur les processus connexes intéressent les psychologues, les psychiatres et les neuropsychiatres, particulièrement quand une personne souffre d'un dommage au cerveau qui perturbe son fonctionnement quotidien dans les aspects économique, social, personnel, comportemental et émotif. En même temps, plusieurs théories ont été développées pour expliquer les changements observables dans l'identité du moi des personnes avec une blessure au cerveau de même qu'avec divers programmes de réadaptation centrés sur le re-établissement des altérations de l'identité du moi. Le présent article se centre sur ce qui suit: (1) élucider le construit du self dans les formulations actuelles des théories de la personnalité; (2) identifier les effets négatifs majeurs des séquelles au cerveau sur les fonctions cognitive, neurocomportementale, émotionnelle et les fonctions de la personnalité des personnes avec une blessure au cerveau; (3) souligner les fondements conceptuels du point de vue de Kurt Goldstein sur l'effort de réadaptation neuropsychologique; (4) illustrer par divers exemples cliniques qu'il est possible, à la suite d'interventions de réadaptation neuropsychologique, de restaurer le self anéanti de certaines personnes avec une blessure au cerveau; et (5) attirer l'attention sur le nombre croissant de programmes holistiques de réadaptation pour les personnes avec une blessure au cerveau à travers le monde. En guise de conclusion, la séquelle de la blessure au cerveau implique non seulement des altérations dans le processus neurologique et cognitif, mais cela implique aussi des changements dans des aspects de la personnalité. Cependant, le nombre des programmes holistiques est en augmentation. Ces programmes, qui sont un modèle particulier de l'approche holistique à la réadaptation neuropsychologique des personnes ayant une blessure au cerveau, ont été implémentés dans divers pays comme l'Australie, la Belgique, le Danemark, l'Angleterre, la Finlande, la France, l'Allemagne, la Hollande, Israel, l'Italie, l'Afrique du Sud, et les États-Unis. Même si chacun de ces programmes a été modifié pour résoudre les nécessités et les ressources des différents pays, tous implémentent les idées de Kurt Goldstein concernant la réadaptation des personnes avec une blessure au cerveau.

Correspondence should be addressed to David Biderman, PhD, New York University Medical Center, 660 First Avenue, New York, NY 10016, USA (E-mail: david.biderman@nyumc.org).
The authors wish to thank Dr Ben-Yishay and Dr Diller for their helpful suggestions.

 DOI: 10.1080/00207590500345963

Las alteraciones cognitivas son frecuentes en personas con desordenes psiquiátricos y neurológicos. Recientemente se ha incrementado el número de investigaciones del "yo" y procesos psicológicos en personas con daño cerebral. Este daño afecta el funcionamiento cotidiano que impacta aspectos económicos, sociales, personales, conductuales y emocionales. Se han postulado diversas teorías para explicar los cambios observables en la identidad del "yo" en personas con daño cerebral y se han desarrollado programas de rehabilitación centrados en el reestablecimiento de alteraciones del "yo". El presente artículo se enfoca en: (1) elucidar sobre el constructo del "yo" en las formulaciones teóricas actuales de la personalidad: (2) señalar los efectos que tiene el daño cerebral sobre las funciones cognoscitivas, las neuroconductuales, las emocionales y aspectos de la personalidad; (3) destacar los puntos de vista conceptuales de Kurt Goldstein en la rehabilitación neuropsicológica; (4) ilustrar con ejemplos clínicos, las intervenciones en rehabilitación neuropsicológica encaminadas a restaurar el "yo" quebrantado de algunas personas con daño cerebral; y (5) atender al creciente número de programas holísticos de rehabilitación para personas con daño cerebral en todo el mundo. En conclusión, las secuelas del daño cerebral no solo implican alteraciones neurológicas o cognoscitivas, sino también involucran cambios en la personalidad. Se presenta un modelo particular de aproximación holística a la rehabilitación neuropsicológica el cual ha sido implementado en la rehabilitación de personas con daño cerebral en diversos países incluyendo: Australia, Bélgica, Dinamarca, Inglaterra, Finlandia, Alemania, Holanda, Israel, Italia, Sudáfrica, y Estados Unidos. Cada uno de esos programas ha sido adaptado a las necesidades particulares de cada país, se presentan los resultados de estas adaptaciones.

BACKGROUND

The construct of "self"

Personality theorists today have an increased interest in the self and its attendant processes. The construct of self has been invoked to differentiate it from the general term "ego," which has been used to denote different aspects of conscious life and interpreted by different personality theorists to mean different things.

Hilgard (1962) expressed the need for the concept of self so that personality theorists could have "some kind of unifying principle" (p. 491). Carl Rogers (1947), who termed this the self-image, included in this construct "all the ways in which the individual perceives himself... (and) the qualities, abilities, impulses, and attitudes" one attributes to one's personality. But the most elaborate treatment of the construct of self has been that of Erik Erikson, who termed it ego-identity (1950, 1958, 1959). The Eriksonian concept of ego-identity has a multiplicity of meanings, which have been systematically described by Yankelovich and Barret (1970).

Accordingly, the concept of ego-identity has three distinguishing components: (1) identity as the synthesis of all the imitations; (2) identity as the persistence of the sense of sameness within oneself through life; and (3) identity as self-definition. Each component is briefly described below.

Identity as imitation. The imitative aspects of ego-identity are routed in the psychological mechanism of the young child: For example, when the 2-year-old girl puts on her mother's hat or her shoes, and declares "I am mommy!" As the child matures, the imitations become more complex, such as "when a (4–5 years old) little girl scolds her doll in the way she herself is scolded, but without adopting her mother's (voice or her) mannerisms" (Yankelovich & Barret, 1970, p. 123), and so on. As the child reaches adolescence, the various imitations become fused "by the (process of) synthesizing ego (which) consolidates them and forges them into a unity and transforms them to create the unique sense of self known as ego-identity" (p. 124). Following adolescence, the process of imitation assumes increasingly more subtle forms, such as the imitative dress "codes" and mannerisms of teenagers, or the—similarly emulative—declarations by college students of their allegiance to various social or political values.

Identity as a sense of continuity. The second component of ego-identity is the experience of "the sense of a persistent sameness within one self," i.e., the subjective sense of coherent memories of one's "self as a stable structure that endures in time" (Yankelovich & Barret, 1970, p. 127). This sense of continuity enables the individual to claim that it has always been the same "me" through the years; from childhood to adulthood.

Identity as self-definition. According to Erikson, as the person reaches adulthood, the ego-identity metamorphoses into two complementary versions of self-definition. One version of self-definition is quite similar to what Jean Paul Sartre meant by the now well-known assertion: "First a person exists and then he defines himself." This notion of self-definition also fits in well with the view of Epictetus the Greek Stoic philosopher (1st and 2nd century AD), who declared: "You should explicitly identify the kind of person you aspire to become. What are your personal ideas? Whom do you admire? What are their special traits that you would make your own?" (Lebell, 1994). The second—the transcendent version of self-definition according to Erikson (1950), was exemplified by George Bernard Shaw's assertion that his identification was always with the "mighty dead," by which he meant to say that he identified with and wished to emulate famous historical figures. Yankelovich and Barrett (1970) thus summarized this aspect of Erikson's ego-identity as "a form of transcendence, a way of reaching beyond one's own self and even beyond the limits of one's own times and culture" (p. 133).

However, though normally the ego-identity can and does endure over time, Erikson (1956) cautioned us not to take this sense of continuity for granted. For, under certain pathologic conditions, it can be disrupted. He cited his experiences during World War II with persons who suffered from what, at the time, was identified as "combat fatigue." Erikson wrote: "what impressed me most was the loss in these men of a sense of identity. They knew who they were ...But it was as if subjectively their lives no longer hung together—and never would again" (p. 38).

Similar to Erikson's notion concerning the dissolution of ego-identity is Laing's (1962) observation that certain individuals with psychiatric conditions exhibit what he termed "ontological insecurity." This is characterized by generalized feelings of unreality; a blurred sense of selfhood; a lack of temporal continuity; diminished awareness of personal cohesiveness; feelings of being partly divorced from one's body; and feelings of "emptiness."

Whether or not an individual has a positive or negative ego-identity (or self-image) is consequential in terms of important aspects of life. Thus, Tucker-Ladd (1996), in his comprehensive review of the literature from the positive psychology movement, repeatedly points out the correlations between positive self-concept and wellness. Cross and Morris (2003) have shown that college students with high relational self-construal (i.e., those whose sense of self depends on the quality and quantity of relationships with others) possessed a greater ability to predict how their roommates felt. They also tended to be more optimistic in nature than did students whose self-construal was based on nonrelational factors. Similarly, Kling, Ryff, Love, and Essex (2003) reported the existence of strong relationships between openness, extraversion, and self-esteem and positive or negative aspects of adjustment to changes in specific life circumstances. Examining the role of positive self-image in psychotherapy, with non-brain-injured individuals, Kelly (2000) pointed out that one of the most important factors in the ability to benefit from psychotherapy is in clients whose self-identity indicates the perception that their therapist has a favourable view of them. Likewise, Hemenover (2003) reported that writing about a traumatic life event increased positive self-perception and self-acceptance; and it decreased distress.

But aspects of ego-identity also play a role in "optimizing" recovery from illness. Thus, for example, Thorpe and Barsky (2001) called attention to the fact that the capacity for self-reflection contributed to the healing of sick women. Whitmarsh, Koutantji, and Sidell (2003) reported that the best predictor of attendance in cardiac rehabilitation was the belief of the person that they could control certain events by their actions. Similarly, Dantas, Motzer, and Ciol (2002) examined the relationships between the sense of coherence (of the self) and the self-esteem and quality of life of these patients after coronary artery bypass surgery.

Sequelae of brain impairment

Although the precise person variables and the conditions under which the ego-identity will become negatively affected by acquired brain injuries is yet to be established, clinical experience as well as research have shown that brain injuries have a major impact on the ego-identity. Depending on the locus, nature, and severity of brain injury, a multiplicity of deficits will occur in different permutations. Ben-Yishay and Prigatano (1989) have listed the most commonly occurring generic impairments of brain functioning, each of which can produce different symptomatic manifestations. The most common generic impairments are: (1) disturbances in the balance between excitatory and inhibitory processes; (2) disturbances in basic attentional functions; (3) impairments of perceptual–spatial–integrative functions; (4) impairments in the speed and efficiency of information processing; (5) impairments in language and communications skills; (6) thinking disorders; (7) inadequate awareness; (8) affective disturbances; and (9) damaged self-esteem and ego-identity.

Several studies are relevant in this context. Kay, Newman, Cavallo, Ezrachi, and Resnick (1992) reported that even after mild traumatic brain injury a shallow sense of self would typically be observed. This shallow sense of self is usually associated with the loss of predictability (of the person's future) and the impairment of the sense of control over one's self and the environment. Secrest and Zeller (2003) have likewise shown that strong relationships could be demonstrated between the experience of continuity of the sense-of-self of persons who sustained a stroke; and also that the sense of continuity correlated with the degree of independence, control, and relatedness of the patients with others. Hill (1999) articulated the notion that one of the tasks of rehabilitation should be to assist the brain-injured individual to rebuild his or her sense of identity based on exploring the individual's new possibilities and capacities, rather than focusing on attempts to restore the pre-injury ego-identity of those individuals. Similarly, Taylor, Swedlung, and Nosek (2004) have found that it was possible to enhance the self-esteem of women with various physical disabilities by means of special interventions. Finally, Nochi (2000) argued that self-narratives of coping ability of individuals with brain injuries have helped improve their self-image.

Kurt Goldstein's ideas about the rehabilitation process

Goldstein (1942, 1952, 1959), who was described as "the father of modern neuropsychology," had some definite ideas about the rehabilitation of individuals who sustained brain injuries. These can be summarized as follows:

1. When it is impossible to restore the organism to its full, preinjury integrity, providing the individual with structure and order will minimize the chances that the person will experience catastrophic responses. This will make it possible for the person to feel that he or she is "healthy."
2. A catastrophic response has all the characteristics of severe anxiety.
3. To achieve the feeling that one is healthy requires a transformation of personality that enables the injured individual to accept the need for living with restrictions, without feeling victimized, and to emerge feeling that life is worth living.
4. Living in an environment that has been structured and ordered by others limits, by necessity, both that person's functional autonomy and his or her lifestyle. Acceptance of living with such restrictions, thus, can be achieved only if the individual makes a conscious and voluntary choice to do so.
5. It is therefore the rehabilitation professional's task to help the individual realize that, in order to attain the feeling that he or she is healthy, the individual must accept living with restrictions (i.e., limitations of his or her freedom to engage in certain activities, or make certain life choices).
6. Due to the impairments of both the cognitive and emotional functions of the person with brain injury, a particular task of therapy is to help the person become aware of and understand the nature and the functional consequences of his or her problems as much as is possible. Awareness and understanding of one's limitations can help motivate the individual to participate in the therapy (i.e., rehabilitative activities) and to accept the limitations that have resulted from the brain injury.
7. A further consequence for therapeutic interventions is that, in attempting to rehabilitate the brain-injured person, we must decide which symptoms can be remedially tackled and which should be left alone.
8. Finally, it is important to examine which of the many psychotherapeutic approaches and techniques that have been found to be useful with neurologically intact individuals are also suitable for individuals with brain impairments.

Possibility of restoring the ego-identity following neuropsychological rehabilitation

Goldstein's (1942, 1952, 1959) concepts have been the guiding principles of the New York University Medical Center, Rusk Institute's day program for holistic neuropsychological rehabilitation, which was founded and articulated by Ben-Yishay and associates (Ben-Yishay, 1996, 1999; Ben-Yishay & Diller, 1981; Ben-Yishay & Gold, 1990; Ben-Yishay et al., 1977, 1985; Ben-Yishay & Lakin, 1989; Ben-Yishay & Prigatano, 1989; Prigatano & Ben-Yishay, 1999; Zide & Ben-Yishay, 1999).

The basic premise of this brain-injury rehabilitation program is that to achieve success, i.e., to optimize the outcomes of the neurorehabilitative process, interventions should proceed in a definite order. Thus, the clinical "landmarks" of this systematic approach are as follows:

1. The patient is helped to become aware of and capable of understanding the impact of his or her various deficits on his or her functional life.
2. The patient is actively assisted (and trained) to become optimally malleable to the interventions of trained rehabilitation specialists (and, later on, of significant others).
3. The patient undergoes intensive cognitive remedial training procedures and specially adapted, psychotherapeutic intervention aimed at helping them to achieve optimal levels of compensation (for those impairments that lend themselves to remediation).
4. The patient undergoes specific therapeutic interventions capable of aiding in the process of reconstituting his or her impaired ego-identity; hence, to find new meaning in life at the cessation of the rehabilitation process.

Three persons who, prior to sustaining severe, incapacitating brain injuries, had achieved highly successful professional careers illustrate the possibility of reconstituting one's ego-identity and finding new meaning in life after a brain injury. These three individuals underwent intensive rehabilitation, over a period of 1 year, in a therapeutic community type of program. They have each attained self-acceptance and have volunteered to serve as peer counsellors (i.e., role models) to new patients who have just began their rehabilitation.

Each of these persons' narratives is summarized by excerpts from their videotaped assertions in front of a patient peer group.

Case illustration 1: Martin (not his real name)

Martin was a 46-year-old physician whose severe brain injuries were the result of encephalitis of unknown aetiology.

Understanding the nature and functional sequelae of his brain impairments. "My injury occurred about 4 years ago ... At the time, I was practicing medicine in my private practice and became abruptly ill ... My illness was an encephalitis of some sort, an inflammation of the brain (which was never determined precisely why it happened) ... At any rate, my illness caused many disabling problems which made it necessary that I enter different rehabilitation programs..."

Self-definition. "First of all, I am the same person who is sitting in front of you ... I feel, in general, that I am a whole person. I don't look at myself as somebody who has a brain injury ... I don't look at myself as separate from the person I was in the past ... As a result of (my rehabilitation) there has been a synthesis ... I have been able to learn enough to function as best I can, both cognitively and interpersonally ... I feel OK."

Finding new meaning in his present life. "... I think (that) I am fortunate in having a loving and supportive family ... Being able to function with my wife and my two children, gives the ultimate meaning to my life as it is today ... However, that would not be successful without employing all the compensations I learned here ... The second part (of what gives meaning to my life) is the opportunity to ... function as a peer counsellor ... that I am able to (share) the knowledge that (I gained) with others that are struggling to (regain their) self-esteem and the ability to function ... (Being a peer counsellor) gives a lot back to me ... the ability to help somebody else ... supports my own self-esteem."

Case illustration 2: Robert (not his real name)

Robert was a 57-year-old successful attorney and a highly respected community leader. He became disabled following several successive strokes.

Understanding the nature and functional sequelae of his brain impairments. "I was a practicing lawyer and I had two hobbies I loved. The first was skiing. The second was fishing. Six year ago, while I was skiing, I had a stroke on the slopes ... but that (was) a minor stroke (only) ... That should have been a warning, but I did not heed it. A year later, I was on my boat ... fishing (and) I had my second stroke ... (which) disabled me physically and also mentally somewhat ... The consequences were that I have a left-sided paresis and dysarthria which prevents me to speak clearly ... I went through several types of rehabilitation programs ... But ... I felt that some things were missing. So, one day ... I heard about this program. I came, visited and said: this is it for me ... They take care of the whole person. Not just the arm, the leg, or the speech (but) the whole person."

Self-definition. "To answer the question (who I am today), we have to go back to who I was before. In a way I am the same person. I still seek happiness, but in a different way. Before the stroke, I used to look for happiness in a material way. I had a boat, went skiing, and travelled as much as (was) possible ... the basic thing is (that) I am still seeking for happiness (but now) I realize that happiness does not come from things. It comes from within (from the satisfaction of being a peer counsellor (which is the reason I come here) because coming here helps me to feel happy."

Finding meaning in his present life. "I find that as I progress in life, I find a need to fulfil myself. I need to be of service. And being a peer counsellor serves that need ... I take this program very seriously because it is very important to me ... I devote all my energies to my 'job' of peer counsellor. (For if) I did not stick to it, I would be cheating myself ... (so) it makes me happy to (be of) service."

Case illustration 3: Carl (not his real name)

Carl was a 40-year-old successful corporate lawyer. He suffered a severely incapacitating stroke.

Understanding the nature and functional sequelae of his brain injury. "While I was on a leave of absence from my job ... I had a sudden aneurism which turned into a massive stroke ... I have no recollection of the stroke. I only remember waking up from a coma ... The immediate consequences were on the physical level, a left-sided paresis. And, cognitively, I was very deficient in a number of ways."

Self-definition. "Carl is somebody who is functioning (on) two different (levels) at the same time. On the spiritual plane, Carl is beyond definition (He is) not a lawyer, not a peer counsellor, not a rehabilitant. The Carl that was, is, and will always be ... is not different from other (human beings) ... On a more physical plane, on the real-life plane, Carl is an individual who ... realizes that 'everything I need is right here in the moment. I happen to be very fortunate in having an opportunity to spend a lot of my time with people who are doing some very honourable work ... I have a functional life, I manage my affairs quite competently, I have a variety of interests ... I am a happy guy'."

Finding meaning in his present life. "Meaning does not come from external circumstances ... I have been through too many difficult external (situations) ... Meaning (to me) comes from simply being relaxed as (to) who I am ... Right now I happen to be in a pleasant (atmosphere), I am healthy, I have a 'job' (i.e., that of peer counsellor), I have friends ... and these provide meaning in my life at present."

CONCLUSION

The growing number of holistic programs in the world

During the past two decades the New York University Rusk Institute Day Program (which serves as the model of the holistic approach to the neuropsychological rehabilitation of brain-injured persons) has inspired the establishment of similar programs in many countries, such as (in alphabetic order): Australia, Belgium, Denmark, England, Finland, France, Germany, Holland, Israel, Italy, South Africa, and in several other locations in the United States.

Although each of these programs has been modified to accommodate the needs and resources of the different countries, they all subscribe to Kurt Goldstein's ideas concerning the rehabilitation of persons with brain injuries.

REFERENCES

Alport, G. W. (1961). *Pattern and growth in personality.* New York: Holt Rinehart & Winston.

Ben-Yishay, Y. (1996). Reflections on the evolution of the therapeutic milieu concept. *Neuropsychological Rehabilitation, 6*, 327–343.

Ben-Yishay, Y. (1999). Postacute neuropsychological rehabilitation. In A. L. Christensen & B. Uzzell (Eds.), *International handbook of neuropsychological rehabilitation* (pp. 131–139). New York: Kluwer Academic/Plenum.

Ben-Yishay, Y., Ben-Nachum, Z., Cohen, A., Gross, Y., Hoffien, D., Rattock, J., & Diller, L. (1977). Digest of a two-year comprehensive clinical research program for out-patient head-injured Israeli veterans. In Y. Ben-Yishay (Ed.), NYU Medical Center *Rehabilitation Monographs, 59*, 1–66.

Ben-Yishay, Y., & Diller, L. (1981). Rehabilitation of cognitive and perceptual defects in people with traumatic brain damage. *International Journal of Rehabilitation Research, 4*, 208–210.

Ben-Yishay, Y., & Diller, L. (1993). Cognitive remediation in traumatic brain injury: Update and issues. *Archives of Physical and Medical Rehabilitation, 74*, 204–213.

Ben-Yishay, Y., & Gold, J. (1990). Therapeutic milieu approach to neuropsychological rehabilitation. In R. L. Wood (Ed.), *Neurobehavioural sequelae of traumatic brain injury* (pp. 194–215). London: Taylor & Francis.

Ben-Yishay, Y., & Lakin, P. (1989). Structured group treatment for brain-injury survivors. In D. W. Ellis & A. L. Christensen (Eds.), *Neuropsychological treatment after brain injury* (pp. 271–295). Boston: Kluwer Academic.

Ben-Yishay, Y., & Prigatano, G. (1989). Cognitive remediation. In M. Rosenthal, E. R. Griffith, M. R. Bond, & J. D. Miller (Eds.), *Rehabilitation of the adult and child with traumatic brain injury*. Philadelphia: F. A. Davis.

Ben-Yishay, Y., Rattock, J., Lakin, P., Piasetsky, E., Ross, B., Silver, S. L., Zide, E., & Ezrachi, O. (1985). Neuropsychological rehabilitation: The quest for a holistic approach. *Seminars in Neurology*, *5*, 252–259.

Cross, S. E., & Morris, M. L. (2003). Getting to know you: The relational self-construal, relational cognition, and well being. *Personality and Social Psychology Bulletin*, *29*, 512–523.

Dantas, R. A., Motzer, S. A., & Ciol, M. A. (2002). The relationship between quality of life, sense of coherence and self-esteem in persons after coronary artery bypass graft surgery. *International Journal of Nursing Studies*, *39*, 745–755.

Erikson, E. H. (1950). *Childhood and society*. New York: W. W. Norton.

Erikson, E. H. (1958). *Young man Luther*. New York: W. W. Norton.

Erikson, E. H. (1959). Identity and the life cycle. *Psychological Issues*, *1*, 102–110. New York: International University Press.

Goldstein, K. (1942). *After-effects of brain injuries in war: Their evaluation and treatment*. New York: Grune & Straton.

Goldstein, K. (1952). *The effects of brain damage on the personality*. Presented at the annual meeting of the American Psychoanalytic Association, Atlantic City, NJ.

Goldstein, K. (1959). Notes on the development of my concepts. *Journal of Individual Psychology*, *15*, 5–14.

Hemenover, S. H. (2003). The good, the bad and the healthy: Impacts of emotional disclosure of trauma on resilient self-concept and psychological distress. *Personality and Social Psychology Bulletin*, *2*, 1236–1244.

Hilgard, E. R. (1962) *Introduction to psychology* (3rd ed.). New York: Harcourt, Brace & World.

Hill, H. (1999). Traumatic brain injury: A view from the inside. *Brain Injury*, *13*, 839–844.

Kay, T., Newman, B., Cavallo, M., Ezrachi, O., & Resnick, N. (1992). Towards a neuropsychological model of functional disability after mild traumatic brain injury. *Neuropsychology*, *6*, 371–385.

Kelly, A. E. (2000). Helping construct desirable identities: A self-presentational view of psychotherapy. *Psychological Bulletin*, *126*, 475–494.

Kling, K. C., Ryff, C. D., Love, G., & Essex, M. (2003). Exploring the influence of personality on depressive symptoms and self-esteem across a significant life transition. *Journal of Personality and Social Psychology*, *85*, 922–932.

Laing, R. O. (1962). *Ontological insecurity in psychoanalysis and existential philosophy*. New York: E. P. Dutton.

Lebell, S. (1994). *A manual for living. Epictetus—a new interpretation*. San Francisco: Harper.

Nochi, M. (2000). Reconstructing self-narratives in coping with traumatic brain injury. *Social Science and Medicine*, *51*, 1795–1804.

Prigatano, G., & Ben-Yishay, Y. (1999). Psychotherapy and psychotherapeutic interventions in brain-injury rehabilitation. In M. Rosenthal (Ed.), *Rehabilitation of the adult and child with traumatic brain-injury*. (3rd ed.). Philadelphia: F. A. Davis.

Rogers, C. R. (1947). Some observations on the organization of personality. *American Psychologist*, *2*, 358–368.

Secrest, J. S., & Zeller, A. (2003). Measuring continuity and discontinuity following stroke. *Journal of Nursing Scholarship*, *35*, 243–247.

Taylor, H. B., Swedlung, N., & Nosek, A. (2004). Enhancing self-esteem in women with physical disabilities. *Rehabilitation Psychology*, *49*, 295–302.

Thorpe, K., & Barsky, J. (2001). Healing through self-reflection. *Journal of Advanced Nursing*, *35*, 760–768.

Tucker-Ladd, C. E. (1996). Psychological self-help. *Mental Health Net*. http://www.mentalhealth.net/psyhelp/

Whitmarsh, A., Koutantji, M., & Sidell, K. (2003). Illness perceptions, mood and coping in predicting attendance of cardiac rehabilitation. *British Journal of Health Psychology*, *8*, 209–221.

Yankelovich, D., & Barrett, W. (1970). *Ego and instinct*. New York: Random House.

Zide, E., & Ben-Yishay, Y. (1999). Therapeutic milieu day program. In A. L. Christensen & B. Uzzell (Eds.), *International handbook of neuropsychological rehabilitation*. New York: Kluwer Academic/Plenum.

Holistic neuropsychological rehabilitation in Finland: The INSURE program—a transcultural outgrowth of perspectives from Israel to Europe via the USA

Jaana M. Sarajuuri and Sanna K. Koskinen

Käpylä Rehabilitation Centre, Helsinki, Finland

Given the interaction of cognitive, behavioural, psychological, and physical factors resulting from traumatic brain injury (TBI), a comprehensive, multidisciplinary, and neuropsychologically oriented rehabilitation could prove to be particularly promising and efficacious in the neuropsychological rehabilitation of post-acute brain-injured individuals. Kurt Goldstein, an eminent pioneer in the development of holistic rehabilitation, stated that brain-injured patients need environments that help them to avoid catastrophic reactions. In his view, the tasks of rehabilitation are to create, for the brain-injured individual, an environment that will minimize the chances for the occurrence of catastrophic responses. In this environment, the individual can engage optimally in various remedial activities, which will gradually culminate in the individual finding new meaning in life after rehabilitation. Yehuda Ben-Yishay incorporated many of Goldstein's ideas and developed a milieu or holistic rehabilitation program in 1978 in New York. The emerging role of psychotherapy for patients and their family members was characteristic of the Neuropsychological Rehabilitation Program that Prigatano established in 1980 in Oklahoma. In Europe, Anne-Lise Christensen, who was also influenced by the work of A. R. Luria, started a holistic program at Copenhagen University in 1985. Based on these pioneering programs, several similar programs were established in Europe. A Finnish program, INSURE, was established in 1993 in Helsinki. The INSURE program is a post-acute, interdisciplinary, 6-week rehabilitation program for selected groups of TBI patients. The core of the program is neuropsychological rehabilitation and psychotherapy with vocational interventions, and follow-up support. In recent years, a holistic rehabilitation program was also established in Turku for children with acquired brain injury. The European Holistic Working Group was founded in 2001, and the authors will also discuss their personal experiences and future of holistic neurospychological rehabilitation in terms of ongoing research work, computer-administered cognitive remediation, and quality of life assessment.

Les lésions cérébrales traumatiques du cerveau LCT se traduisent par une interaction de facteurs cognitifs, comportementaux, psychologiques, et physiques. Par conséquent, une réadaptation compréhensive, multidisciplinaire et orientée vers la neuropsychologie pourrait mieux servir les personnes avec LCT. En effet, la réadaptation neuropsychologique semble particulièrement prometteuse et efficace chez les individus avec une blessure au cerveau en état post-aigu. Kurt Goldstein, un pionnier éminent dans le développement de la réadaptation holistique, a déclaré que les patients ayant une blessure au cerveau ont besoins d'environnements qui les aident à éviter les réactions catastrophiques. Selon lui, les tâches de la réadaptation sont de créer, pour les personnes avec une blessure au cerveau, un environnement qui minimisera les chances d'émergence de réponses catastrophiques. Dans cet environnement, l'individu peut s'engager de manière optimale dans diverses activités thérapeutiques qui culmineront graduellement dans la découverte par l'individu d'un nouveau sens a sa vie après la réadaptation. Yehuda Ben-Yishay a incorporé beaucoup des idées de Goldstein et a développé un milieu ou un programme de réadaptation holistique en 1978 a New York. Le rôle émergent de la psychothérapie pour les patients et les membres de leur famille était une caractéristique du Pogramme de Réadaptation Neuropsychologique établi en 1980 par Prigatano in Oklahoma. En Europe, Anne-Lise Christensen, influencée elle aussi par les travaux de A.R. Luria, a commencé un programme holistique à l'Université Coppenhagen en 1985. En se fondant sur ces programmes pionniers, de similaires programmes ont été établis en Europe. Un programme finlandais, INSURE, a été établi en 1993 à Helsinki. Le programme INSURE est un programme de

Correspondence should be addressed to Jaana Sarajuuri, Käpylä Rehabilitation Centre, Nordenskiöldinkatu 18 B, PO Box 103, FIN-00251 HELSINKI, Finland (E-mail: jaana.sarajuuri@invalidiliitto.fi).

The authors thank Prof. Yehuda Ben-Yishay, PhD, Rusk Institute of Rehabilitation Medicine, NYU Medical Center, New York, for his support and very helpful comments on the manuscript.

 DOI: 10.1080/01650250500346103

réadaptation poste-aigu, interdisciplinaire et d'une durée de 6 semaines destiné à des groupes sélectes de patients LCT. La réadaptation neuropsychologique et la psychothérapie avec des interventions vocationnelles et avec un soutien de suivi sont au cœur de ce programme. Dans les dernières années, un programme de réadaptation holistique a été également établi en Turquie pour les enfants souffrant d'une lésion cérébrale acquise. Le Groupe de Travail Européen holistique a été fondé en 2001. Dans le cadre de ce groupe de travail, les auteurs vont aussi discuter de leurs expériences personnelles et de l'avenir de la réadaptation holistique neuropsychologique en termes de travaux de recherche en cours, du traitement cognitif administré par ordinateur et de l'évaluation de la qualité de vie.

En los traumatismo craneoencefálico (TCE), se presenta una interacción de factores cognoscitivos, conductuales, psicológicos y físicos. Los programas de rehabilitación comprensivos, multidisciplinarios y orientados neuropsicológicamente son los mas efectivos para la rehabilitación neuropsicológica de individuos con daño cerebral posagudo. Kurt Goldstein, un pionero en el desarrollo de rehabilitación holística, estableció que los pacientes con daño cerebral requieren un medio ambiente controlado que les ayuden a evitar las reacciones catastróficas. Es por ello que los programas de rehabilitación incluyen: un ambiente en el que se minimicen las oportunidades de respuestas catastróficas y en donde el individuo pueda participar óptimamente en varias actividades remediales que gradualmente culminen en la creación de un nuevo sentido de vida después de la rehabilitación. Yehuda Ben-Yishay incorporó muchas de las ideas de Goldstein y desarrolló un programa de rehabilitación holístico en 1978 en Nueva York. El papel emergente de la psicoterapia para pacientes y sus familiares fue característico del Programa de Rehabilitación Neuropsicológico que Prigatano estableció en 1980 en Oklahoma. En Europa Anne-Lise Christensen, basándose en el trabajo de A.R. Luria, inició un programa holístico en la Universidad de Copenhague en 1985. El programa Finlandés, INSURE, se estableció en 1993 en Helsinki. INSURE, es un programa de rehabilitación interdisciplinario con duración de 6 semanas. Este programa fue diseñado para grupos seleccionados de pacientes con TCE. Su propósito es la rehabilitación neuropsicológica y la psicoterapia con intervenciones vocacionales, y con apoyo de seguimiento. En años recientes, un programa similar para niños con daño cerebral adquirido se estableció en Turku. El Grupo de Trabajo Holístico Europeo fue fundado en 2001.Los autores discuten sus experiencias personales y el futuro de la rehabilitación neuropsicológica que incorpora tanto la rehabilitación cognoscitiva computarizada como la evaluación de la calidad de vida.

BACKGROUND

Traumatic brain injury (TBI) is a heterogeneous disorder, and different forms of rehabilitation are needed for different subgroups of patients and at different phases over the course of recovery in order to optimize outcomes (Consensus Conference,1999; Cope, 1995; Eames & Wood, 1989). During the past 25 years, there have been considerable improvements in TBI rehabilitation services.

Given the interaction of cognitive, behavioural, psychological, and physical factors resulting from TBI, a convincing argument has been made that persons with TBI are best served by a comprehensive, multidisciplinary, and neuropsychologically oriented rehabilitation. In the practice of neuropsychological rehabilitation we need to help patients with the following challenges: understanding the nature of their neuropsychological disturbances; remediating cognitive and neurobehavioural impairments, thus compensating for functional deficits that were caused by the brain injury; and making choices that will enhance the quality of their lives. To adequately address these issues, neuropsychological rehabilitation should be holistic (Prigatano, 2004).

The main elements of holistic programs consist of creating a therapeutic milieu within which individual and group remedial and therapeutic interventions, including family education and guidance, are followed by supported work trials. Then, after discharge from active rehabilitation, rehabilitants are followed up and their adjustment is systematically monitored. The effectiveness of systematic and holistic neuropsychologically oriented TBI rehabilitation programs in enhancing patients' productivity status has been supported by uncontrolled studies and a few studies with control groups (Ben-Yishay, Silver, Piasetsky, & Rattok, 1987; Christensen, Pinner, Moller Pedersen, Teasdale, & Trexler, 1992; Prigatano et al., 1994; Sarajuuri, Kaipio, Koskinen, Niemalä, Servo, & Vilkki, 2005). A comprehensive review article by Cicerone and associates (2000) formed the basis of evidence-based recommendations for neuropsychological rehabilitation. The authors have singled out the holistic approach as being particularly promising and efficacious in the neuropsychological rehabilitation of post-acute brain-injured individuals.

In the history of holistic neuropsychological rehabilitation, Kurt Goldstein can be said to be the eminent pioneer. While working with brain-injured soldiers during World War I he built up a renowned clinic for them in Germany. He stated that brain-injured patients need environments that help them to avoid catastrophic reactions. A catastrophic response is the behavioural manifestation of the brain-injured person's experience of failure to cope in particular situations. It bears all the hallmarks of severe anxiety. In Goldstein's view, therefore, the tasks of rehabilitation are to create an environment for the brain-injured individual that will minimize the chances for the occurrence of catastrophic responses. Within such an environment, the individual could engage optimally in various remedial activities, which will gradually culminate in the individual's finding new meaning in life after rehabilitation (Goldstein, 1942, 1959).

Yehuda Ben-Yishay incorporated many of Goldstein's ideas and developed a milieu or holistic rehabilitation program—the New York University Head Trauma Program—which has been in existence since 1978. Even before that he had the opportunity to translate the idea of holistic rehabilitation into practice with Israeli soldiers who had sustained head injuries in the early 1970s (Ben-Yishay, 1996). In his holistic day program, patients undergo intensive, systematic, and well-coordinated remedial and therapeutic interventions (modified to the brain-injured patient's needs and abilities) designed to restore their ability to function, as well as to help them deal with intrapersonal and interpersonal difficulties (Ben-Yishay, 2001; Ben-Yishay & Daniels-Zide, 2000; Ben-Yishay et al., 1985).

The emerging role of psychotherapy for patients and their family members was characteristic of the Neuropsychological Rehabilitation Program, which Prigatano established in 1980 in Oklahoma and after that in Phoenix in 1986 (Prigatano, Fordyce, Zeiner, Roueche, Pepping, & Wood, 1986).

In Europe, Anne-Lise Christensen, who was also influenced by the work of A. R. Luria, started a holistic program at Copenhagen University in 1985 (Christensen, 2000).

Based on these pioneering programs a Finnish program was established in 1993 in the Käpylä Rehabilitation Centre in Helsinki. The INSURE program (Individualized Neuropsychological Subgroup Rehabilitation Program) is a post-acute, interdisciplinary, 6-week rehabilitation program for selected groups of TBI patients. The core of the program is neuropsychological rehabilitation and psychotherapy (Kaipio, Sarajuuri, & Koskinen, 2000). In recent years, a holistic rehabilitation program was established in Turku, Finland, for children with acquired brain injury. In the HOPE program, rehabilitation of children aims at activating the resources needed for building their future. Skills needed in everyday life are rehearsed individually and in small groups. Rehabilitation tries to strengthen self-knowledge, social, and learning skills, and also supports age-appropriate development. Solution-oriented and family therapeutic methods, as well as psychological counselling and neuropsychotherapy, are applied (Mäki & Honkinen, 2004).

Based on the pioneering programs of Ben-Yishay, Prigatano, and Christensen, several similar programs were established in Europe. To exchange ideas, to compare outcome results, and to share novel approaches to treatment, the European Holistic Working Group was founded in 2001 on the occasion of the 10th anniversary of the German-Asklepios program. The second meeting took place in 2003 in the Netherlands, where the Rehabilitation Centre of Amsterdam celebrated the 5th anniversary of its program. Then, in 2004, another meeting was organized by the Käpylä Rehabilitation Centre in Helsinki on the occasion of the 10th anniversary of its INSURE program. In 2005 the meeting of the European Holistic Working Group took place in Copenhagen, when the Danish CRBI program had its 20th anniversary.

THE INSURE PROGRAM

The INSURE has been under development since 1991, and has been used in its present form since 1993. It has been described in detail elsewhere (Kaipio et al., 2000). The INSURE population forms a subgroup of around 220 TBI patients treated annually in the Käpylä Rehabilitation Centre, which is a nationwide rehabilitation centre for neurological patients. For other TBI patients not selected for the INSURE program, various other kinds of rehabilitation services are available and the patients receive information and recommendations regarding appropriate rehabilitation. The INSURE program is recommended for TBI patients who have the potential to resume productive lives and to achieve stable psychological adjustment. Referrals for the program come from hospitals, insurance companies, the public health care system, and private clinics throughout Finland. The INSURE is a post-acute treatment program, which means that in general the patients start the rehabilitation program at least 1 year after their injury.

Four separate INSURE subgroups are formed each year for the 6-week rehabilitation program. The subgroups are small, normally consisting of five to six patients, which ensures intense working conditions. Special care is taken in the selection process of the patients to ensure that the groups are as homogenous as possible in terms of age, education, severity of the injury, and socio-economic status. Homogeneity facilitates peer solidarity and support. Also emphasized in the selection of group members are social appropriateness and motivation to learn healthy ways of communal adaptation. The critical nature of personal commitment is emphasized during the recruitment interview, which is conducted by two senior neuropsychologists from the program. Patients are independent in their daily life activities and their physical disabilities are only slightly incapacitating. Applicants average from 20 to 55 years of age. The time between the selection interview to starting the program ranges from a few months to 1 year, depending on the final formation of the homogenous subgroups. It is noteworthy that the very knowledge of being selected as a participant in the program has salutary effects on the behaviour and attitudes of candidates who are waiting to commence treatments.

Members of the interdisciplinary rehabilitation team consist of two neuropsychologists, two neurologists, a rehabilitation nurse, two social workers, two speech and language pathologists, and a physical therapist. Consistency of treatments and uniformity of adherence to the realization of clinical objectives is ensured when the staff membership is comprised of professionals who realize the need for and are committed to the development of a common way of formulating, assessing, and implementing treatments. Medical consultations are arranged, usually with specialists in neuropsychiatry, neuroradiology, and physiatry. The staff work closely together to foster consistency among the various rehabilitation activities. The importance of therapeutic alliance, which refers to the patient and therapist working together to achieve certain goals, is also emphasized. The program is directed by a clinical neuropsychologist. Each patient is assigned a primary therapist—a neuropsychologist—whose task is to coordinate and monitor the implementation of the treatment plan.

The program simulates the stress of working days and the challenges of social interaction required in everyday life. It starts at 8.30 am and ends at 4.00 pm on weekdays. Patients are treated in group and individual rehabilitation formats. Many typical symptoms reveal themselves only in group settings, during interaction with others. Every morning begins with an Orientation group, led by a neuropsychologist, in which the members determine individual goals for the day, for the program, and for the future. It aims also to promote both psychological and physiological arousal, and to foster personal orientation.

The Neuropsychological Psychotherapy group is the heart of the program. It meets 4 days a week. The guided group sessions focus on such themes as understanding the nature of the typical TBI sequelae and their impact on the lives of the patients; understanding how and why these deficits affect their personal emotions and social lives; learning to cope with these deficits and stress; etc. The participants also have individual neuropsychotherapy sessions three or four times per week. The patients are taught to assess their goals for work and education realistically, bearing in mind the post-injury changes in their resources. The psychotherapeutic process is vital for helping patients to achieve a sense of identity, to learn to behave in their own best self-interests, and to reconstruct life after brain injury (Prigatano, 1999).

The Cognitive group-remedial sessions are held twice a week. The aim is to help the patients to: (1) understand the rationale for cognitive remedial training procedures that are capable of ameliorating the interferences of attentional disorders, poor information processing abilities, and memory problems with higher-level reasoning functions; (2) practise compensatory skills capable of enhancing cognitive skills; and (3) translate lessons learned from the rehabilitation setting to life away from the program.

Group activities of various kinds are used to reinforce and enrich the program. Enjoyment of life, motivation, and the pleasures of friendship and society are emphasized in planning activities and in forming relationships. In the Pragmatic group-communication sessions, patients are guided by speech and language therapists to communicate their thoughts more effectively. The "Pictures-of-Self" workshop enables patients to express their emotions and feelings about the changes in their lives that were caused by the brain injury. These sessions help them also in the process of self-examination by means of collages made up of different materials such as photos, fabrics, and mosaics. The patients are able to focus on meaningful childhood memories, express feelings about their families, point to personally meaningful achievements, and examine their progress in their rehabilitation. As they review their presentations in the group to each other, they may gain better insights into and control over their lives, which may in turn help them to further diminish their confusion and the psychological stress related to the injury and its consequences. The Quality-of-Life group sessions deal with practical issues concerning everyday life and well-being. The Sport, Relaxation, and Jogging groups aim to encourage the members to start or restart sport activities. Particular attention is also paid to possible TBI-associated injuries or symptoms, such as cervical injuries, pain, sleep disturbances, and posttraumatic stress disorders.

Participation of the significant others is a crucial part of the program. A 2-day INSURE seminar is held in the latter part of the program. Patients, their significant others, and employers, as well as professionals from the public health-care system, are called together to share information and to learn about experiences following TBI. During the seminar, individuals' plans for the next step in their rehabilitation are reviewed and operationalized. It is also during these seminars that former participants in the INSURE program are invited to present their experiences post-discharge. Such presentations offer the current participants concrete examples of adjustment after rehabilitation; the most successful previous patients are viewed by the other participants as positive role models.

Supported and individually tailored vocational interventions are also essential elements in the INSURE program. They help the patients to find productive activities that fit their interests and abilities. When it is considered to be an adapted and practical goal, patients are encouraged to have supported work trials in the general market, where they could possibly continue after the program.

These interventions are worked out with the local social and healthcare units and the system liable for the care in each case. Once a suitable work trial placement is finalized, the patient receives tailor-made neuropsychological supports to ensure his or her success and stable emotional adjustment. The follow-up support is arranged through the public or private healthcare services. Most patients continue with individual neuropsychological rehabilitation for different periods following completion of the program. On completion of an INSURE program, patients should have substantial knowledge about TBI, giving them a sound basis for understanding and coping with TBI-related changes, and for participating in productive living according to their own best self-interests. On the whole the INSURE program is designed to be reasonable in cost and length to make it appealing and possible to patients with different sources of reimbursement.

COMPUTER-ADMINISTERED COGNITIVE REMEDIATION IN A FRAME OF HOLISTIC NEUROPSYCHOLOGICAL REHABILITATION: FORAMENREHAB PROGRAMS

Cognitive rehabilitation is traditionally considered to be an important part of rehabilitation of the brain-injured patient. Cognitive rehabilitation is defined as a systematic, functionally oriented service, which consists of therapeutic activities that are based on assessment and understanding of the patient's brain-behavioural deficits (Cicerone et al., 2000). Specific interventions may have various approaches, including attempting via restitutive training to restore impaired functions; strengthening preserved but weakened functions; teaching ways of bypassing or compensating for impaired functions that do not lend themselves to remediation; utilizing external compensatory devices, e.g., memory aids; helping the patient to become aware and understand his or her assets as well as weaknesses. Regardless of the form of intervention, the aim of cognitive rehabilitation is to improve the person's functioning in their everyday life.

According to the recommendations of evidence-based studies, computer-based interventions that include active therapist involvement to foster insight into cognitive strengths and weaknesses, to develop compensatory strategies, and to facilitate the transfer of skills into real-life situations, may be used as part of a multimodal intervention for cognitive deficits (Cicerone et al., 2000). Cognitive retraining is also seen as one of the elements of the holistic neuropsychological rehabilitation.

Due to the lack of theoretically and clinically based cognitive rehabilitation software in the Finnish language, we started a project aiming at developing tools for computer-administered cognitive remediation. FORAMENRehab cognitive software is a tool for cognitive rehabilitation to be used as part of a holistic neuropsychological rehabilitation approach. In the Cognitive group of the INSURE program this software is systematically used. FORAMENRehab software provides an easy-to-handle and efficient graphical user interface operating in a Windows environment. The menu structure, toolbar, and icons are illustrative, and the help screens provide information, so the program is usable even without the help of the clinician. Each program has a clear written instruction on the screen as well as a model animation. The parameters of each program can be modified to adjust to a particular user. The results are presented both in written and graphical forms, and they can be printed. They can also be saved to file and compared with the previous results. The first module, which was published in 2000, was designed for disturbances of attention. In 2004 we published the second module for the remediation of memory disturbances. At the moment our team is working on the modules for disturbances of visual perception and problem solving. The clinical experiences of the applicability of FORAMENRehab software in Finnish TBI and stroke patients have been promising (Koskinen & Sarajuuri, 2004).

In addition to developing the cognitive rehabilitation software, our team has developed a computer-based modification of an examination technique to evaluate executive functioning (Sarajuuri, Koskinen, & Vilkki, 2003). Deficits in executive functioning and mental programming manifest themselves in novel situations as perseverative, impulsive, or ineffective performance, or problems in attention. Although routine operative skills may be intact, their application is inappropriate. These deficits appear in anterior cerebral lesions and in traumatic brain injuries. Executive functioning is an essential factor in mastering one's psychosocial life and recovering after brain injury. The Spatial Sequence Learning task (SSLT) is a neuropsychological test for assessing executive functioning. The method is based on the Corsi Block-tapping test and further developed by Professor Juhani Vilkki. The validity of SSLT has been proved in studies predicting psychosocial recovery after head injury (Vilkki, 1992; Vilkki, Ahola, Holst, Öhman, Servo, & Heiskanen, 1994). However, standardized presentation of the manual version of the method is difficult to perform, often leading to invalid results. We hope that the computer-administered version will increase the validity and usability of the method.

EXPERIENCES AND FUTURE REMARKS

Our holistic rehabilitation program has been going since 1993, but it has been open to continuous development according to the advances in neurosciences and also the cumulating experience of the staff. Ongoing scientific research of the team members has made it possible to critically investigate different aspects and methods of the program. It has also been important to maintain an inspiring rehabilitation effort.

A 2-year follow-up study was designed to evaluate the outcome of the INSURE program. In this study the productivity of patients who underwent the rehabilitation program was compared to that of matched control patients who received conventional clinical care and rehabilitation. The results have been encouraging and quite consistent with those reported in previous studies on the efficacy of holistic rehabilitation programs (Sarajuuri et al., 2005).

Ben-Yishay and Daniels-Zide (2000) have pointed out that the conventional way of viewing outcomes of rehabilitation methods of brain-injured persons in terms of return to competitive work or to the ability of the patient to perform work-related tasks (less than full job descriptions) misses the bigger picture of rehabilitation. For, as they have shown, patients who proved capable of attaining an examined self, i.e., who recaptured their ego-identity, made better functional as well as subjective adjustments to their disabilities compared to patients who have not achieved a self-examined status. Thus, by looking at how the brain-injured patient views his inner world, we may develop meaningful ways of measuring how far a patient may have come towards realizing his or her potential for rehabilitation. Furthermore, these authors have stated that we should begin to think seriously about developing quality of life (QoL) targets in the field of neuropsychological rehabilitation, as well as valid tools capable of measuring progress toward those targets.

We conducted a pilot study in which the goal was to evaluate the QoL of TBI patients and their significant others 2 to 4 years after being discharged from the INSURE program (Koskinen Sarajuuri, & Jokitalo, 2004). The subjects were 19 (16 men, 3 women) TBI patients who had participated in the INSURE program. Their mean age at the time of the injury was 30.5 years, the mean time since injury to the program was 3.5 years, and the mean Glasgow coma scale score at injury was 7.9. The QoL and strain were evaluated by a questionnaire (life satisfaction: global, self-care/ADL, leisure, togetherness/friends, togetherness/family, marriage/courtship, sexuality). Almost 80% of the patients reported being at least *rather satisfied*. Ratings of satisfaction were highest for togetherness/friends and for the self-care/ADL items, and lowest for the marriage/courtship and the sexuality items. All the significant others reported being at least *rather satisfied* in life. About 70% of them reported experiencing mild stress and about 30% moderate stress. No relation was found between satisfaction in life and the severity of the injury, age at the injury, chronicity, or the severity of neuropsychological symptoms. The high estimate of the QoL is in accordance with an earlier study using the same questionnaire (Koskinen, 1998). However, satisfaction with social relationships was much higher in the INSURE group, referring to the importance of a comprehensive holistic rehabilitation program and peer support. The instrument used in this study takes into consideration many of the important aspects of QoL but neglects the cognitive aspects. In recent years, international group consensus meetings concluded that there is a need for further investigations and development of tools to measure QoL issues following TBI rehabilitation (Bullinger, 2002).

In this context, it is important to note the commencement in 2003 of a multicentre study aimed at developing a new instrument for measuring QoL after TBI. The QOLIBRI study has been undertaken by an international consortium of professional societies (Euroacademia Multidisciplinaria Neurotraumatologica, European Brain Injury Society, National Brain Injury Research Training and Treatment Foundation, and European Brain and Behaviour Society) (Truelle, 2004). Its coordinator is Professor Jean-Luc Truelle from Paris. At the current time, field testing to identify the best performing items is ongoing. The objective is to test a minimum of 200–300 patients for each language of the participating countries. The participating countries are: Argentina, Belgium, Brazil, Denmark, Finland, France, Germany, Greece, Italy, the Netherlands, Spain, Switzerland, Sweden, Taiwan, United Kingdom, and United States.

According to Evans and Ruff (1992), it is no longer sufficient to consider such outcomes of rehabilitation as improvement in range of motion, mobility, memory quotients, and the like as the sole, or even the most important, indices of the efficacy of rehabilitation. Rather, rehabilitation services, and healthcare services in general, must gauge the impact of their efforts upon all involved consumer groups (patient, family, and financial provider). Assessment of long-term psychosocial outcome has focused mainly on the perspective of the family or carers, who usually report that personality changes in the TBI person are their greatest concern (Brooks, Campsie, & Symington, 1987; Koskinen, 1998). Less is known, however, about the outcomes of rehabilitation as viewed subjectively by head-injured individuals, except for data derived from rating scales that evaluate the patient's emotional status or the degree to which pathognomonic symptoms persist (Van Zomeren & Van Den Burg, 1985). In our study, 38 consecutive INSURE patients served as the study subjects. Two years after completing the rehabilitation program the patients and their significant others were asked to evaluate on an open-ended questionnaire how the rehabilitation program has affected their subsequent lives, particularly in the areas that were singled out for remedial interventions while these patients attended the program. The significant others of these patients were also asked to share their own perspective on their loved one's functioning during the elapsing 2 years. The analysis of the data is presently ongoing and the results will be published later.

CONCLUSION

Neuropsychological rehabilitation should address many aspects of a brain-injured individual, with appropriate therapeutic interventions for cognitive, emotional, and interpersonal skills while increasing the awareness and understanding of the new self. Holistic neuropsychological rehabilitation programs aim to help patients to understand their underlying cognitive deficits and to learn how to cope with them. They also help patients to deal with their suffering and to re-establish meaning in their life.

While a scientific approach is necessary for neuropsychology and brain-injury rehabilitation, it may fail to address certain important aspects of human existence, e.g., the role of the patient's subjective experience in rehabilitation and their related search for meaning in life (Prigatano, 1989). According to Prigatano (1999, p. 337) "holistic neuropsychological rehabilitation combines the strength and insight of science with the wisdom of the humanities."

We would like to conclude by presenting a story told in neuropsychological group psychotherapy by a woman, a nurse, who was 50 years of age at the time of her injury. She was hit by a bus while walking on a street and suffered a significant diffuse brain injury. The symbolic story describes her phenomenological experience after TBI from despair to the state where she could make peace with her situation in the phase of her brain injury. She refers to a story written by a famous Finnish writer Tove Jansson in the book *Tales from Moominvalley* (1962).

Tove Jansson has written a story about an invisible child, a little girl, who had transformed herself into someone so insignificant that she could no longer be perceived at all. Gradually Moominmamma's tender care helped her slowly recuperate her connection with the rest of the world. At first, only the girl's shoes could be seen, then her socks, then her dress, etc. In the INSURE program there was something of this process. After my TBI I disappeared just like that little girl. Unfortunately though, no-one else could understand that. The problems that the new situation had created got new names and were noticed only by myself. Sometimes they went unnoticed even by me. Like in a nightmare, things that were totally unimaginable before my disability started happening in my life. I had entered into a world with new laws. The INSURE has helped me to see and understand who I am now. It has also defined me to others. My nightmare has transformed itself into reality that can be coped with and controlled. It has transformed my life into something significantly easier. Finally, it has given me the chance to live my life as something possible.

REFERENCES

Ben-Yishay, Y. (1996). Reflections on the evolution of the therapeutic milieu concept. *Neuropsychological Rehabilitation*, *6*, 327–343.

Ben-Yishay, Y. (2001). Cognitive rehabilitation of TBI patients: The holistic, therapeutic milieu approach. *The Japanese Journal of Rehabilitation Medicine*, *38* (Suppl), 6465–6482.

Ben-Yishay, Y., & Daniels-Zide, E. (2000). Examined lives: Outcomes after holistic rehabilitation. *Rehabilitation Psychology*, *45*, 112–129.

Ben-Yishay, Y., Rattok, J., Lakin, P., Piasetsky, E. B., Ross, B., Silver, S., Zide, E., & Ezrachi, O. (1985). Neuropsychologic rehabilitation: Quest for a holistic approach. *Seminars in Neurology*, *5*, 252–259.

Ben-Yishay, Y., Silver, S. M., Piasetsky, E., & Rattok, J. (1987). Relationship between employability and vocational outcome after intensive holistic cognitive rehabilitation. *Journal of Head Trauma Rehabilitation*, *2*, 35–48.

Brooks, D. N., Campsie, L., & Symington, C. (1987). The effects of severe head injury on patient and relative within seven years of injury. *Journal of Head Trauma Rehabilitaton*, *2*, 1–13.

Bullinger, M. (2002). TBI Consensus group. Quality of life in patients with traumatic brain injury. Basic issues, assessment and recommendations. *Restorative Neurology and Neuroscience*, *20*, 1–14.

Christensen, A.-L. (2000). Neuropsychological postacute rehabilitation. In A.-L. Christensen & B. Uzzell (Eds.), *International handbook of neuropsychological rehabilitation* (pp. 151–163). New York: Kluwer Academic/Plenum.

Christensen, A.-L., Pinner, E. M., Moller Pedersen, P., Teasdale, T. W., & Trexler, L. E. (1992). Psychosocial outcome following individualized neuropsychological rehabilitation of brain damage. *Acta Neurologica Scandinavica*, *85*, 32–38.

Cicerone, K. D., Dahlberg, C., Kalmar, K., Langenbahn, D. M., Malec, J. F., Bergquist, T. F., Felicetti, T., Giacino, J. T., Harley, J. P., Harrington, D. E., Herzog, J., Kneipp, S., Laatsch, L., & Morse, P. A. (2000). Evidence-based cognitive rehabilitation: Recommendations for clinical practice. *Archives of Physical Medicine and Rehabilitation*, *81*, 1596–1615.

Consensus Conference. (1999). Rehabilitation of persons with traumatic brain injury. NIH Consensus Development Panel on Rehabilitation of Persons with Traumatic Brain Injury. *JAMA*, *282*, 974–983.

Cope, D. N. (1995). The effectiveness of traumatic brain injury rehabilitation: A review. *Brain Injury*, *9*, 649–670.

Eames, P., & Wood, R. Ll. (1989). The structure and content of a head injury rehabilitation service. In R. Ll. Wood & P. Eames (Eds.), *Models of brain injury rehabilitation* (pp. 31–47). London: Chapman & Hall.

Evans, R. W., & Ruff, R. M. (1992). Outcome and value: A perspective on rehabilitation outcomes achieved in acquired brain injury. *Journal of Head Trauma Rehabilitation*, *7*, 24–36.

Goldstein, K. (1942). *After-effects of brain injuries in war: Their evaluation and treatment*. New York: Grune & Stratton.

Goldstein, K. (1959). Notes on the development of my concepts. *Journal of Individual Psychology*, *15*, 5–14.

Jansson, T. (1962). *Tales from Moominvalley*. New York: Farrar, Straus & Giroux.

Kaipio, M.-L., Sarajuuri, J., & Koskinen, S. (2000). INSURE program and modifications in Finland. In A.-L. Christensen & B. Uzzell (Eds.), *International handbook of neuropsychological rehabilitation* (pp. 247–258). New York: Kluwer Academic/Plenum.

Koskinen, S. (1998). Quality of life 10 years after a very severe traumatic brain injury (TBI). *Brain Injury*, *12*, 631–648.

Koskinen, S., & Sarajuuri, J. (2004). Computer-administered cognitive remediation in a frame of holistic neuropsychological rehabilitation: FORAMENRehab programs. *Svensk Neuro-psykologi*, *4*, 10–11.

Koskinen, S., Sarajuuri, J., & Jokitalo, P. (2004, May). *Quality of life after a holistic neurorehabilitation program*. Paper presented at the 9th Congress of the Euroacademia Multidisciplinaria Neurotraumatologica, Bucharest, Romania.

Mäki, H., & Honkinen, O. (2004, August). *Holistic rehabilitation of children with aquired brain injury—preliminary experiences from the HOPE-program in Finland*. Paper presented at the 8th Nordic Meeting in Neuropsychology, Turku, Finland.

Prigatano, G. (1989). Work, love, and play after brain injury. *Bulletin of Menninger Clinic*, *53*, 414–431.

Prigatano, G. (1999). *Principles of neuropsychological rehabilitation*. New York: Oxford University Press.

Prigatano, G. (2000). A brief overview of four principles of neuropsychological rehabilitation. In A.-L. Christensen & B. Uzzell (Eds.), *International handbook of neuropsychological rehabilitation* (pp. 115–125). New York: Kluwer Academic/Plenum.

Prigatano, G. (2004, May). *Science and symbolism in neuropsychological rehabilitation*. Paper presented at the International Symposium on Holistic

Rehabilitation—INSURE Program 10 years, Helsinki, Finland.

Prigatano, G. P., Fordyce, D. J., Zeiner, H. K., Roueche, J. R., Pepping, M., & Wood, B. C. (1986). *Neuropsychological rehabilitation after brain injury.* Baltimore: The Johns Hopkins University Press.

Prigatano, G. P., Klonoff, P. S., O'Brien, K. P., Altman, I. M., Amin, K., Chiapello, D., Shepherd, J., Cunningham, M., & Mora, M. (1994). Productivity after neuropsychologically oriented milieu rehabilitation. *Journal of Head Trauma Rehabilitation, 9*, 91–102.

Sarajuuri, J., Kaipio, M.-L., Koskinen, S., Niemalä, M., Servo, A., & Vilkki, J. (2005). Outcome of a comprehensive neurorehabilitation program for patients with traumatic brain injury. *Archives of Physical Medicine and Rehabilitation, 86*, 2296–2302.

Sarajuuri, J., Koskinen, S., & Vilkki, J. (2003). Assessing executive functioning: The computer-administered spatial sequence learning task. *Brain Injury, 17* (Suppl 1), 155–156.

Truelle, J. L. (2004, May). *QOLIBRI.* Paper presented at the 9th Congress of the Euroacademia Multidisciplinaria Neurotraumatologica, Bucharest, Romania.

Van Zomeren, A. H., & Van Den Burg, W. (1985). Residual complaints of patients two years after severe head injury. *Journal of Neurology, Neurosurgery and Psychiatry, 48*, 21–28.

Vilkki, J. (1992). Cognitive flexibility and mental programming after closed head injury and anterior or posterior cerebral excisions. *Neuropsychologia, 30*, 807–814.

Vilkki, J., Ahola, K., Holst, P., Öhman, J., Servo, A., & Heiskanen, O. (1994). Prediction of psychosocial recovery after head injury with cognitive tests and neurobehavioral ratings. *Journal of Clinical and Experimental Neuropsychology, 16*, 325–338.

INTERNATIONAL JOURNAL OF PSYCHOLOGY, 2006, 41 (5), 371–384

Postnatal adjustment of Chinese parents: A two-wave panel study in Taiwan

Luo Lu

National Central University, Taiwan, ROC

This study focused on examining the relationships between stress, resources, and adjustment of Chinese married mothers and fathers following childbirth. Guided by a generic theoretical model of parenthood transition, the aim of the current study was threefold. First, longitudinal data were collected to clarify the impact of parenthood from 6 weeks postnatal (*Time 1*) to 6 months postnatal (*Time 2*). A diachronic design is more advantageous in making causal inferences as baseline levels of mental health and marital satisfaction can be controlled. Second, a gender-balanced design was adopted to examine the transition processes for both men and women to overcome our shortcomings in understanding men's experiences. Third, this study was conducted in a Chinese society to examine the transition to parenthood as embedded in this particular cultural context. A total of 483 parents (253 females, 230 males) took part in this two-wave panel study. Hierarchical multiple regression analyses and structural equation modelling techniques were used to test for direct, moderation, and mediation effects of marital congruence and social support as resources. Results showed that (a) parental stress had negative effects on mental health and marital satisfaction, and these relationships were robust across time and gender; (b) marital congruence and social support had direct as well as mediation effects on adjustment; (c) marital congruence also had moderation (stress buffering) effects on the stress/mental health relationship; (d) over the half-year period, there were no significant changes in stress and adjustment outcomes, yet marital congruence and social support significantly declined, and this trend was the same for both sexes; (e) although males and females did not differ in marital congruence and social support, women reported higher stress, more psychological symptoms, and lower marital satisfaction than men. These gender differences did not change over time. These results were discussed in relation to existing theories and research, as well as the distinct characteristics of the contemporary Chinese society.

Cette étude visait à explorer le processus d'adaptation suivant la naissance d'un enfant chez des mères et des pères chinois mariés. Au total, 483 parents (253 femmes et 230 hommes) ont pris part à cette étude menée en deux temps, soit à 6 semaines et à 6 mois après la naissance de l'enfant. Des analyses de régressions hiérarchiques multiples et la technique de modélisation par équations structurelles ont été employées pour tester les effets directs, modérateurs et médiateurs. Les résultats ont montré que (a) le stress parental a eu des effets négatifs sur la santé mentale et la satisfaction conjugale, et que ces relations étaient stables à travers le temps et les genres; (b) l'harmonie conjugale et le soutien social ont montré des effets directs et médiateurs sur l'adaptation; (c) l'harmonie conjugale a également présenté des effets modérateurs (facteur de protection) sur la relation entre le stress et la santé mentale; (d) au cours de cette période de 6 mois, il n'y a pas eu de changement significatif du stress et de l'adaptation, alors que l'harmonie conjugale et le soutien social ont significativement diminué, cette tendance étant la même pour les deux genres; (e) quoique les hommes et les femmes ne différaient pas quant à l'harmonie conjugale et au soutien social, les femmes ont rapporté plus de stress, plus de symptômes psychologiques et moins de satisfaction conjugale que les hommes. Ces différences reliées au genre n'ont pas changé à travers le temps. Ces résultats ont été discutés en relation avec les théories et la recherche existantes, tout en tenant compte des caractéristiques distinctes de la société chinoise contemporaine.

Este estudio se centró en el examen de la relación entre el estrés, los recursos y el ajuste de madres y padres chinos después del nacimiento de un hijo. Guiados por un modelo teórico genérico de transición a la paternidad, el propósito del presente estudio fue triple. Primero, se recogió datos longitudinales para aclarar el

Correspondence should be addressed to Professor Luo Lu, Institute of Human Resource Management, National Central University, No.300, Jhongda Rd, Jhongli City, Taoyuan County 32001, Taiwan, ROC (E-mail: luolu@mgt.ncu.edu.tw).
This research was supported by a grant from the National Science Council, Taiwan, ROC, NSC89-2413-H-037-008.

 DOI: 10.1080/00207590500345328

impacto de la paternidad a las 6 semanas después del nacimiento (Momento 1) y a los 6 meses después del nacimiento (Momento 2). El diseño diacrónico es el que ofreció más ventajas para la realización de inferencias causales, dado que es posible controlar los niveles de línea base de la salud mental y de la satisfacción marital. Segundo, se adoptó un diseño que equilibró el género para explorar los procesos de transición tanto en hombres como en mujeres para superar las limitaciones que entraña el entender las experiencias masculinas. En tercer lugar, se condujo el estudio en una sociedad china para examinar la transición a la paternidad dentro de ese contexto cultural en particular. Un total de 483 padres (253 mujeres, 230 hombres) participaron en este estudio panel de dos ondas. Se empleó tanto análisis de regresión múltiple como la técnica de modelamiento de ecuaciones estructurales para someter a prueba los efectos directos, moderadores y mediadores de la congruencia marital y el apoyo social como recursos. Los resultados muestran que (a) el estrés de los padres ejerce efectos negativos sobre la salud mental y la satisfacción marital, y que esas relaciones son robustas en el tiempo y el género; (b) la congruencia marital y el apoyo social mostraron tanto efectos directos como mediadores sobre el ajuste; (c) la congruencia marital también mostró efectos moderadores (amortigua el estrés) sobre la relación estrés/salud mental; (d) a lo largo del periodo de medio año, no hubo cambios significativos en los resultados de estrés y ajuste, no obstante la congruencia marital y el apoyo social se redujeron significativamente, y esta tendencia fue la misma para ambos sexos; (e) a pesar de que no hubo diferencia entre hombres y mujeres en cuanto a congruencia marital y apoyo social, las mujeres manifestaron más estrés, más síntomas psicológicos y menos satisfacción marital que los hombres. Estas diferencias de género no cambiaron con el paso del tiempo. Se discuten estos resultados en relación con las teorías y la investigación existentes, así como las características distintivas de la sociedad china contemporánea.

INTRODUCTION

At the turn of the century, the traditionally conservative East Asia is undergoing profound economic and societal modernizations. As a consequence, the divorce rate has skyrocketed in this region. Even though Taiwan is a prototypical Chinese society with a strong Confucian family tradition, the latest official estimate indicates that for every three new marriages one ends in divorce (Executive Yuan, 2004). Research has suggested that problems leading to marital dissolution begin early in relationships (Thornes & Collard, 1979). Transition to parenthood has been described as a "crisis" for both men and woman (Cowan et al., 1985). The present study thus aimed to explore the adjustment of married mothers and fathers following childbirth. The extant research on parenthood adjustment, however, has been heavily influenced by the dominant societal ethos of parenting being a "women's issue" and, consequently, little attention has been paid to men's adjustment following childbirth. Thus, one thrust of the present study was its inclusion of fathers. The two-wave panel design also allowed considerations of both the earlier (6 weeks) and later (6 months) stages of parenting. As it is not a foregone conclusion that Western research findings can be generalized to such a vastly different culture as the Chinese, this study with Chinese parents is both theoretically and practically important.

Impact of parenthood: Mental health and marital satisfaction

Becoming a parent might be a stressful transition (Santrock, 1995) that can incur costs to personal well-being. Abbott and Brody (1985) noted that having a young child aged between 0 and 2 years has the most adverse effect on the mother's physical and mental health. In the West, much extant work has focused on maternal postpartum depression; however, empirical evidence is inconclusive. Cooper, Campbell, Day, Kennerley, and Bond (1988), for example, found that antenatal and postnatal women were no more likely to be depressed than a general population sample of nonpuerperal women. On the other hand, Osofsky (1979) has suggested that postnatal anxiety may affect bonding between mother and child, but this suggestion has not been closely examined.

In contrast to the extensive study on women's postpartum depression, men's physical rather than mental health seems to have received more attention in scientific research. Ferketich and Mercer (1989) found that men's perception of their health was that it was significantly poorer at 8 months postnatal than during their partners' pregnancy. Furthermore, Quill, Lipkin, and Lamb (1984) found that men visited doctors more in the year after their children were born than during their partner's pregnancy. The strong relationship between physical and mental health (Lu, Tseng, & Cooper, 1999; Marks, Goldberg, & Hillier, 1979) suggests that men experiencing a high level of physical symptoms may actually be having difficulties adjusting to their new role as a father. Thus, the present study expanded the scope of mental health to include depression, anxiety, and somatic symptoms in examining the impact of parenthood transition.

Transition to parenthood has also been found to be associated with a decline in marital satisfaction (Argyle, 1987). This adverse effect on marriage of the arrival of a child is probably caused by the competition for limited resources between parenthood and marriage (Belsky, 1990). However, previous work has focused almost exclusively on mother's reports of marital satisfaction; consequently, we know very little about men's psychological experiences in their transition to fatherhood. One study did examine reports of both men and women, and found that while women's marital satisfaction declined 6 months after childbirth, men's marital satisfaction declined between 6 and 18 months after their children were born (Cowan et al., 1985). It may be speculated that women are more sensitive to the impact of parenthood on their marital relationship, and detect early warning signs; men, on the other hand, may feel the impact of their role change in other ways, such as financial strain at the early parenthood stage (Atkinson & Blackwelder, 1993), and only later recognize that fatherhood may also have affected their marital relationship.

To sum up, extant literature in the West has suggested that the parenthood transition may incur costs on mental health and may suppress marital satisfaction. Specifically, it was hypothesized that *parental stress would be positively related to psychological symptoms and negatively related to marital satisfaction, when stress and outcomes were assessed at the same time, and after the baseline levels of mental health or marital satisfaction were controlled.*

Resources for coping with parenthood stress

Although becoming a parent can be a potentially stressful life event for both men and women, as we have reviewed earlier, new parents still have various resources to help them meet the challenge of parenthood. Social networks are often mobilized to help people cope with the impending or newly acquired status of being a parent, especially women. Previous research has noted that the frequency of contacts with families of origin and with other parents tends to increase over time from pregnancy through 9 months postpartum. Further, the amount of emotional and material support received from families and friends is likely to be the greatest at 3 months postpartum, especially for first-time parents. Other services, such as babysitting, were also provided in some cases (Belsky & Rovine, 1984). While evidence supporting the beneficial effect of social support on well-being is unequivocal (e.g., Wortman & Dunkel-Schetter, 1987), a lack of social support was linked to postpartum depression among women (Howell-White, 1991).

However, men and women may have different experiences of social support during their transition to parenthood. Compared to men, women more actively solicit social support (Lu & Argyle, 1992), and indeed receive more support from others (Lu, 1995). More specifically, mothers more than fathers seek social support as a means of adjusting to parenthood (Ventura & Boss, 1983). Furthermore, as mothers are more often the focus of social support provision, men's needs for understanding and support have largely been neglected (Sullivan-Lyons, 1998).

Within the conjugal system, the psychological sense of unity, alliance, and partnership have been found to play a particularly central role in the adjustment to parenthood. Couples who have close/confiding marriages, compared to those who are unhappily married, are more likely to be warm and sensitive parents and to hold positive attitudes about their babies and their parenting roles (Owen, Lewis, & Henderson, 1989). For women, high levels of marital intimacy are also associated with a reduced level of postpartum depression (Stemp, Turner, & Noh, 1986). Previous work has suggested that the single best predictor of postpartum marital adjustment is the level of marital adjustment during a pregnancy (Harriman, 1986), and better adjustment has been linked to cohesive and satisfying couple bonds (Belsky & Pensky, 1988).

In the present study, marital congruence was conceptualized as an indicator of the positive quality of a marital relationship. Marital congruence refers to the extent of conjugal agreement on important issues in life, such as finance, affection, and outlook of life, which has been found to relate to marital satisfaction (Locke & Wallace, 1959). In the context of parenthood transition, research has found that how couples deal with the allocation of childcare and other household chores was a strong predictor of adaptation. Issues such as paternal involvement (Levy-Shiff, 1994), violated expectations for the sharing of responsibilities (Hackel & Ruble, 1992), and the process of decision-making (Osofsky & Culp, 1989) are all predictive of marital satisfaction for both sexes.

The present study thus focused on both social support and marital congruence as resources in the context of adjustment to parenthood. Specifically, it was hypothesized that *both social support and marital congruence would be negatively related to psychological symptoms and positively related to marital satisfaction, when assessed at the same time, and after the baseline levels of mental health or marital satisfaction were controlled.* It was further hypothesized that in addition to these direct effects, *both social support and marital congruence would moderate stress/mental health and stress/marital satisfaction relationships.*

Parenting in a Chinese cultural context

As noted by Phoenix and Woollett (1991), motherhood and fatherhood are socially and culturally constructed; becoming a parent in a Chinese society thus entails some distinct experiences. Confucian philosophy has constructed family and filial piety as the central cultural values that are transmitted and reinforced through social institutions and socialization practices in Chinese societies (Yeh & Bedford, 2003). Traditionally, the ultimate purpose of a marriage is to produce an heir to carry on the family line. The Confucian teachings regard the failure to produce offspring as the gravest violation of filial piety, which still has a normative influence on people's views of parenthood in contemporary Chinese societies (Yue & Ng, 1999).

It is thus important to recognize that, in a Chinese cultural context, becoming a parent is to fulfil a vitally important social duty and obligation as well as to contribute to the collective well-being (Lu, 2001). The stresses and challenges of transition to parenthood, blended with joy and accomplishment, are immense. Furthermore, as first pointed out by the famous anthropologist Francis Hsu (1953), the traditional Chinese culture regards the father son (child) axis as the primal relationship in the society, so far more energy and resources are allocated to childcare while sacrificing conjugal needs, and the impact of the birth of a child on the Chinese marital relationship is likely to be much greater than in a Western society.

Recent empirical studies in Taiwan have indeed found that Chinese couples view the parent–child relationship as more important than the conjugal relationship (Chen, 1978), and women more than men give higher ratings to the importance as well as to the stress of parental roles (Lu & Lin, 1998). Furthermore, for both men and women, parental stress is detrimental to personal well-being (Lu & Lin, 1998). Chong (1995) followed up 36 pairs of Chinese parents from when they first knew about the conception of their children for 4 consecutive years. Repeated in-depth interviews revealed the underlying theme of the overriding importance of childcare roles above personal and conjugal needs.

In addition, the close-knit social network of a Chinese society is rather active in providing various kinds of support to the young parents-to-be. Today, though, such help could be a potential source for conflict as young couples may hold very different views regarding childrearing practices to those of their elderly relatives. All these distinct cultural and social characteristics must be taken into account in our effort to understand the transition to parenthood among the Chinese people.

To this end, a generic model of parenthood stress, resources, and adjustment (see Figure 1) was purported, and we have already completed a longitudinal analysis of parenthood transition by following a panel of Chinese parents for a half-year period through the pre- and post-parenthood comparison (Lu, in press). This study, with data from a representative sample of 364 parents in Taiwan, has provided strong support for parts of the model in Figure 1: (a) in cross-sectional analyses, parenthood stress had consistent negative effects on mental health and marital satisfaction (paths 1 & 3); (b) in prospective analyses, stress still had adverse effects on postnatal mental health or marital satisfaction after controlling for their prenatal baseline levels (paths 8–3); (c) social support and marital congruence had beneficial effects on the parenthood adjustment (paths 2 & 4); and (d) compared to men, women reported higher stress, more psychological symptoms, and lower marital satisfaction than men, but received more social support. Another publication (Lu, 2004) reported results of a rigorous dyadic analysis based on a subsample of 90 married couples from the present database; it also confirmed the pattern of sex differences in the timeframe of post-parenthood adjustment.

Like other researchers (Fergusson, Horwood, & Thorpe, 1996; Ferketich & Mercer, 1989), the above study (Lu, in press) focused on adjustment *during* the actual transition of parenthood and examined trajectories from 6 weeks prenatal to 6 weeks postpartum. The present study, however, aimed to trace the impact of parenthood in a continuing manner, focusing on adjustment *after* the transition to parenthood.

The same generic model was adopted, though it was fitted to a different time frame. The aim of the current study was threefold. First, longitudinal

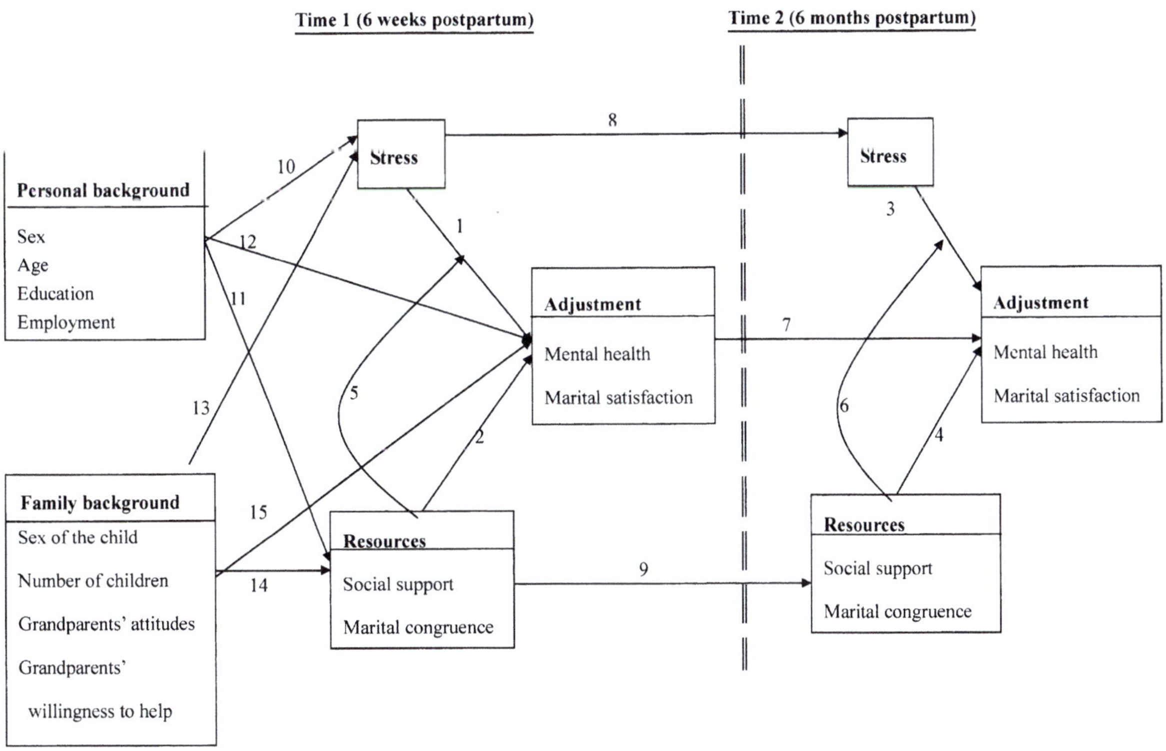

Figure 1. A generic framework of parenthood transition.

data were collected to clarify the impact of parenthood from 6 weeks postnatal (*Time 1*) to 6 months postnatal (*Time 2*). A diachronic design is *more* advantageous in making causal inferences as baseline levels of mental health and marital satisfaction can be controlled. Second, a gender-balanced design was adopted to examine the transition processes for both men and women to overcome our shortcomings in understanding men's experiences. Third, this study was conducted in a Chinese society to examine the transition to parenthood as embedded in this particular cultural context.

More specifically, a two-wave panel study was conducted to examine stress, resources, and adjustment at 6 weeks and 6 months after childbirth. A test of the full generic model in Figure 1 is clearly beyond the scope of a single empirical study, and most personal and family background variables (except gender) were found ineffective in the parenthood transition (Lu, in press). The present study thus focused on examining the relationships between stress, resources and adjustment.

METHODS

Participants

The target population for the present study was parents who had a child born in a particular month and resided in Kaohsiung, the second largest city in Taiwan. Using the random sampling procedure, parents listed in the Kaohsiung Municipal Birth Registration were invited by phone to participate in the study. As a two-wave panel study, each consenting participant answered a structured questionnaire twice, once when his/her child was 6 weeks old, and another when the child was 6 months old. Participation was anonymous. A total of 483 parents (253 F and 230 M) with newly born children returned completed questionnaires at least once (response rate = 63%). This response rate is comparable to the reported average of mail surveys using the general population (60% ± 20) (Baruch, 1999).

Two hundred and four participants had data for both Time 1 and Time 2, and 90 pairs were married to each other. Data attrition for Time 2 was due to various causes such as residence change, incorrect contact information, and refusal. Analyses revealed *no* systematic differences between those who initially declined to participate/those who did not participate at Time 2 and those who stayed throughout the study, in terms of gender distribution, age, education attainment, and employment status. However, self-selection bias could not be completely ruled out and results should still be read with due caution.

Analyses reported in the present paper came from data of 230 fathers (47.6%) and 253 mothers

(52.4%). The mean age of participants was 30.02 (SD = 4.86). Most of our participants had senior high school education (47.4%), and a further 48.9% had at least some higher education. Almost all fathers were working (96.4%), but only half of the mothers (53.2%) had paid jobs. These participants in the present study were *roughly* representative of Taiwan's young married population and their family characteristics in terms of gender distribution, age, education attainment, and employment status (Executive Yuan, 2004).

Instruments

The structured questionnaire included the following scales and measures.

Stress of parenthood. The Perceived Stress Scale (Cohen, Kamarck, & Mermelstein, 1983) was used in the present study to measure the stress of parenthood transition. Participants were specifically instructed to rate each statement regarding their *parenting experiences* in the last month. Five-point scales were used for rating the frequency of a particular stress feeling (0 = *never*, 4 = *very often*), a high score indicating a higher level of perceived stress. Sample items are "How often have you been upset because of something that happened unexpectedly?" and "How often have you felt confident about your ability to handle your personal problems?" (reverse scored). The Cronbach's α was .81 in the present study.

Mental health. Three subscales, depression, anxiety, and somatic symptoms from the SCL-90-R (Derogatis, Rickels, & Rock, 1976), were used to assess mental symptoms. Three-point rating scales were used, and a high score indicates more mental symptoms, hence *worse* health. The Cronbach's α was .91 in the present study.

Social support. The Inventory of Socially Supportive Behaviors (Barrera, 1981) was used to assess actual received support, which includes emotional, tangible, and informational support, and companionship. Four-point rating scales were used for rating the frequency of receiving a particular form of help (0 = *not at all*, 3 = *very often*), a high score indicating more received support. The Cronbach's α was .93 in the present study.

Marital congruence. Eight items from the Marital Adjustment Scale (Locke & Wallace, 1959) were used to assess conjugal agreement on important life domains (e.g., finance, affection, and outlook on life). Six-point rating scales were used for rating the degree of conjugal agreement (1 = *always disagree*, 6 = *always agree*), a high score indicating greater marital congruence. The Cronbach's α was .85 in the present study.

Marital satisfaction. This was rated by participants in reference to the marriage *as a whole.* A 7-point scale (1 = *very dissatisfied*, 7 = *very satisfied*) was used; a high score indicating greater satisfaction with the marriage. Previous research has demonstrated that single-item global measures of satisfaction are acceptable, and may even be more indicative than the summation of facets (Scarpello & Campbell, 1983; Wanous, Reichers, & Hudy, 1997).

RESULTS

As there were 90 pairs of married couples in the present sample, the assumption that participants could be treated as independent might be in question. All analyses were conducted twice, once with these 90 pairs taken out and once with them included. Results were generally similar, thus those with the entire sample of 483 participants are reported below.

Gender differences

Gender differences were examined with t-tests, and results are presented in Table 1. At both 6 weeks and 6 months postpartum, men perceived less parental stress than women. They also reported better mental health and higher marital satisfaction.

Temporal changes

Longitudinal correlations were computed by correlating scores of the same measures taken at different times. As can been seen in Table 2, these Pearson correlation coefficients ranged from .45 to .57. Such magnitude of longitudinal correlation implied fluctuation over time. Paired t-tests were then conducted to compare means of each construct over the 5-month interval. Results showed that stress, mental health, and marital satisfaction were not significantly different at 6 weeks and 6 months postpartum. However, the amount of social support declined over the period, $t(192) = 3.70, p<.01$, as did marital congruence, $t(196) = 3.86, p<.001$. It seems that while stress and its outcome stayed unchanged, resources were actually shrinking over time following the transition to parenthood.

TABLE 1
t-tests for gender differences postpartum

	Male		*Female*			
	Mean	*SD*	*Mean*	*SD*	*df*	*t*
6 weeks						
Stress	22.89	6.09	25.06	6.41	449	−3.68***
Mental health	24.82	5.72	27.19	6.53	467	−4.19***
Marital satisfaction	5.05	1.29	4.58	1.53	464	3.66***
Social support	21.44	8.77	22.11	9.71	451	−0.78
Marital congruence	37.02	4.97	36.19	5.90	459	1.63
6 months						
Stress	23.25	5.90	24.99	6.24	199	−2.03*
Mental health	24.84	5.16	26.41	5.35	204	−2.14*
Marital satisfaction	5.47	1.26	4.71	1.45	208	4.01***
Social support	18.44	7.96	19.67	9.96	205	−0.99
Marital congruence	35.71	5.63	34.81	6.74	205	1.04

*$p<.05$; **$p<.01$; ***$p<.001$.

Direct effects of stress and resources on adjustment

Pearson correlations were computed among the main research variables and a full correlation matrix is presented in Table 2.

Several findings are worth attention. First, stress significantly correlated with mental health and marital satisfaction. Simultaneous correlations (stress, mental health, and satisfaction measures taken at the same time) were generally higher than cross-lagged correlations (the above three measures taken at different times). Second, social support significantly correlated with mental health and marital satisfaction in terms of simultaneous correlations. However, cross-lagged correlations were not significant. Third, marital congruence significantly correlated with mental health and martial satisfaction, in terms of both simultaneous and cross-lagged correlations.

The two-wave data offered an opportunity to better explore the direct effects of stress and resources on adjustment after controlling for baseline measures. Regression models were tested predicting mental health and marital satisfaction at 6 months postpartum, while controlling for their "baseline" levels at 6 weeks postpartum. Hierarchical multiple regression analyses were conducted, and the results are presented in Table 3. At Step 1, sex (coded 1 for *male* and 2 for *female*) was entered as there were gender differences on stress, mental health, and marital satisfaction (see Table 1). At Step 2, the "baseline" measure at Time 1 (mental health or marital satisfaction) was entered. At Step 3, stress, social support, and marital congruence at Time 2 were entered.

In predicting mental health at Time 2 (6 months postpartum), all five variables accounted for a total of 45% of variance. Stress and marital congruence were significantly related to mental health at Time 2 even when mental health at Time 1 (6 weeks postpartum) was controlled for.

In predicting marital satisfaction at Time 2 (6 months postpartum), all five variables accounted for a total of 45% of variance. Marital congruence was significantly related to marital satisfaction at Time 2 even when marital satisfaction at Time 1 (6 weeks postpartum) was controlled for.

Moderating effects of resources on adjustment

Paths 5 and 6 in Figure 1 represented hypothesized *moderating* effects of resources on the stress/adjustment relationship. To test for these indirect effects of resources, a series of hierarchical regression analyses as suggested by Cohen and Cohen (1983) were conducted, and results are presented in Table 4. Following Cohen and Cohen's 3-step procedure, the moderating effect can be demonstrated by the statistical significance and form of the main and interaction terms in a hierarchical regression analysis. In the present study, there were four dependent variables: mental health at Times 1 and 2, and marital satisfaction at Times 1 and 2. There were two proposed moderators: social support and marital congruence. Therefore, a total of eight hierarchical regression analyses were needed. The entry of variables into the equation followed the same sequence: (1) stress; (2) moderator; (3) the product term representing stress × moderator. All variables were standardized before the regression analyses, and unstandardized regression coefficients are reported from the final equation.

TABLE 2
Pearson correlations among the main research variables

Variables	*1*	*2*	*3*	*4*	*5*	*6*	*7*	*8*	*9*	*10*
1. Stress (1)	1.00									
2. Mental health (1)	.57***	1.00								
3. Marital satisfaction (1)	−.33***	−.37***	1.00							
4. Social support (1)	−.24***	−.19***	.35***	1.00						
5. Marital congruence (1)	−.34***	−.45***	.51***	.18***	1.00					
6. Stress (2)	.47***	.27***	−.16*	−.08	−.17*	1.00				
7. Mental health (2)	.34***	.49***	−.24***	.03	−.24***	.52***	1.00			
8. Marital satisfaction (2)	−.29***	−.26***	.49***	.11	.40***	−.34***	−.41***	1.00		
9. Social support (2)	−.09	−.09	.26***	.57***	.06	−.18*	−.14*	.21**	1.00	
10. Marital congruence (2)	−.14	−.24***	.35***	−.05	.45***	−.23***	−.37***	.53***	.11	1.00

TABLE 3
Hierarchical regression analyses testing for direct effects of stress and resources

Dependent variable	*Step*	*Entered variables*	*β*	*R^2*	*F*	*Dependent variable*	*Step*	*Entered variables*	*β*	*R^2*	*F*
Mental health (2)	1	Sex	−.01			Marital satisfaction (2)	1	Sex	−.17**		
	2	Mental health (1)	.33***				2	Marital satisfaction (1)	.26**		
	3	Stress (2)	.36***				3	Stress (2)	−.13		
		Support (2)	−.01					Support (2)	.08		
		Marital congruence (2)	−.17*	.45	25.49***			Marital congruence (2)	.36***	.45	20.61***

TABLE 4
Hierarchical regression analyses testing for moderation effects of resources

Dependent variable	*Step*	*Entered variables*	*B*	*R^2*	*F*	*Dependent variable*	*Step*	*Entered variables*	*B*	*R^2*	*F*
Mental health (1)	1	S (1)	.55***			Marital satisfaction (1)	1	S (1)	−.59***		
	2	SS (1)	−.01				2	SS (1)	.45***		
	3	S (1) × SS (1)	−.29	.33	68.34***		3	S (1) × SS (1)	.01	.19	32.03***
Mental health (1)	1	S (1)	.47***			Marital satisfaction (1)	1	S (1)	−.41***		
	2	MC (1)	−.30***				2	MC (1)	.12***		
	3	S (1) × MC (1)	−.75***	.42	102.17***		3	S (1) × MC (1)	.01	.29	58.57***
Mental health (2)	1	S (2)	.44***			Marital satisfaction (2)	1	S (2)	−.73***		
	2	SS (2)	−.01				2	SS (2)	.25**		
	3	S (2) × SS (2)	−.01	.27	24.13***		3	S (2) × SS (2)	.15	.16	11.96***
Mental health (2)	1	S (2)	.38***			Marital satisfaction (1)	1	S (2)	−.52***		
	2	MC (2)	−.20***				2	MC (2)	.10*		
	3	S (2) × MC (2)	−.99***	.38	39.23***		3	S (2) × MC (2)	.13	.35	34.01***

$p<.05$; $**p<.01$; $***p<.001$. S = Stress; SS = Social support; MC = Marital congruence.

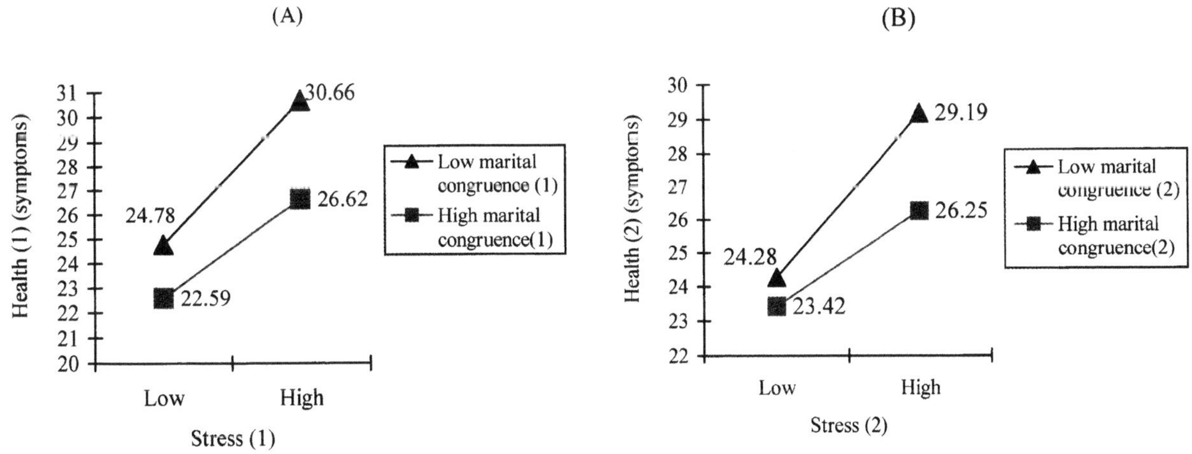

Figure 2. Moderating effects of marital congruence on the stress–health relation.

As can be seen in Table 4, stress contributed significantly to mental health and marital satisfaction at both times postpartum. Marital congruence too seemed to have a stable relationship with mental health and marital satisfaction across time. More importantly, marital congruence had a reliable moderating effect on the stress/mental health relationship at both times. These moderating effects are plotted in Figure 2(A) and (B). As can be clearly seen, marital congruence buffered or alleviated the impact of parental stress on mental health.

Mediating effects of stress and resources on adjustment

Another kind of indirect effect: *Mediation* was implied in the theoretical framework depicted in Figure 1. For instance, previous stress and resources may influence later adjustment through their carry-over effects on later stress and resources (paths 8–3, 9–4). Also, stress and resources at Time 1 may influence mental health at Time 1, which has a carry-over effect on mental health at Time 2 (paths 1–7, 2–7). To test for such mediating effects, structural equation modelling (SEM) techniques are needed. As stated earlier, the model in Figure 1 was useful only as a generic framework to organize specific studies, thus was not testable as a SEM model. Furthermore, moderating effects (paths 5 & 6) were already tested using moderated regression analyses. Instead we focused on the carry-over effects of stress (path 8–3), resources (path 9–4) and mediating effects of prior adjustment (paths 1–7, 2–7), as depicted in Figure 1. To facilitate understanding of mechanisms of two distinct aspects of adjustment, separate models were tested for mental health and marital satisfaction rather than a full saturated one. For exploratory purposes, model modification procedures were followed to construct the best-fitting models (Raykov, Tomer, & Nesselroade, 1991).

The initial "mental health model" was constructed to include paths 8–3, 9–4, 1–7, and 2–7 in Figure 1. This model was evaluated with the Maximum Likelihood technique provided by AMOS 3.06, and modified by eliminating nonsignificant paths. As a result, marital congruence at Time 2 was taken out, as the path linking it with mental health at Time 2 was not significant. Three other paths were also omitted (stress1→mental health2, support1→mental health1, marital congruence1→mental health2) for the same reason. The final model is presented in Figure 3, with all paths statistically significant at the level of $p = .05$ and above.

Model evaluation is usually not a simple procedure, and no single descriptive index seems to be superior to the others and impeccable in this regard (Bentler, 1990; Raykov et al., 1991). Basically, evaluating a model is to strike a balance between simplicity vs complexity (reflected in the parsimony indexes), and good fit vs poor fit (reflected in the fit indexes). The "mental health model" reached statistical nonsignificance, χ^2 (11, N = 204) = 18.06, p = .08. The model also showed an acceptable level of fit, GFI = 0.98, AGFI = 0.94, RMR = 2.39. In addition, the comparative fit index (CFI) is relatively robust across sample size compared to other fit indexes (Bentler, 1990), and a value at the upper .90s indicates an acceptable fit (CFI = .98 in the present model). RMSEA is a measure of discrepancy per degree of freedom, with a value below .05 to .08 indicating a close fit (RMSEA = .06 in the present model).

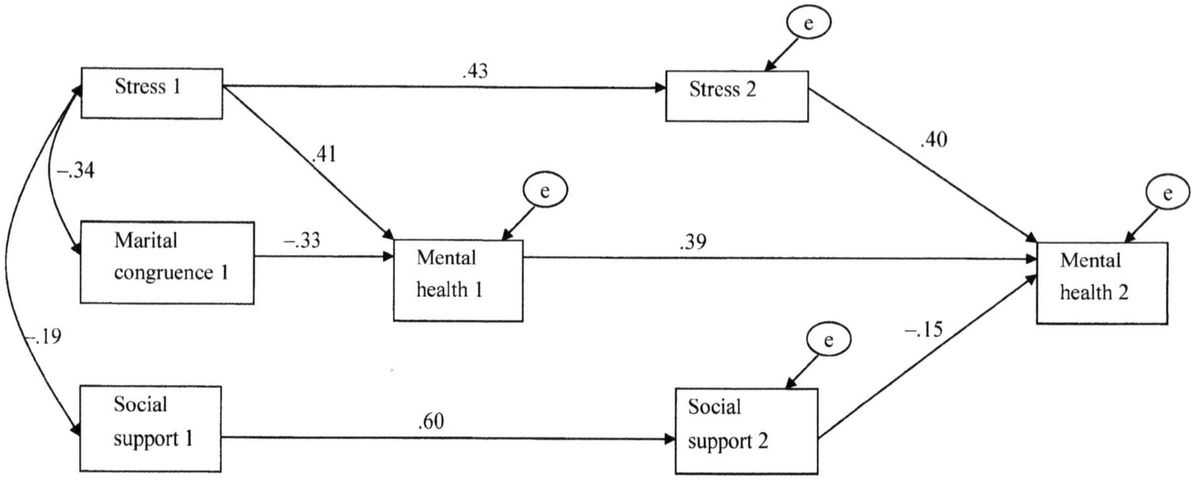

Figure 3. A structural model of mental health.

Taken together, the results of the present model showed an acceptable value of fit.

Exactly the same procedures were followed to construct, modify, and test the "marital satisfaction model." During the model trimming process, social support at Time 2 was taken out, as the path linking it with marital satisfaction at Time 2 was not significant. Three other paths were also omitted (stress1→marital satisfaction2, support1→marital satisfaction2, marital congruence1→marital satisfaction2) for the same reason. The final model is presented in Figure 4 with all paths statistically significant at the level of p = .05 and above.

The "marital satisfaction model" did not reach statistical nonsignificance, χ^2 (11, N = 204) = 26.51, p = .005. The fit indices were very good (GFI = 0.97, AGFI = 0.91), and residuals were small (RMR = 1.82, RMSEA = 0.08). In addition, the comparative fit index (CFI) of .95 was very good. Taken together, our model showed an acceptable level of fit to the data.

DISCUSSION

The present study was set against the Chinese cultural background. Adopting a panel study design, longitudinal data were collected at two points of time following childbirth, from a representative sample of both men and women. With these methodological strengths, results from the present study warrant serious reflection and careful consideration for researchers and practitioners alike. The following discussion will be organized around three major themes: impact of parenthood, roles of resources, and gender differences.

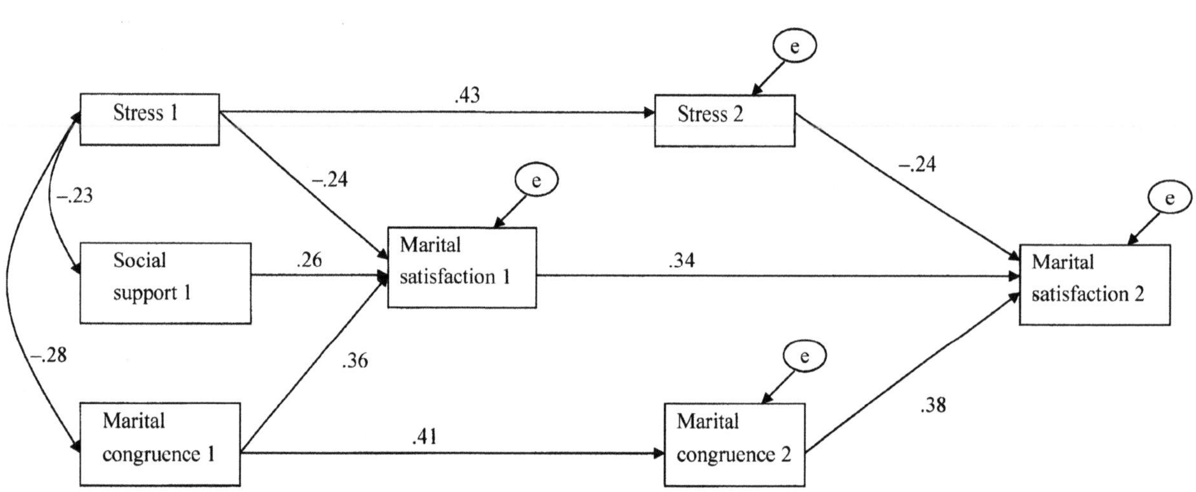

Figure 4. A structural model of mental satisfaction.

Gender differences in parenthood transition

Most extant research relating to the transition of parenthood has focused on maternal distress and adjustment. Consequently, we know very little about men's experiences of fatherhood. The present study was thus rare in drawing a community sample with men and women equally represented. Our results have revealed a stable pattern of gender differences over a half-year period after the child was born. Women consistently reported higher stress, worse mental health, and lower marital satisfaction than men. This pattern of gender differences was more rigorously examined and confirmed using the subset of 90 pairs of husband–wife dyadic data (Lu, 2004).

Our finding of women's or wives' heightened stress and poorer mental health is consistent with existing research on maternal distress and adjustment (Brody, 1985; Cowan et al., 1985). In particular, the Chinese culture places great emphasis on the continuation of the family line, and places the responsibility of childrearing squarely on the shoulders of women (Kao & Lu, 2001; Lu, Gilmour, & Kao, 2001; Yang, 1988). Becoming a mother is not only the most salient role for women (Lu & Lin, 1998), but also culturally sanctioned as a women's legitimate occupation (Chen, 1978). It is thus understandable that becoming a mother may be far more salient and stressful than becoming a father. However, men's experiences of fatherhood are also changing fast in a modern society. Traditionally, the Chinese fathers are sole wage earners and have little to do with childcare. Contemporary fathers, though, are expected to share household duties including childcare responsibilities, especially when mothers are working too (Lu & Lin, 1998). Although women still assume a greater share of homemaking activities, the pressure of being "a new good man" is increasing (Lu, Hwang, & Kao, 2005). As can be seen in the present study, parenthood stress was detrimental to both men's mental health and their marital happiness. Previous research has even found that husbands report the greater degree of unhappiness (Cowan et al., 1985). However, a longer follow-up phase is needed to identify sensitive points for the change and turning point in mental health and marital adjustment. For the time being, it is already clear that both men and women feel the negative effects of having a child on their mental health and marital relationship. Hence scientific research and intervention should better address the needs and concerns of both genders.

Impact of parenthood: Immediate vs long-lasting effects

Existing theories and research have suggested that becoming a parent can be a challenge that may have profound effects on both the individual and the developing family (Abbott & Brody, 1985; Argyle, 1987; Cowan et al., 1985; Sullivan-Lyons, 1998). The present study focused on the adjustment *after* the transition to parenthood and examined trajectories of post-parenthood adjustment for both men and women. Parenthood stress was found to have a negative impact on mental health 6 months following childbirth after controlling for the "baseline" level. Psychological distress is, therefore, more than the spillover of previous distress, and parental stress is the antecedent of psychological symptoms.

Our SEM models depicted more clearly the relationship between parental stress and adjustment. Where mental health is concerned, parental stress has three routes to assert its impact (see Figure 3). First, stress has a direct effect on concurrent mental health. Second, it has an indirect effect on later mental health through its impact on concurrent mental health. Third, stress has another indirect effect on later mental health through its carryover effect on later stress. Similar mechanisms also apply to marital satisfaction (see Figure 4). Taken together, the above results have supported paths 1, 3, 8–3, 1–7 in the generic framework (Figure 1).

With its methodological strengths, the present study has extended the current understanding of parenthood transition in several ways. First, as stress, mental health, and marital satisfaction were measured twice, data at Time 1 and Time 2 can serve as a cross-validation for each other. The pattern of relations between stress, mental health, and marital satisfaction was identical in both sets of data (Table 2). As a further check, the entire sample was randomly split into two equivalent parts and the two SEM models (Figures 3 and 4) were cross-validated. They fitted the two subsamples equally well. The robustness of this finding adds weight to our claim about the adjustment process to parenthood transition.

Second, there was moderate temporal stability regarding perceived stress, mental health, and marital satisfaction from 6 weeks to 6 months following childbirth. This suggests that conditions over this substantial period were quite stable. In other words, the impact of becoming a parent is of a stable and continuing nature. Furthermore, parental stress did not lessen over the 6 months period following childbirth. Consequently, mental health and marital satisfaction did not improve either. Furthermore, additional analyses revealed no gender difference in this pattern. Corroborating previous findings (e.g., Fergusson et al., 1996; Ferketich & Mercer, 1989), it can be concluded that the stressful impact of parenthood may be both immediate and long-lasting for both men and women.

Third, the mental health measure in the present study included not only depression, but also anxiety and common somatic symptoms. The above findings, therefore, went beyond the existing research on postnatal depression and provided a wider scope for the appreciation of mental health issues related to the transition to parenthood.

Finally, the stressful impact of parenthood found in the present study also corroborates the results of previous studies among the Chinese (Chong, 1995; Lu & Lin, 1998). It is clear now that, although the Chinese culture places great emphasis on the family and socially sanctioned parenthood as a divine obligation, becoming a parent is still a stressful transition for both men and women. In a time of rising divorce rate and heightened general life stress, young parents deserve more scientific recognition and understanding of the stress associated with parenthood. Hopefully, more concerted and effective help such as community intervention can be provided to people at such a crossroads of family life (Lu, in press).

Role of resources: Social support vs marital congruence

Although entering parenthood is indeed challenging and stressful, there are still quite considerable individual differences in dealing with this transition. The two structural models (Figures 3 and 4) revealed some adjustment mechanisms involving social support. Where mental health is concerned, support has an indirect effect on later mental health through its carryover effect on later support. Those who receive more support earlier on tend to retain their support, which protects them from distress. Where marital satisfaction is concerned, support has an indirect effect on later satisfaction through its contribution to concurrent satisfaction. Social support helps to enhance marital satisfaction, which is maintained over time. Taken together, the above results have supported paths 2, 4, 9–4, 2–7 in the generic framework (Figure 1).

Marital congruence, too, has demonstrated an unequivocal beneficial effect in the transition to parenthood. For both mental health and marital satisfaction, the protective effect of marital congruence was reliable and robust (see Tables 2 and 3).

In addition to these direct effects, marital congruence also demonstrated a reliable moderating effect on the stress/mental health relationship at 6 weeks and 6 months postpartum (see Table 4 and Figure 2). Furthermore, mediation effects of marital congruence on adjustment were also found (Figures 3 and 4). Where mental health is concerned, marital congruence has an indirect effect on later mental health through its contribution to concurrent mental health. Marital congruence protects mental health, which is maintained over time. Where marital satisfaction is concerned, marital congruence has two routes of effect. First, marital congruence has an indirect effect on later satisfaction through its contribution to concurrent satisfaction. Marital congruence helps to enhance marital satisfaction, which is maintained over time. Second, marital congruence has an indirect effect on later marital satisfaction through its carryover effect on later marital congruence. Taken together, the above results have supported paths 2, 4, 9–4, 2–7 in the generic framework (Figure 1).

It is clear that in the crucial transition to parenthood, resources within the conjugal system are indeed very important and effective. Previous study has noted that for women, high levels of marital intimacy are associated with a reduction in the degree of postpartum depression (Stemp et al., 1986). The above results extend the protective role of marital satisfaction to a much wider scope of adjustment for both men and women.

Limitations

It should be kept in mind that these data came from a cross-sectional self-report design. One cannot draw causal conclusions, and there is the concern about possible percept–percept bias. Arguing against this possibility are the findings that 20% of the correlation coefficients and one third of regression coefficients were nonsignificant (see Tables 2 and 4). This suggests that there was no pervasive underlying bias inflating these relationships. Nonetheless, one should still be cautious in interpreting this data, as well as data from other studies using similar designs.

One more limitation of the present study was the use of a one-item measure for marital satisfaction. A multi-item scale would strengthen the validity of findings. Type I errors also cannot be completely ruled out when multiple analyses were run.

The other limitation of the present study is that the analysis was limited to parents *after* childbirth. Ideally, the same participants should be studied prior to childbirth and followed afterwards for a substantial period of time to plot trajectories of parenthood adjustment. A separate sample of expecting parents ($N = 364$) were studied twice at 6 weeks before and 6 weeks after childbirth, and can act as a comparison group (Lu, in press). Using the same measures as those in the present study, at 6 weeks prenatal, fathers reported stress at 21.95, and mothers at 23.03; at 6 weeks postnatal, fathers reported stress at 21.64, and mothers at 23.93. The present sample did seem to report somewhat inflated levels of stress, though comparisons with clinical samples were not possible.

Manuscript received December 2004
Revised manuscript accepted August 2005

REFERENCES

Abbott, D. A., & Brody, G. H. (1985). The relation of child age, gender, and number of children to the marital adjustment of wives. *Journal of Marriage and the Family*, *47*, 77–84.

Argyle, M. (1987). *The psychology of happiness*. London: Methuen.

Atkinson, M. P., & Blackwelder, S. P. (1993). Fathering in the 20th century. *Journal of Marriage and the Family*, *55*, 975–986.

Barrera, M. (1981). Social adjustment in the pregnant adolescents: Measurement issues. In B. H. Gottlieb (Ed.), *Social networks and social support* (pp. 69–96). London: Sage.

Baruch, Y. (1999). Response rate in academic studies: A comparative analysis. *Human Relations*, *52*, 421–438.

Belsky, J. (1990). Children and marriage. In F. D. Fincham & T. N. Bradbury (Eds.), *The psychology of marriage: Basic issues and applications* (pp. 119–134). New York: Guilford Press.

Belsky, J., & Pensky, E. (1988). Marital change across the transition to parenthood. *Marriage and Family Review*, *12*, 133–156.

Belsky, J., & Rovine, M. (1984). Social-network contact, family support, and transition to parenthood. *Journal of Marriage and the Family*, *46*, 455–467.

Bentler, P. M. (1990). Comparative indexes in structural models. *Psychological Bulletin*, *107*, 238–246.

Brody, E. M. (1985). Parent care as a normative family stress. *Gerontologist*, *25*, 19–29.

Chen, J. F. (1978). *Marital role behavior and marital satisfaction*. Master's dissertation, National Taiwan University.

Chong, S. J. (1995). *Personality and attitude changes during the transition to parenthood* (Tech. Rep. NSC842413-H-004-004). Taipei, Taiwan: National Science Council.

Cohen, J., & Cohen, P. (1983). *Applying multiple regression/correlation analysis for the behavioral sciences* (2nd ed.). Hillsdale, NJ: Lawrence Erlbaum Associates Inc.

Cohen, S., Kamarck, T., & Mermelstein, R. (1983). A global measure of perceived stress. *Journal of Health and Social Behavior*, *24*, 385–396.

Cooper, P. J., Campbell, E. A., Day, A., Kennerley, H., & Bond, A. (1988). Nonpsychotic psychiatric disorder after childbirth. *British Journal of Psychiatry*, *152*, 799–806.

Cowan, C., Cowan, P., Heming, G., Garrett, E., Coysh, W., Curtis-Boles, H., & Boles, A. (1985). Transitions to parenthood: His, hers and theirs. *Journal of Family Issues*, *6*, 451–482.

Derogatis, L. R., Rickels, K., & Rock, A. F. (1976). The SCL-90MMPI: A step in the validation of a new self-report scale. *British Journal of Psychiatry*, *128*, 280–289.

Executive Yuan. (2004). *Report on the nation's family life*. Taipei: Author.

Fergusson, D. M., Horwood, L. J., & Thorpe, K. (1996). Changes in depression during and following pregnancy: ALSPAC Study Team, Study of pregnancy and children. *Paediatric and Prenatal Epidemiology*, *10*, 279–293.

Ferketich, S. L., & Mercer, R. T. (1989). Men's health status during pregnancy and early fatherhood. *Research in Nursing and Health*, *12*, 137–148.

Hackel, L. S., & Ruble, D. N. (1992). Changes in the marital relationship after the first baby is born: Predicting the impact of expectancy disconfirmation. *Journal of Personality and Social Psychology*, *62*, 944–957.

Harriman, L. C. (1986). Marital adjustment as related to personal and marital changes accompanying parenthood. *Family Relations*, *35*, 233–239.

Howell-White, S. (1991). *The relationship of locus of control to postpartum depression*. Paper presented at the meeting of the American Sociological Association, Cincinnati, OH, USA.

Hsu, L. G. (1953). *The Chinese and the Americans: Two ways of life*. New York: Henry Schuman.

Kao, S. F., & Lu, L. (2001). The relationship between parental rearing attitudes and the perceived stress of JHSEE among junior high school students. *Research in Applied Psychology*, *10*, 221–250.

Levy-Shiff, R. (1994). Individual and contextual correlates of marital change across the transition to parenthood. *Developmental Psychology*, *30*, 591–601.

Locke, H. J., & Wallace, K. M. (1959). Short marital-adjustment and prediction tests: Their reliability and validity. *Marriage and Family Living*, *21*, 251–255.

Lu, L. (1995). Correlates of social support: Personal characteristics and social resources. *Counseling Psychology Quarterly*, *8*, 173–181.

Lu, L. (2001). Understanding happiness: A look into the Chinese folk psychology. *Journal of Happiness Studies*, *2*, 407–432.

Lu, L. (2004). Sex differences and conjugal interdependence on parenthood stress and adjustment: A dyadic longitudinal Chinese study. *Marriage and Family Review*, *36*, 75–93.

Lu, L. (in press). The transition to parenthood: Stress, resources and gender differences in a Chinese society. *Journal of Community Psychology*.

Lu, L., & Argyle, M. (1992). Receiving and giving support: Effects on relationships and well-being. *Counselling Psychology Quarterly*, *5*, 123–133.

Lu, L., Gilmour, R., & Kao, S. F. (2001). Culture values and happiness: An East–West dialogue. *Journal of Social Psychology*, *141*, 477–493.

Lu, L., Hwang, M. T., & Kao, S. F. (2005). The bi-directional conflict of work and family: Antecedents, consequences and moderators. *Research in Applied Psychology*, *27*, 133–166.

Lu, L., & Lin, Y. Y. (1998). Family roles and happiness in adulthood. *Personality and Individual Differences*, *25*, 195–207.

Lu, L., Tseng, H. J., & Cooper, C. L. (1999). Managerial stress, job satisfaction and health in Taiwan. *Stress Medicine*, *15*, 53–64.

Marks, J., Goldberg, D. P., & Hillier, V. F. (1979). Determinants of the ability of General Practitioners to detect psychiatric illness. *Psychological Medicine*, *11*, 535–550.

Osofsky, J. D. (1979). *Handbook of infant development*. New York: Wiley.

Osofsky, J. D., & Culp, R. E. (1989). Risk factors in the transition to fatherhood. In S. H. Cath, A. Gurwitt, & L. Gunsberg (Eds.), *Fathers and their families* (pp. 145–165). Hillsdale, NJ: Analytic Press.

Owen, M. T., Lewis, J. M., & Henderson, V. K. (1989). Marriage, adult adjustment, and early parenting. *Child Development*, *60*, 1015–1024.

Phoenix, A., & Woollett, A. (1991). Motherhood, social construction and psychology. In A. Phoenix, A. Woollett, & E. Lloyd (Eds.), *Motherhood: Meanings, practices and ideologies* (pp. 13–27). London: Sage.

Quill, T. E., Lipkin, M., & Lamb, G. S. (1984). Health seeking by men in their spouse's pregnancy. *Psychosomatic Medicine*, *46*, 277–283.

Raykov, T., Tomer, A., & Nesselroade, J. R. (1991). Reporting structural equation modeling results in psychology and aging: Some proposed guidelines. *Psychology and Aging*, *6*, 499–503.

Santrock, J. W. (1995). *Life-span development* (5th ed.), Madison, WI: Brown & Benchmark.

Scarpello, V., & Campbell, J. P. (1983). Job satisfaction: Are all the parts there? *Personnel Psychology*, *36*, 577–600.

Stemp, P. S., Turner, M. A., & Noh, S. (1986). Psychological distress in the postpartum period: The significance of social support. *Journal of Marriage and the Family*, *48*, 271–277.

Sullivan-Lyons, J. (1998). Men becoming fathers: 'Sometimes I wonder how I'll cope'. In S. Clement (Ed.), *Psychological perspectives on pregnancy and childbirth*. London: Churchill-Livingstone.

Thornes, B., & Collard, J. (1979). *Who divorces?*. London: Routledge & Kegan Paul.

Ventura, J. N., & Boss, P. G. (1983). The family coping inventory applied to parents with new babies. *Journal of Marriage and the Family*, *45*, 867–875.

Wanous, J. P., Reichers, A. E., & Hudy, M. J. (1997). Overall job satisfaction: How good are single-item measures? *Journal of Applied Psychology*, *82*, 247–252.

Wortman, C. B., & Dunkel-Schetter, C. (1987). Conceptual and methodological issues in the study of social support. In A. Baum & J. E. Singer (Eds.), *Handbook of psychology and health* (pp. 63–107). Hillsdale, NJ: Lawrence Erlbaum Associates Inc.

Yang, K. S. (1988). A conceptual analysis of filial piety among the Chinese people. In K. S. Yang (Ed.), *Psychology of the Chinese people*. Taipei: Laurent.

Yeh, K. H., & Bedford, O. (2003). A test of the Dual Filial Piety model. *Asian Journal of Social Psychology*, *6*, 215–228.

Yue, X., & Ng, S. H. (1999). Filial obligations and expectation in China: Current views from young and old people in Beijing. *Asian Journal of Social Psychology*, *2*, 215–226.

INTERNATIONAL JOURNAL OF PSYCHOLOGY, 2006, 41 (5), 385–396

Immunization and facilitation produced by predictable and controllable aversive events alternating with different duration unpredictable and uncontrollable aversive events

Francisco Vicente, Pilar Ferrándiz, and Cristina Díaz-Berciano

Universidad Complutense de Madrid, Spain

This investigation examined whether immunization to learned helplessness is more effective through predictable and controllable events alternating with inescapable and unpredictable events of different duration, than through experiences with only controllable and predictable events. Prior experience with intermittent success resulted in greater immunization than experience with consistent success. Forty-two male Wistar rats were distributed at random to one of the six groups ($n = 7$ each). In groups M-20, M-40, and M-80, uncontrollable and unpredictable episodes of shocks with three levels of duration were intermixed with controllable and predictable events: short mixed immunization, 20 trials; moderate mixed immunization, 40 trials; and long mixed immunization, 80 trials. Group C-U received immunization treatment with only controllable and predictable events; C-NT was the control group and received controllability training but with no uncontrollable and unpredictable footshock; and group NT-U received basic learned helplessness treatment. In the test phase, all the subjects were exposed to escape/avoidance training. The results demonstrated the greater efficacy of immunization in groups M-20 and M-40 (short and moderate mixed immunization), in terms of significant differences in latency of response relative to groups M-80 (long mixed immunization) and C-U (standard immunization), while the behaviour of groups M-80 and C-U was similar. All immunization (mixed and standard) groups presented a shorter latency than group NT-U (no immunization). These data were discussed according to the "dual-expectancy hypothesis," the "interference hypothesis," the "anxiety hypothesis," and the "reactance theory."

Cette recherche a examiné dans quelle mesure l'immunisation à la résignation acquise est plus efficace lors d'événements prédictibles et contrôlables alternant avec des événements inévitables et non prédictibles, de différentes durées, que lors d'événements contrôlables et prédictibles seulement. Une expérience précédente menant à un succès intermittent a résulté en une plus grande immunisation qu'une expérience menant à un succès constant. Quarante-deux rats Wistar males ont été répartis au hasard dans six groupes (n = 7 chacun). Pour trois groupes, des épisodes incontrôlables et non prédictibles de chocs ont été mélangés avec des événements contrôlables et prédictibles, avec trois niveaux de durée pour le premier traitement: immunisation courte mixte de 20 essais (groupe M-20), immunisation modérée mixte de 40 essais (groupe M-40) et immunisation longue mixte de 80 essais (groupe M 80). En ce qui a trait aux trois autres groupes, un a reçu un traitement d'immunisation avec seulement des événements contrôlables et prédictibles (groupe C-U); un autre fut considéré comme groupe contrôle et a reçu un entraînement de contrôlabilité mais sans recevoir de choc incontrôlable et non prédictible (groupe C-NT) et; un dernier groupe a reçu un traitement de base de résignation acquise (groupe NT-U). Dans la phase de test, tous les sujets ont été exposés à un entraînement de fuite/évitement. Les résultats ont démontré une plus grande efficacité de l'immunisation dans les groupes M-20 et M-40 comparativement aux groupes M-80 et C-U, en termes de différences significatives dans la latence de réponse, tandis que les comportements des groupes M-80 et C-U étaient similaires. Tous les groupes ayant reçu une immunisation (M-20, M-40, M-80 et C-U) ont présenté une latence plus courte que le groupe sans immunisation (NT-U). Ces données ont été discutées en lien avec l'hypothèse de double attente, l'hypothèse d'interférence, l'hypothèse d'anxiété et la théorie de la réactance.

Correspondence should be addressed to F. Vicente or C. Díaz-Berciano, Departamento de Psicología Básica I (Procesos Básicos), Facultad de Psicología, Universidad Complutense de Madrid, Campus de Somosaguas, 28223 Madrid, Spain (E-mail: fvicente@psi.ucm.es or cdiazberciano@psi.ucm.es).

This research was supported by a research grant from the Complutense University of Madrid.

In memoriam of Pilar Ferrándiz.

 DOI: 10.1080/00207590500411344

La presente investigación ha examinado si la inmunización frente a la indefensión aprendida es más efectiva cuando se alternan sucesos predecibles y controlables con sucesos impredecibles e incontrolables, de diferente duración, que cuando se presentan sólo sucesos predecibles y controlables. Se ha comprobado que el efecto de inmunización es mayor cuando la experiencia previa es con sucesos intermitentes que con continuos. Se utilizaron cuarenta y dos ratas Wistar macho que fueron distribuidas al azar a uno de los seis grupos (n = 7 por grupo). Los grupos M-20, M-40 y M-80 recibieron entrenamiento mixto con sesiones impredecibles e incontrolables alternando con sesiones predecibles y controlables, siendo la duración del tratamiento anterior de tres niveles: inmunización mixta corta de 20 ensayos, inmunización mixta moderada de 40 ensayos, e inmunización mixta larga de 80 ensayos; el grupo C-NT fue el grupo control y no recibió entrenamiento con descargas impredecibles e incontrolables; el grupo C-U recibió tratamiento de inmunización sólo con sucesos controlables y predecibles; y el grupo NT-U recibió el tratamiento básico de indefensión aprendida. En la fase de prueba todos los sujetos fueron expuestos a un entrenamiento de escape / evitación. Los resultados mostraron la eficacia de la inmunización en los grupos M-20 y M-40 (inmunización mixta corta y moderada), existiendo diferencias significativas en la latencia de respuesta respecto a los grupos M-80 (inmunización mixta larga) y C-U (inmunización estándar), mientras que la conducta de los grupos M-80 y C-U fue similar. Todos los grupos inmunizados (de forma mixta o estándar) presentaron una menor latencia que el grupo NT-U (no inmunización). Las comparaciones múltiples mostraron que la latencia de respuesta de los grupos M-20, M-40 y C-NT (control) fue menor que la del resto de los grupos. Estos datos han sido discutidos de acuerdo con la "hipótesis de expectativa dual," la "hipótesis de la interferencia," la "hipótesis de la ansiedad," y la "teoría de la reactancia."

Pre-exposure to a series of inescapable shocks or noncontingent events has been shown to produce deficits in a variety of later situations and has been called *learned helplessness*; such behaviour reflects the interference produced by uncontrollable shocks (Seligman & Maier, 1967). Experimental animals showed three kinds of deficits comprising a syndrome: (1) the animal failed to reliably initiate responses in the presence of shocks—a motivational deficit; (2) they failed to show learning after having experienced a reinforced escape response—an associative or cognitive deficit; (3) they showed anxiety followed by depression—an affective/emotional deficit (Overmier & Seligman, 1967). The original theory proposed that uncontrollability was the critical determinant. Later, Overmier (1985) proposed that the helplessness syndrome is not a unitary phenomenon but is multidimensional, being the product of different causal factors; helplessness was modulated by both controllability and predictability (e.g., Dess, Linwick, Paterson, Overmier, & Levine, 1983; Jackson & Minor, 1988; Overmier & LoLordo, 1998; Overmier, Murison, Taklo, & Espelid, 1994). Furthermore, Overmier (1985) suggested that uncontrollability of the aversive event produces the motivational deficit, whereas unpredictability produces the cognitive deficit. There is growing evidence in favour of such separation of causal factors, which suggests that uncontrollability on its own does not adequately account for the observed phenomena (Ferrándiz, 1989; Ferrándiz & Pardo, 1990; Ferrándiz & Vicente, 1997). For this reason, predictable and controllable events were studied in this experiment.

There are a variety of alternative explanations as to why animals exposed to inescapable shocks later failed to learn to escape, including behavioural, cognitive, and neurochemical factors. In the same way that different points of view exist concerning the acquisition of the deficits that appear in the phenomenon of learned helplessness, different points of view occur, logically, regarding the phenomenon of "immunization" against helplessness, which is the object of this study.

The relationship between behaviour and outcomes may affect the acquisition of later operant responses, which suggests a means to prevent or immunize against the interference effect caused by exposure to unpredictable, inescapable shocks.

There has been a great deal of research done on the mechanisms that reduce the helplessness deficits. These include: (1) the presentation of predictable stimuli (Jackson & Minor, 1988); (2) immunization phases with escapable and predictable stimuli (Ferrándiz & Pardo, 1990; Troisi, Bersh, Stromberg, Mauro, & Whitehouse 1991); (3) administration of certain drugs prior to exposure to uncontrollable events (Drugan, Ryan, Minor, & Maier, 1984; Scheggi, Masi, Tagliamonte, Gambarana, Tolu, & De Montis, 2000; Woodson, Minor, & Job, 1998); (4) agonistic behaviour during unavoidable stress that prevents the development of pathological changes in adaptive behaviour (learned helplessness) and changes in the endocrine system (Zhukov & Vinogradova, 1998); (5) feedback stimuli for responses during the testing (Warren, Rossellini & Maier, 1989); and (6) prevention training in human identification of automatic negative thoughts, distraction techniques, behavioural activation strategies, etc. (Seligman, Schulman, DeRubeis, & Hollons, 1999).

The similarity between the learned helplessness phenomenon and learned irrelevance, i.e., that in both paradigms, noncontingent relationships of two events (a CS and a US or a response and an outcome) cause interference with subsequent learning, has led some researchers to suggest that the prevention of general learned irrelevance (Imada & Kitaguchi, 2002; Nakajima, Nakajima, & Imada, 1999; Overmier, 2002) would prevent learned helplessness. The prevention or immunization in both phenomena is that the experience of a positive relationship could attenuate the deficit in the test phase.

Immunization or prevention is one of the subjects of positive psychology (Seligman & Csikszentmihalyi, 2000). In the past decade, psychologists have become concerned with prevention, and this was the main theme of the 1998 American Psychological Association convention in San Francisco. Prevention researchers have discovered that there are human strengths that act as buffers against mental illness; the question is, how? However, at the current time, what seems to happen more frequently in real life has not yet been investigated; i.e., that one is normally subjected to uncontrollable and unpredictable situations of varying duration alternating with predictable and controllable situations. In these situations, individual subjects are perhaps immunized more than if they were only subjected to situations of continuous control and prediction.

From our point of view, there are four hypotheses that explain why immunization to helplessness might be more effective through alternating inescapable and unpredictable events with predictable and controllable events than only through experiences of control and prediction.

First, according to the "interference hypothesis" of immunization, Seligman and Maier (1967) and Seligman (1992) proposed that when an animal was initially exposed to response-contingent escapable shocks, learned helplessness effects should be completely eliminated. This is because if an animal has initially learned control over an aversive event, this ought to interfere with its subsequent learning of a noncontingent relation when it encounters inescapable shocks. An initial positive contingency experience like this might reduce the animal's tendency to expect future noncontingency. In human research, people can be immunized against the effects of uncontrollable events by providing them with previous experience with controllability (e.g., Altmaier & Happ, 1985; Dyck & Breen, 1978; Eckelman & Dyck, 1979). Studies have also demonstrated that humans, like animals, can be immunized against learned helplessness effects by being exposed to controllable events beforehand (Mikulincer, 1994).

Second, agreeing with the "anxiety hypothesis," the degree of behavioural control that a human or an animal has over a stressor is one of the most potent variables determining the behavioural, physiological, and neural impact of the stressor. Its controllability is not a physical property of the stressor, but is a characteristic of the stressor about which the organism must learn. The effect of helplessness is produced by the more substantial and chronic fear engendered by unsignalled inescapable shocks compared with escapable and predictable shock (Minor, Dess, & Overmier, 1991; Overmier & Murison, 2000; Steciuk, Kram, Kramer, & Petty, 1999). Chorpita and Barlow (1998) emphasize the importance of early experience of uncontrollable and unpredictable events in the development of anxiety. Early experience with uncontrollable events may be thought of as a primary pathway to the development of anxiety, because such experiences may foster an increased likelihood of processing events as "not within one's control." However, the effects of stressors are not straightforward, as their long-term effects on development are not necessarily harmful. In fact, the negative impact of stressors appears to be closely tied to their interpretations and one's ability to control these stressors. When control is possible, environmental challenges and the associated distress may potentially lead to adaptive functioning over time. There is evidence with rats and mice that shows that early exposure to stressful manipulations such as a controllable shock can actually lead to a less fearful animal when it is exposed to subsequent uncontrollable events. Controllable trauma can actually immunize animals against later helplessness. Taking into account the role of control, or the belief that one has control, in reducing anxiety, this explanatory mechanism—the anxiety hypothesis—could accommodate immunization.

Jones, Nation, and Massad (1977) found that immunization procedures interacted definitively with schedules of reinforcement. Specifically, partial success pretraining was found to prevent the development of learned helplessness and, as a consequence, the performance deficits characteristic of subjects exposed to uncontrollable events did not occur. Subjects who received continuous success training failed to demonstrate comparable immunization effects. Nation and Massad (1978) found that both partial and continuous reinforcement are efficacious procedures for reversing learned helplessness; however, the partial success schedule produced greater response persistence in escape extinction. Subjects immunized with partial success continue to display active escape responses, refusing to relent to the debilitating effects of exposure to inescapable stimuli. These findings concerning immunization effects against helplessness in both investigations provides the key support base for the present research.

Finally, according to the "reactance theory," in some studies when subjects are in an uncontrollable situation, reactance effects appear rather than helplessness, depending on the amount of experience with uncontrollability. The reactance-helplessness integration has several virtues and can explain immunization effects (Peterson, Maier, & Seligman, 1993). When the amount of experience with uncontrollable events is systematically varied, less experience with uncontrollability leads to facilitation of problem solving, whereas more experience with uncontrollability leads to impairment. On the other hand, Anderson, Crowell, DePaul, and McEachin (1997) propose that longer duration inescapable shocks come to have a greater degree of total aversiveness, and thereby should have more deleterious effects on subsequent test performance than shocks of shorter duration.

The purpose of the present investigation has been to prove how immunization to helplessness is made more effective by alternating inescapable and unpredictable with predictable and controllable events in an previous phase, than by having initial experiences of only control and prediction.

METHOD

Subjects

Forty-two albino male, experimentally naive Wistar rats were used (supplied by CAI Animalario of the Complutense University of Madrid); mean body weight at the beginning of the experiment was about 350 g. The rats were kept in individual boxes with a constant temperature (22° ± 2°C), with free access to water and food. They were maintained with the light-dark cycle of 12:12 hours. The animals were maintained in accordance with RD 223/1988 normative guidelines for care.

The animals stayed 7 days in laboratory housing colony conditions to acclimatize to the new conditions before beginning the experimental phase. There were assigned randomly to six equal-sized groups of seven rats each.

Apparatus

A two-way shuttle-box (Letica, LI-900), of 50 × 25 × 25 with an acrylic frontal wall and steel floor bars was used. The shuttle-box consisted of two identical adjacent chambers (25 × 25 × 25 cm), separated by a plastic barrier with an open arch in the bottom (9 × 9 cm). The floor grid of each compartment had 18 bars. The shuttle-box was put inside a soundproofed chamber equipped with a ventilator in the side wall for air renewal, which produced a background noise (72dB "Alpha"). In the front wall of the soundproof box there was a white light (24V), which remained lit throughout the experiment. An audio generator (LI100-26 Audio Gen), and a Shock Manager with scrambler were used (LI100-26-Shocker). Experimental events were controlled automatically through a personal computer using specific software.

Procedure

The rats were weighed daily from the beginning until the end of the experiment. The experiment was carried out in a suitable soundproofed room close to the housing colony. The animals were allowed to acclimatize for 2 minutes in the experimental box before each training session commenced. After the experimental session, the substrate of the bottom box was changed and fresh sawdust was used. The inside of the experimental box was cleaned with a soap and water solution to take away any trace of the smell of the animal.

The experiment consisted of three phases: (1) immunization phase, (2) pre-treatment phase, and (3) test phase (see Table 1).

1. *Immunization phase*: During this phase the groups M-20, M-40, and M-80 received training with uncontrollable, unpredictable aversive events alternating with controllable, predictable aversive events. The duration of the treatment with controllable events was greater than the training with uncontrollable events (relationship 3:1 days).

On day 1, the groups M-20, M-40, and M-80 received training with uncontrollable, unpredictable footshock (AC, 1 mA of intensity, 5 s of duration). The inter-trial interval varied by 60 s (range: 30–90 s). The duration of the treatment was different for each of the three groups. The group M-20 received 20 trials (short mixed immunization group), the group M-40 received 40 trials (moderate mixed immunization group), and the group M-80 received 80 trials (long mixed immunization group). The groups C-NT

TABLE 1
The experimental protocol is shown: *20, 40,* and *80* mean the number of uncontrollable shocks per session; *us* means uncontrollable shocks; *no treat* means no treatment

	Immunization phase				*Pre-treatment phase*	*Test phase*
Groups	*Day 1*	*Days 2–4*	*Day 8*	*Days 9–11*	*Day 15*	*Days 16–18*
M-20	20 us	Esc/avoid	20 us	Esc/avoid	80 us	Esc/avoid
M-40	40 us	Esc/avoid	40 us	Esc/avoid	80 us	Esc/avoid
M-80	80 us	Esc/avoid	80 us	Esc/avoid	80 us	Esc/avoid
C-NT	No treat	Esc/avoid	No treat	Esc/avoid	No treat	Esc/avoid
C-U	No treat	Esc/avoid	No treat	Esc/avoid	80 us	Esc/avoid
NT-U	No treat	No treat	No treat	No treat	80 us	Esc/avoid

(control-no treatment group), C-U (controllable-uncontrollable or standard immunization group), and NT-U (no treatment-uncontrollable or no-immunization group) were introduced in the experimental box for 30 minutes without receiving any treatment. In this phase the rats could go from one compartment to the other; the barrier was coloured beige and the light of the experimental box was white.

On days 2, 3, and 4, the groups M-20, M-40, M-80, C-NT, and C-U received escape/avoidance training (80 trials, AC, 0.6 mA of intensity, and 10 s maximum duration). Each trial consisted of the following events. The tone was presented for 8 s (800 Hz, 90 dB "Alpha") and then, after 1 s of silence, the footshock was presented. The subjects could avoid or escape the shock. The maximum duration of the shock was 10 s if the subject did not escape. During these days, the group NT-U (no-immunization group) was introduced into the experimental box without receiving any treatment. During the escape-avoidance training the light of the box was red, and the barrier between compartments was also red.

After the last training day, all the subjects remained in their boxes in the colony for a period of 72 hours without receiving treatment to prevent excessive stress.

The 4 days of treatment accomplished during the first week were repeated again in the following week. Thus, on day 8 the groups M-20, M-40, and M-80 received training with uncontrollable, unpredictable aversive events, and the groups C-NT, C-U, and NT-U were introduced to the experimental box without receiving any treatment. On days 9, 10 and 11 all the groups, except group NT-U, received training with controllable, predictable aversive events. Again, after the 4 consecutive days of treatment, all the animals remained in the housing colony for 72 hours.

2. *Pre-treatment phase*: On day 15 of the experimental period, the groups M-20, M-40, M-80, C-U, and NT-U received uncontrollable, unpredictable footshock treatment (80 trials, 1 mA of intensity, and 5 s of duration). The group C-NT was introduced into the experimental box for 30 minutes without receiving any treatment (controllable events group). During this phase the light of the box was white and the central barrier was beige.

3. *Test phase*: All the groups received 80 escape/avoidance trials training (0.6 mA of shock intensity, 10 s of maximum duration), over 3 consecutive days on days 16, 17, and 18. The subjects received the tone (800 Hz, 90 dB "Alpha") for 8 s and, after 1 s of silence, the footshock appeared. The animals could avoid or escape the shock. During this phase the lateral walls of the box had six black horizontal lines and six white lines (each 2 cm in width). The light of the box was red and the central barrier was also red.

During the escape/avoidance test days, latency of response (highest value was 19 s), total number of responses, and number of avoidance responses were registered for testing the short- and mid-term immunization effect.

Kruskal-Wallis and Friedman tests were used to assess the variance of the behavioural measures over different treatment groups. Subsequently, appropriate paired comparisons were carried out using Mann-Whitney U-test (α = .05).

RESULTS

Test phase

The Friedman test showed differences in latency of response in all groups on different test days, H(2) = 2628.2, $p<.001$. Multiple comparisons showed a higher latency of response on day 1 compared to day 2, U = 5179295, $p<.001$, and day 3, U = 4981948, $p<.001$. Furthermore, subjects on day 2 showed a higher latency than on day 3,

U = 5430043, $p<.05$. No differences were found in total number of responses and avoidance responses factors between days.

First test day. Groups differed significantly in latency of response, H(5) = 640.769, $p<.001$ (see Figure 1). The multiple comparisons showed that group M-20 (short mixed immunization) presented a shorter latency than the rest of the groups (M-20<M-40, M-80, C-NT, C-U, and NT-U). Group M-40 showed a shorter latency than M-80, C-U, and NT-U. Groups M-80 and C-U presented a shorter latency than the NT-U group. Group C-NT showed a shorter latency than groups C-U and NT-U. All immunization (mixed or standard) groups presented a shorter latency than group NT-U (no immunization). Groups M-20 and M-40 (short and moderate mixed immunization) showed a shorter latency than group C-U (standard immunization). Also, group M-20 showed a shorter latency than the control group (C-NT). No differences were found between long mixed immunization (M-80 group) and standard immunization (C-U group).

The Kruskal-Wallis test showed differences in the total number of responses in all groups over the test days, H(5) = 18.17, $p<.05$. All groups showed a higher total number of responses than group NT-U, except group M-80 (M-20, M-40, C-NT, and C-U>NT-U) (see Figure 2). Group M-20 presented a higher total number of responses than group C-U. These results showed that the immunization groups (except the long immunization group) presented a higher activity level than the no immunization group. The short mixed immunization group had a higher activity level than the standard immunization group.

The Kruskal-Wallis test showed differences in the number of avoidance responses in all groups over the test days, H(5) = 18.98, $p<.05$. All groups showed a higher number of avoidance responses than group NT-U, except group C-U (M-20, M-40, M-80, and C-NT>NT-U) (see Figure 3). Group M-20 presented a higher number of avoidance responses than group C-U. These results showed that the mixed immunization groups presented a higher associative capacity than the no immunization group.

Second test day. Groups differed significantly in latency of response, H(5) = 213.350, $p<.001$. The multiple comparisons showed that the latency of response in groups M-20, M-40, C-NT, and C-U was smaller than the latency of group NT-U. The latency of response of groups M-20, M-40, and C-NT was smaller than that of the M-80 and C-U groups.

Groups differed significantly in total number of responses, H(5) = 14.48, $p<.05$. The multiple comparisons showed that the total number of responses in groups M-20, M-40, and C-NT was higher than in the NT-U group. Furthermore, the total number of responses in group M-20 was higher than in the M-40, M-80, and C-U groups.

Groups differed significantly in number of avoidance responses, H(5) = 13.05, $p<.05$. The

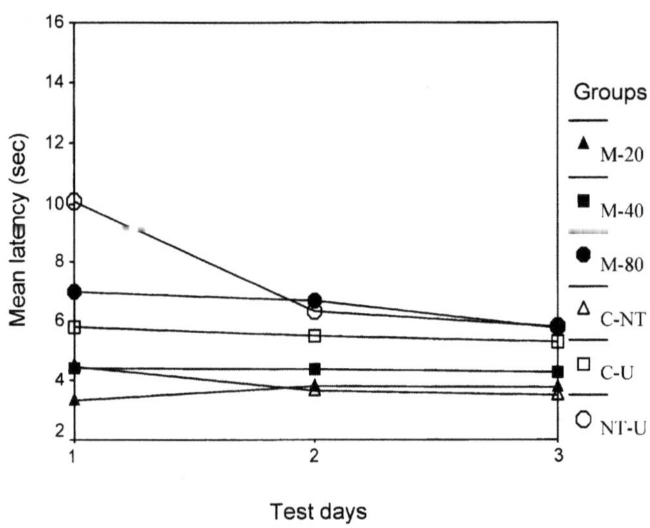

Figure 1. Mean latency of response in the test phase for the different groups. The groups M-20, M-40, and M-80 received mixed immunization training (light, moderate, and severe respectively). The groups C-NT and C-U received only controllable aversive events treatment in the immunization phase (control group and standard immunization group respectively). The group NT-U was not immunized (no immunization group).

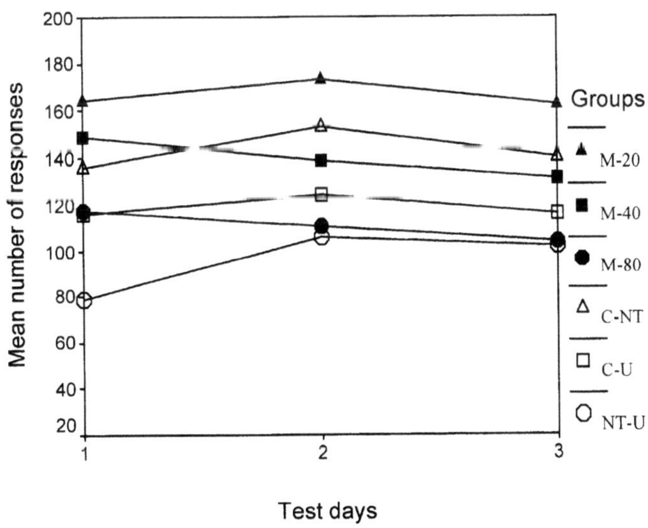

Figure 2. Mean number of responses in the test phase for the different groups.

multiple comparisons showed that the number of avoidance responses in groups M-20, M-40, and C-NT was higher than in group NT-U.

Third test day. Groups differed significantly in latency of response, H(5) = 173.263, p<.001. The multiple comparisons showed that the latency of response of groups M-20, M-40, M-80, and C-NT was smaller than the latency of group NT-U. The latency of response of groups M-20, M-40, and C-NT was smaller than the latency of groups M-80, C-U, and NT-U. Group M-20 differed from all of the groups except the C-NT group. Groups M-20 and M-40 did not differ, and group M-80 did not differ from group C-U.

The no immunization group (NT-U group) showed a longer latency than the groups with mixed immunization treatment (M-20, M-40, M-80 groups), and the group with standard immunization treatment (C-U group). These data indicated a significant immunization effect of mixed immunization treatment on subsequent learning, and it was similar or better than immunization treatment using controllable and predictable events. When the uncontrollable aversive events training immunization treatment was short or moderate (M-20 and M-40 groups), learning was as good in the C-NT group (control group). The shorter the uncontrollability length in the mixed immunization treatment, the better the subsequent learning. Also, when the uncontrollable aversive events training in the mixed immunization treatment was high (M-80 group), the latency of response was similar to that of the group immunized with controllable and predictable aversive events (C-U group).

There were significant differences for the total number of responses produced during the test phase, H(5) = 17.611, *p*<.05. Multiple comparisons showed that the total number of responses for group M-20 was bigger than for groups M-40, M-80, C-U, and NT-U. Considering that this variable represents the subject's motivational level, we could affirm that mixed immunization treatment produced a similar effect to that seen in control groups (there were no differences in groups M-40, M-80, C-NT, and C-U). When the uncontrollability duration in the mixed immunization treatment is short, the subject's motivation is higher than the motivation of groups trained with controllable events (M-20>C-U).

There were no significant differences between groups for the avoidance responses during the third test day. This tendency can be seen in Figure 3.

Development of the performance through the test days. The Kruskal-Wallis test showed differences in latency of response in all groups over the test days, H(2) = 74.03, *p*<.001; group, H(5) = 551.61, *p*<.001, and Group × Days interaction, H(17) = 1116.828, *p*<.001. The M-20 and M-40 groups did not vary their latency of response over the test days (see Figure 4). Group M-80 presented some changes over the test days, H(2) = 8.18, *p*<.05, and there were differences between the third test day and both the first and the second test days. We found statistically significant differences in group C-NT over the test days, H(2) = 17.81, *p*<.05, and these differences existed between the first and the second days, and between the first and the third days. In group C-U there were statistically significant differences between the first and the third days, H(2) = 8.68, $p<.05$. Group NT-U presented differences between the first and the second days, the first and the third days, and the second and the third days, H(2) = 330.68, $p<.05$. In all cases, the differences involved a decrease of latency of response over the test days.

No differences due to the test days were found in the total number of responses and number of avoidance responses.

Development of performance through the immunization days. With respect to the changes in latency of response through the six controllability sessions, statistically significant differences were found in the day of training, H(5) = 3222.17, $p<.001$, group, H(4) = 538.83, $p<.001$, and Day × Group interaction, H(29) = 3984.02, $p<.001$.

Groups C-NT and C-U showed significant differences in latency of response to the three mixed immunization treatment groups, H(4) = 581.49, $p<.001$; H(4) = 185.63, $p<.001$, respectively, on days 1 and 2 of controllability training (C-NT, C-U<M-20, M-40, M-80) (see Figure 4). On days 3, 4, and 5 differences appeared between groups C-NT and C-U, and groups M-40 and M-80, H(4) = 54.67, $p<.001$; H (4) = 60.56, $p<.001$; H(4) = 184.63, $p<.001$, respectively (C-NT, C-U<M-40, M-80). On day 6 differences have only been found between groups C-NT and C-U and group M-80, H(4) = 74.49, $p<.001$ (C-NT,

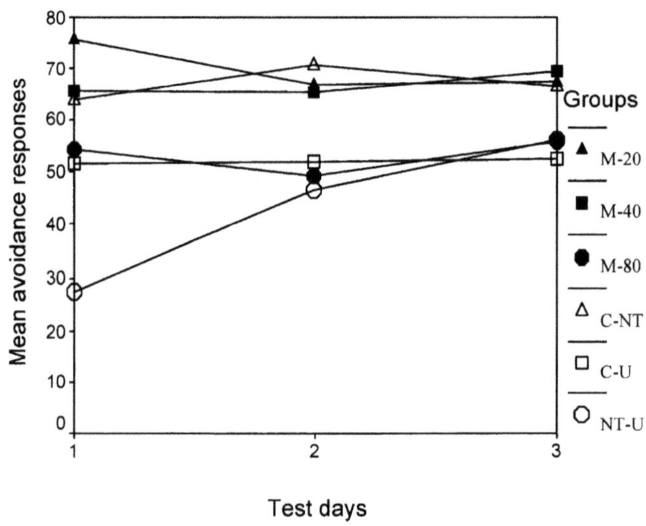

Figure 3. Mean number of avoidance responses in the test phase for the different groups.

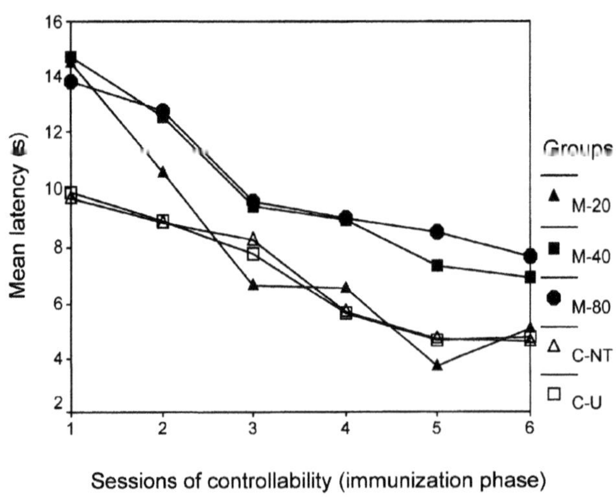

Figure 4. Mean latency of response in the immunization phase for the different groups. Because the group NT-U was not immunized it does not appear.

C-U<M-80). These results show that when the days of short and moderate mixed immunization treatment increased, the differences between these and the control groups (C-NT and C-U) decreased with respect to the latency of response. Therefore, when the mixed treatment was short, the differences disappeared after the third day. When the mixed treatment was moderate, the differences disappeared after the sixth day, and when the mixed treatment was long, the differences remained over the 6 days of controllability training.

Furthermore, group M-20 showed a shorter latency of response than groups M-40 and M-80 from days 2 to 5 of controllability training (M-20<M-40, M-80). On day 6 there were differences between groups M-20 and M-40 with M-80 (M-20, M-40<M-80). Also, group M-20 showed a shorter latency of response than groups C-NT and C-U on days 3 and 5 of training: The lower the level of uncontrollability in mixed immunization training, the shorter the latency of response.

On day 1 of the controllability sessions, groups C-NT and C-U showed a higher number of responses than the mixed immunization groups, $H(4) = 15.16$, $p<.05$ (C-NT, C-U>M-20, M-40, M-80) (see Figure 5). On days 2, 3, and 4 there were no differences between groups. On day 5, group M-20 showed a higher number of responses than the rest of the groups, $H(4) = 13.36$, $p<.05$ (M-20>M-40, M-80, C-NT, C-U). On day 6, group M-20 showed a higher number of responses than groups M-80, C-NT, and C-U, $H(4) = 11.16$, $p<.05$ (M-20>M-80, C-NT, C-U).

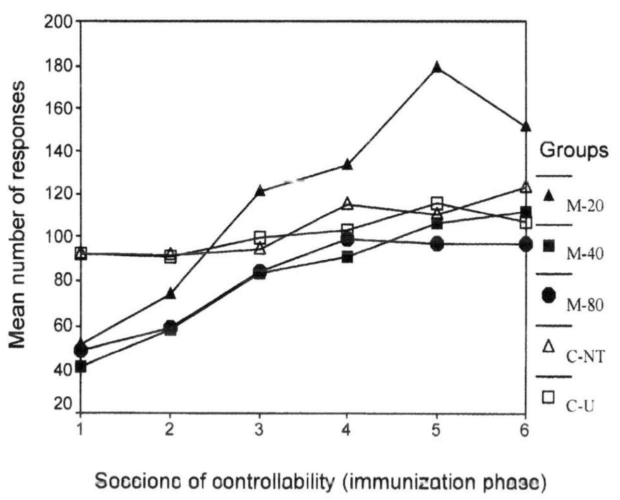

Figure 5. Mean number of responses in the immunization phase for the different groups. Because the group NT-U was not immunized it does not appear.

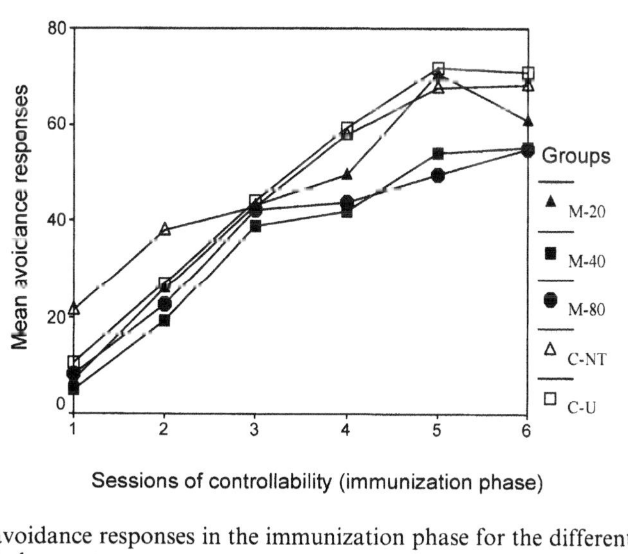

Figure 6. Mean number of avoidance responses in the immunization phase for the different groups. Because the group NT-U was not immunized it does not appear.

No differences between groups in the number of avoidance responses were found. This tendency can be seen in Figure 6.

DISCUSSION

The present research was guided by the presumption that it is possible to immunize animals from the exposure to inescapable aversive stimuli. The prototype for immunization is the research of Seligman and Maier (1967), who trained some of their subjects (dogs) to perform the test response prior to shock treatment to prevent the development of independence response reinforcement. However, according to the present results, there are some differences between our experiment and prior studies; only the animals that were subjected to uncontrollable and unpredictable short and moderate aversive stimuli (groups M-20, and M-40) alternating with controllable and predictable aversive stimuli, behaved in a similar way to the control group during the test period.

The present experiment demonstrated that the application of uncontrollable and unpredictable aversive stimuli, short and moderate, alternating with controllable and predictable aversive stimuli, could immunize, and therefore influence proactive interference, lessening the effects produced by learned helplessness. When all the organisms, except the control group, are exposed to long inescapable and unpredictable situations, the subjects that had previously had experiences with uncontrollable and unpredictable short and moderate events perform better than those that had never had similar experiences.

There are a number of interesting comments to be made about the results obtained here. From a theoretical point of view, our results are partly in accord with the hypothesis of the interference of the pre-treatment phase with the test phase due to the expectations of the subject (Seligman & Maier, 1967). This hypothesis differs from that seen in the introduction, as the hypothesis of interference proposes that previous experience of the control to the phase of helplessness interferes with later noncontingent learning. The results confirm that alternating situations of lack of control and prediction with controllable and predictable situations produce better immunization. This was demonstrated in the shorter latency (M-20 long latency reflects equally the lack of motivation to respond and the cognitive difficulty in finding the correct response) in groups M-20, M-40, and C-NT, as opposed to group M-80, and the same occurs in the number of responses of escape/avoidance.

The results of this experiment agree with the dual-expectancy hypothesis of Bolles (1972), which assumes that animals learn expectancy of response-reinforcement dependence and independence, and so they can perform in accordance with both situations (controllability and uncontrollability). Expectancy is under contextual discriminative control. Extending treatment increases the strength of expectancy. So, the subjects with short and moderate mixed training have appropriate expectancies in every situation, and they perform better than subjects previously trained only with controllable events. The severe mixed training has less immunizing effect, maybe because the expectancy of uncontrollability is too strong.

According to the "hypothesis of anxiety," Maier (1990, 1993), Maier and Watkins (1998) and Minor (1990) propose that the inescapable, long shock produces conditioned fear that is then transferred to the following phase. Anderson et al. (1997) and Lehmann et al. (1999) postulate that exposure to a series of inescapable and long events produce motivational and neurochemical disorders that can influence a variety of future learning. The anxiety hypothesis argues that exposure to inescapable shock produces chronic fear (Rowe, 2003).

In the experiment, groups M-20 and M-40, which during the pre-treatment phase had received inescapable and unpredictable shocks alternated with escapable and predictable shocks, exhibited less fear in response to the shock than animals that, in the pre-treatment phase, had been subjected only to controllable and predictable events, as it is the first time that they have been subjected to this new situation. The present data may reflect also the proposal of Minor et al. (1991), which states that shock treatment intensifies neophobic responses. For groups M-20, M-40, and M-80 the second phase is not new. Following the arguments of Overmier (1988), we also propose that inescapable shocks are considered an M-20 stressing condition that influences future situations, and many possible conditions, like M-20 shock escape contingency, may modulate the behavioural and/or biophysiological consequences of the stressor. In the phase of immunization, inescapable and unpredictable shocks in groups M-20 and M-40 were also added.

This investigation demonstrated that the lack of control and short and moderate prediction (groups M-20 and M-40), combined with situations of predictable and controllable escape/avoidance, immunize the subjects, a situation that does not occur when the lack of prediction is longer (group M-80). These results could be interpreted in the frame of the reactance theory. As some studies have found, when the amount of experience with uncontrollable events is systematically varied, less experience with uncontrollability leads to an M-20 facilitation of problem solving at the test task, whereas more experience with uncontrollability leads to impairment (e.g., Mikulincer, Kendem, & Zilkha-Segal, 1989).

According to Mikulincer (1994), in a situation of short or moderate failure, strategies centred on the problem are activated and there is improvement in the subsequent learning. On the other hand, when the pre-treatment is longer, strategies of avoidance and reorganization are activated, which produce helplessness and deficit in subsequent learning. In our case, perhaps reactance is an immediate reaction in groups M-20 and M-40, and as it is followed by escapable and avoidable situations, subjects do not perceive the situation as completely uncontrollable, and therefore helplessness is not produced. This does not occur in group M-80.

According to the "punishment intensification effect" (Goddard, 1999), pre-exposure to prolonged inescapable shock facilitates the ability of brief shock to punish responding. There is evidence that the punishment intensification effect results because shock onset is made more aversive due to its pairing with the delivery of prolonged shock. According to the present account, the duration of inescapable shock may be an important factor in any subsequent escape/avoidance learning deficit. Crowell and Anderson (1981) showed greater impairments in escape learning when rats were exposed to 10 s, rather than 5 s, inescapable shocks. It is possible that in group M-80 (prolonged inescapable shock) this effect appears, but it does not in groups M-20 and M-40.

The major conclusion of this research represents the first empirical demonstration of the possibility of obtaining immunization with aversive uncontrollable and unpredictable events of short and moderate duration, alternating with escapable and predictable events. The potential importance of these data applied in immunization areas may represent the greatest contribution made by the present study. The present findings implicate failure as a necessary component for an immunization program; it may be crucial that failure is an integral part of our lives to permit the formation of perceptions of the contingencies operating in a complex cause and effect environment. Experiences of success intercalated with experiences of failure involve subjects in a discrimination task, in which they learn that some behaviours are reinforced and other behaviours are not.

A likely limitation of this study is that the extended nonreinforced exposure to the context in group NT-U may have contributed to the slower acquisition of learning in the test phase, but it is necessary to prove this idea. A second limitation is that mixed groups differ in overall shock exposure and that might influence the results. Nevertheless, although this could be considered a methodological failing, these conditions are necessary to test our hypothesis, and they do not affect the major conclusion of the experiment.

Manuscript received June 2004
Revised manuscript accepted August 2005

REFERENCES

Altmaier, E. M., & Happ, D. A. (1985). Coping skills training's immunization effects against learned helplessness. *Journal of Social and Clinical Psychology*, *3*, 181–189.

Anderson, D. C., Crowell, C. R., DePaul, M., & McEachin, J. (1997). Intensification of punishment effects through exposure to prolonged, fixed-duration shocks: The role of shocks cues as a stimulus for fear. *Animal Learning and Behavior*, *25*, 68–83.

Bolles, R. C. (1972). Reinforcement, expectancy, and learning. *Psychological Review*, *79*, 394–409.

Chorpita, B. F., & Barlow, D. H. (1998). The development of anxiety: The role of control in the early environment. *Psychological Bulletin*, *124*, 3–21.

Crowell, C. R., & Anderson, D. C. (1981). Influence of duration and number of inescapable shocks on intra-shock activity and subsequent interference effects. *Animal Learning and Behavior*, *9*, 28–37.

Dess, N. K., Linwick, D., Patterson, J., Overmier, J. B., & Levine, S. (1983). Immediate and proactive effects of controllability and predictability on plasma cortisol responses to shocks in dogs. *Behavioral Neurosciences*, *97*, 1005–1016.

Drugan, R. C., Ryan, S. M., Minor, T. R., & Maier, S. F. (1984). Librium prevents the analgesia and shuttle box escape deficit typically observed following inescapable shock. *Pharmacology Biochemistry and Behavior*, *21*, 749–754.

Dyck, D. G., & Breen, L. J. (1978). Learned helplessness, immunization, and importance of task in humans. *Psychological Reports*, *43*, 315–321.

Eckelman, J. D., & Dyck, D. G. (1979). Task- and setting-related cues in immunization against learned helplessness. *American Journal of Psychology*, *92*, 653–667.

Ferrándiz, P. (1989). Immunization, controllability and predictability in no contingent context. In N. W. Bond & D. A. T. Siddle (Eds.), *Psychobiology: Issues and applications* (pp. 481–490). New York: North-Holland/Elsevier Science.

Ferrándiz, P., & Pardo, A. (1990). Immunization to learned helplessness in appetitive no contingent contexts. *Animal Learning and Behavior*, *18*, 252–256.

Ferrándiz, P., & Vicente, F. (1997). The conditioned attention theory and bifactorial theory on the learned helplessness syndrome in appetitive contexts. *International Journal of Psychology*, *32*, 399–408.

Goddard, M. J. (1999). The role of US signal value in contingency, drug conditioning, and learned helplessness. *Psychonomic Bulletin and Review*, *6*, 412–423.

Imada, H., & Kitaguchi, K. (2002). Recent learned helplessness/irrelevance research in Japan: Conceptual framework and some experiments in learned irrelevance. *Integrative Physiological and Behavioral Science*, *37*, 9–21.

Jackson, L. J., & Minor, T. R. (1988). Effects of signalling inescapable shock on subsequent escape learning: Implications for theories of coping and "learned helplessness." *Journal of Experimental Psychology: Animal Behavior Processes*, *14*, 390–400.

Jones, S. L., Nation, J. R., & Massad, P. (1977). Immunization against learned helplessness in man. *Journal of Abnormal Psychology*, *86*, 75–83.

Lehmann, J., Weizman, R., Pryce, C. R., Leschiner, S., Allmann, I., Feldon, J., & Gavish, M. (1999). Peripheral benzodiazepine receptors in cerebral cortex, but not in internal organs, are increased following inescapable stress and subsequent avoidance/escape shuttle-box testing. *Brain Research*, *851*, 141–147.

Maier, S. F. (1990). Role of fear in mediating shuttle escape learning deficit produced by inescapable shock. *Journal of Experimental Psychology: Animal Behavior Processes*, *16*, 137–149.

Maier, S. F. (1993). Learned helplessness, fear and anxiety. In C. Stanford & P. Salmon (Eds.), *Stress: From synapse to syndrome* (pp. 207–243). San Diego, CA: Academic Press.

Maier, S. F., & Watkins, L. R. (1998). Stressor controllability, anxiety, and serotonin. *Cognitive Therapy and Research*, *22*, 595–613.

Mikulincer, M. (1994). *Human learned helplessness: A coping perspective*. New York: Plenum Press.

Mikulincer, M., Kendem, P., & Zilkha-Segal, H. (1989). Learned helplessness, reactance, and cue utilization. *Journal of Research in Personality*, *23*, 235–247.

Minor, T. R. (1990). Conditioned fear and neophobia following inescapable shock. *Animal Learning and Behavior*, *18*, 212–226.

Minor, T., Dess, N., & Overmier, B. (1991). Inverting the traditional view of "learned helplessness." In M. R. Denny (Ed.), *Fear, avoidance and phobias* (pp. 87–134). Hillsdale, NJ: Lawrence Erlbaum Associates Inc.

Nakajima, M., Nakajima, S., & Imada, H. (1999). General learned irrelevance and its prevention. *Learning and Motivation*, *30*, 265–280.

Nation, J. R., & Massad, P. (1978). Persistence training: A partial reinforcement procedure for reversing learned helplessness and depression. *Journal of Experimental Psychology: General*, *107*, 436–451.

Overmier, J. B. (1985). Toward a reanalysis of the causal structure of the learned helplessness syndrome. In F. R. Brush & J. B. Overmier (Eds.), *Affect, conditioning and cognition: Essays on the determinants of behavior* (pp. 211–227). Hillsdale, NJ: Lawrence Erlbaum Associates Inc.

Overmier, J. B. (1988). Psychological determinants of when stressors stress. In D. Hellhammer, I. Florin, & H. Weiner (Eds.), *Neurobiological approaches to human disease* (pp. 236–259). Toronto: Hans Hubee.

Overmier, J. B. (2002). On learned irrelevance. *Integrative Physiological and Behavioural Science*, *37*, 4–8.

Overmier, J. B., & LoLordo, V. M. (1998). Learned helplessness. In W O'Donohue (Ed.), *Learning and behavior therapy* (pp. 352–373). Boston: Allyn & Bacon.

Overmier, J. B., & Murison, R. (2000). Anxiety and helplessness in the face of stress predisposes, precipitates, and sustains gastric ulceration. *Behavioural Brain Research*, *110*, 161–174.

Overmier, J. B., Murison, R., Taklo, T., & Espelid, R. (1994). Effects of traumatic stress on defensive burying: An alternative test of the learned helplessness model of depression and enhanced retrieval of unpleasant memories. *Biological Psychiatry*, *36*, 703–704.

Overmier, J. B., & Seligman, M. E. P. (1967). Effects of inescapable shock upon subsequent escape and avoidance learning. *Journal of Comparative and Physiological Psychology*, *63*, 23–33.

Peterson, C., Maier, S. F., & Seligman, M. E. P. (1993). *Learned helplessness. A theory for the age of personal control*. Oxford: Oxford University Press.

Rowe, M. K. (2003). The role of a compromised energy metabolism in the learned helplessness paradigm. *Dissertation Abstracts International: Section B*, *64*, 458.

Scheggi, S., Masi, F., Tagliamonte, A., Gambarana, C., Tolu, P., & De Montis M., G. (2000). Rats sensitised to morphine are resistant to the behavioral effects of an unavoidable stress. *Brain Research*, *853*, 290–298.

Seligman, M. E. P. (1992). *Learned optimism*. New York: A. Knopf.

Seligman, M. E. P., & Csikszentmihalyi, M. (2000). Positive psychology. *American Psychologist*, *55*, 5–14.

Seligman, M. E. P., & Maier, S. F. (1967). Failure to escape traumatic shock. *Journal of Experimental Psychology*, *74*, 1–9.

Seligman, M. E. P., Schulman, P., DeRubeis, R., & Hollons, S. (1999). The prevention of depression and anxiety. *Prevention and Treatment 2*, 8. Retrieved March 10, 2003 from http://journals.apa.org/prevention/volume2/pre0020008a.html

Steciuk, M., Kram, M., Kramer, G., & Petty, F. (1999). Decrease in stress induced c-Fos like immunoreactivity in the lateral septal nucleus of learned helpless rats. *Brain Research*, *822*, 256–259.

Troisi, J. R., Bersh, P. J., Stromberg, M. F., Mauro, B. C., & Whitehouse, W. G. (1991). Stimulus control of immunization against chronic learned helplessness. *Animal Learning and Behavior*, *19*, 88–94.

Warren, D. A., Rosellini, R. A., & Maier, S. F. (1989). Fear, stimulus feedback, and stressor controllability. In G. Bower (Ed.), *The psychology of learning and motivation, Vol. 24* (pp. 167–207). Orlando, FL: Academic Press.

Woodson, J. C., Minor, T. R., & Job, R. F. S. (1998). Inhibition of adenosine deaminase by erythro-9 (2-hydroxy-3-nonyl) adenine (EJNA) mimics the effect of inescapable shock on escape learning in rats. *Behavioral Neuroscience*, *112*, 399–409.

Zhukov, D. A., & Vinogradova, E. P. (1998). Agonistic behavior during stress prevents the development of learned helplessness in rats. *Neuroscience and Behavioral Physiology*, *28*, 206–210.

A person-centred approach to identifying acculturation groups among Chinese Canadians

Ai-Lan Chia and Catherine L. Costigan

University of Victoria, Victoria, British Columbia, Canada

This study adopted a person-centred approach to explore acculturation groups among Chinese Canadians and to examine the demographic and adjustment profiles associated with each group. A total of 234 Chinese Canadian university students completed measures assessing different aspects of their Chinese and Canadian cultural orientations. Cluster analyses identified five acculturation groups: *Integrated Group, Separated Group, Assimilated Group, Integrated Group without Chinese Practices, and Marginalized Group with Chinese Practices.* Three of the five groups resembled Berry's acculturation model, and the other two groups demonstrated unique constellations of cultural orientations. The differences between the current acculturation groups and Berry's acculturation strategies were due to the differentiation between internal and external domains of cultural orientation, the addition of the domain of ethnic group evaluation, which is not typically included in acculturation research, and the use of cluster analysis, which allows for varying degrees of immersion in multiple domains of acculturation. Expected differences among the five acculturation groups in terms of participants' demographic backgrounds (e.g., length of residence in Canada), language preferences, and psychological adjustment supported the validity of the cluster solution. As expected, members of the Marginalized Group with Chinese Practices, the largest single group in the current sample, reported poorer adjustment than the Assimilated Group and the Integrated Group without Chinese Practices. The results of this study highlight the value of simultaneously considering multiple domains of acculturation and argue against research methods that assume acculturation status based on background factors such as place of birth or language use. Implications of these findings for understanding the cultural adaptation of Chinese Canadians are discussed.

Cette étude a adopté une approche centrée sur la personne pour explorer l'acculturation parmi les Canadiens chinois et pour examiner les profiles démographiques et d'ajustement de chaque groupe. Un total de 234 étudiants universitaires Canadiens chinois ont complété les mesures évaluant différents aspects de leurs orientations chinoise et canadienne. Les analyses par grappes (cluster analysis) ont identifié cinq groupes d'acculturation: *le groupe intégré, le groupe séparé, le groupe assimilé, le groupe intégré sans pratiques chinoises et le groupe marginalisé avec des pratiques chinoises.* Trois des cinq groupes étaient semblables au modèle d'acculturation de Berry. Par contre, les deux autres groupes ont démontré des constellations uniques d'orientations culturelles. Les différences entre les présents groupes d'acculturation et les stratégies d'acculturation de Berry sont dues à la différentiation entre les domaines internes et externes de l'orientation culturelle, à l'addition du domaine de l'évaluation du groupe ethnique qui n'est pas incluse typiquement dans la recherche sur l'acculturation, à l'utilisation de l'analyse par grappes qui permet des degrés variés d'immersion dans de multiples domaines d'acculturation. Des différences attendues entre les cinq groupes d'acculturation en termes d'origine démographique des participants (e.g. durée de la résidence au Canada), de préférence linguistique et d'ajustement psychologique ont appuyé la validité de la solution des grappes. Tel qu'attendu, les membres du groupe marginalisé avec des pratiques chinoises, le seul plus large groupe dans l'échantillon de cette étude, ont rapporté un ajustement plus faible que celui du groupe assimilé et du groupe intégré sans pratiques chinoises. Les résultats de cette étude soulignent l'importance de considérer simultanément les domaines multiples d'acculturation et d'argumenter contre les méthodes de recherche qui présument le statut d'acculturation en se fondant sur les facteurs d'origine comme le lieu de naissance ou l'utilisation d'une langue.

Correspondence should be addressed to Ai-Lan Chia, Department of Psychology, Box 3050 STN CSC, University of Victoria, Victoria, British Columbia, V8W 3P5 Canada (E-mail: achia@uvic.ca).

The first author gratefully acknowledges financial support from the Canadian Institute for Health Research (CIHR) doctoral fellowship. The authors wish to express their gratitude to Jacqueline E. Bush and Jing-Ee Tan for their comments on this article. A part of this manuscript was presented at the biennial meeting of International Society of Study for Behavioural Development, Ottawa, August 2002.

 DOI: 10.1080/00207590500412227

Les implications de ces résultats pour la compréhension de l'adaptation culturelle des Canadiens chinois sont discutées.

Este estudio adoptó un enfoque centrado en la persona para explorar los grupos de aculturación entre canadienses chinos y examinar los perfiles demográficos y de ajuste asociados con cada grupo. Un total de 234 estudiantes universitarios canadienses chinos respondieron a diferentes instrumentos que miden diferentes aspectos de sus orientaciones culturales chinas y canadienses. Los análisis de cúmulos identificaron cinco grupos de aculturación: *Grupo Integrado, Grupo Separado, Grupo Asimilado, Grupo Integrado sin Prácticas Chinas, y Grupo Marginado con Prácticas Chinas.* Tres de los cinco grupos se asemejaron al modelo de aculturación de Berry, y dos más mostraron constelaciones únicas de orientaciones culturales. Las diferencias entre los grupos de aculturación actuales y las estrategias de aculturación de Berry se debieron a la diferenciación entre los dominios interno y externo de orientación cultural, la inclusión del dominio de evaluación del grupo étnico, que generalmente no se incluye en la investigación sobre aculturación, y el uso del análisis de cúmulos, que permite varios niveles de inmersión en dominios de aculturación múltiples. Las diferencias esperadas entre los cinco grupos de aculturación en términos de los antecedentes demográficos de los participantes (por ejemplo, la duración de su residencia en Canadá), las preferencias de lenguaje, y el ajuste psicológicos apoyaron la validez de la solución de los cúmulos. Como se esperaba, los miembros del grupo Marginado con Prácticas Chinas, el grupo más grande en la presente muestra, refirieron menos ajuste que el Grupo Asimilado y el Grupo Integrado sin Prácticas Chinas. Los resultados de este estudio arrojan luz sobre el valor de considerar simultáneamente dominios múltiples de aculturación y argumentan en contra de los métodos de investigación que suponen que el status de la aculturación se basa en factores antecedentes como el lugar de nacimiento y el uso del lenguaje. Se discuten las repercusiones de estos hallazgos en la comprensión de la adaptación cultural de los canadienses chinos.

Acculturation is generally viewed as a process of change that occurs as a consequence of continuous, first-hand contact between two or more distinct cultural groups (Berry, 1980, 2003). Contemporary acculturation research uses an orthogonal two-dimensional model, in which an individual's ethnic cultural orientation is independent of his/her orientation towards the host culture. This is an improvement on earlier research that used a bipolar perspective, in which increased involvement in the host culture was used to indicate decreased engagement with the ethnic culture. The most widely researched two-dimensional model has been Berry's (1980, 2003) model of acculturation strategies. In Berry's model, *integration* involves maintaining one's cultural heritage while also endorsing intergroup relations; *assimilation* involves relinquishing one's cultural heritage and adopting the beliefs and behaviours of the new culture; *separation* involves maintaining one's heritage culture to the exclusion of pursuing intergroup relations; and *marginalization* involves nonadherence to either the old or new culture.

Empirical research generally supports the utility of Berry's model in describing individuals' acculturation experiences. Foreign-born immigrants more strongly identify with their ethnic culture than native-born generations (Cuéllar, Arnold, & Maldonado, 1995; Gim Chung, Kim, & Abreu, 2004; Sanchez & Fernandez, 1993). In addition, a longer length of residence in the host culture and a younger age at the time of immigration are related to a higher level of acculturation into the host culture among immigrants (Lee, Sobal, & Frongillo, 2003; Richman, Gaviria, Flaherty, Birz, & Wintrob, 1987; Ryder, Alden, & Paulhus, 2000). Foreign-born immigrants most commonly prefer an integrated acculturation strategy (Coatsworth, Maldonado-Molina, Pantin, & Szapocznik, 2005; Eyou, Adair, & Dixon, 2000), and seldom prefer an assimilated strategy (Berry, Kim, Power, Young, & Bujaki, 1989); immigrants who do prefer assimilation tend to have the longest length of residence in the host country (Liem, Lim, & Liem, 2000). A fairly consistent pattern emerges when individuals' psychological adjustment is examined in relation to acculturation strategies. Integrated individuals, who are orientated towards both ethnic and host cultures, tend to show fewer psychological problems than individuals who are oriented towards the ethnic or host culture only, and marginalized individuals often report the lowest levels of adjustment (Pawliuk et al., 1996; Sanchez & Fernandez, 1993; Ying, 1995).

Two methods of measurement have commonly been used when Berry's model of acculturation is adopted. First, instruments that include four subscales representing each of the four strategies of integration, assimilation, separation, and marginalization are administered (Berry et al., 1989). This measurement method bridges earlier theorizing and empirical research, and has advanced the understanding of the acculturation experiences of immigrants. However, this measurement method has also been critiqued on conceptual and methodological grounds (Rudmin, 2003; Ryder et al., 2000). For example, items within the same subscale that assess an individual's attitudes toward both ethnic and host cultures are written with a "double-barrelled" quality, which might introduce psychometric problems because they could be interpreted differently by different respondents (Clark & Watson, 1995). Particular concerns have been raised regarding items for the marginalization subscale (e.g., "I cannot worry about something as trivial as furniture when I have so many problems"; Berry et al., 1989), which includes affect-laden or negative mood words, thus possibly superficially inflating relations with adjustment measures such as depression or stress (Clark & Watson, 1995).

The second measurement method used in research adopting Berry's model has been to assess ethnic and host cultural orientations as two separate dimensions, and then apply a specific cut-off score to categorize participants into one of Berry's four acculturation strategies. Typically, researchers use a cut-off score on selected continuous measures to group individuals into "high" and "low" categories. For instance, individuals who score in the "high" category for both ethnic and host identities are labelled "bicultural." From a conceptual perspective, an independent assessment of ethnic and host cultural orientations indeed reflects the theoretical underpinnings of an orthogonal model. However, the cut-off score approach fails to capture the diversity *within* an individual's ethnic or host cultural orientation because it is an all-or-nothing method of categorization. This approach ignores the fact that ethnic minorities may show varying degrees of immersion into ethnic and host cultures (Sanchez & Fernandez, 1993). Furthermore, there is little consistency in the selection of cut-off scores. The majority of studies use either the scale mid-point (e.g., Eyou et al., 2000), the mean for the sample (e.g., Der-Karabetian & Ruiz, 1997), or the proportional distribution of the scores in the sample (e.g., Torres, 1999). Some studies use the discrepancy between one's orientation toward the host culture and the ethnic culture (e.g., Pawliuk et al., 1996), while others do not provide any information about how groups are formed (e.g., Gil, Vega, & Dimas, 1994). Thus, it is unclear how well the findings across studies can be integrated.

Complicating the issue of how to best represent acculturation strategies is the growing recognition that both ethnic and host dimensions of cultural orientations are better understood as consisting of multiple domains (Van de Vijver & Phalet, 2004). For example, changes in both host and ethnic dimensions can occur in domains such as behavioural practices, identity, and values (Birman & Trickett, 2001; Costigan & Su, 2004; Phinney, Horenczyk, Liebkind, & Vedder, 2001). However, rather than assessing multiple domains, most research focuses on only one domain (Tropp, Erkut, Coll, Alarcon, & Garcia, 1999), typically the behavioural domain of the host dimension (such as English language proficiency). It is a difficult task, operationally and conceptually, to categorize participants into acculturation strategies when the cut-off scores of more than two continuous measures are used. However, choosing some, but not all, important domains of ethnic and host cultural orientations as classification criteria may fail to demonstrate the complexity of these two processes and the resultant acculturation strategies. Often, multiple aspects of an individual's cultural orientations interact with one another to collectively formulate the overall pattern of acculturation.

In order to improve upon these conceptual and methodological limitations, the current study adopts a theoretically grounded multidimensional perspective of ethnic and host cultural orientations to form acculturation groups. Instead of using the cut-off score approach, a statistical approach (i.e., cluster analyses) is used that facilitates the identification and examination of acculturation groups among Chinese Canadians. Cluster analysis is a commonly used method to classify participants from one sample into discrete categories in a cross-sectional analysis (Bergman & Magnusson, 1997), but it has rarely been applied in acculturation research (e.g., Lee et al., 2003). Multiple domains of Chinese and Canadian cultural orientations can be simultaneously considered in cluster analyses. These domains are treated as continuous rather than categorical in order to explore the *degree* to which individuals in each cluster identify with the ethnic and host cultures. Thus, individuals' cultural orientations are viewed from a dimensional, rather than an all-or-nothing, perspective.

Formulating acculturation groups via cluster analysis allows us to examine patterns of cultural orientations, to focus on participants as the central unit of analysis, and to explore both the common and rare cultural orientation patterns. Cluster analysis groups together individuals who have responded to items in similar ways across a variety of variables that often do not function independently in influencing attitudes and behaviours. By focusing on identifying patterns across several domains of cultural identification rather than on specific variables as main analytical units, cluster analysis allows us to better understand an individual from a holistic and interactionistic perspective (Bergman & Magnusson, 1997). The final cluster solution reflects participants' experiences without imposing a priori conception regarding how many or what kinds of acculturation groups should emerge.

The theoretical model of acculturation used in the current study is rooted in Berry's orthogonal model (1980, 2003). That is, Chinese and Canadian dimensions of an individual's cultural orientation are assessed separately. In addition, multiple domains are assessed within each dimension. These domains were selected based on the theoretical underpinnings of acculturation. Specifically, both the Chinese and Canadian dimensions were conceptualized as having an internal and an external domain (e.g., Chang, Tracey, & Moore, 2005; Tropp et al., 1999). The *internal domain* refers to the psychological aspects of an individual's cultural orientation, including knowledge of cultural values, identity achievement, and a sense of belonging (Phinney, 1992; The Chinese Culture Connection, 1987). The *external domain* refers to behavioural aspects such as language use and cultural practices (Cuéllar et al., 1995). Research has found that external domains may change more readily following immigration than internal domains (Van de Vijver & Phalet, 2004).

In addition to these four domains, a fifth domain of *ethnic group evaluation* is assessed. This domain refers to individuals' perceptions of how their ethnic group is evaluated by others as well as their own evaluation of their group. Unlike ethnic identity, which refers to a person's internal sense of identification with an ethnic group, ethnic evaluation incorporates a consideration of the broader context in which acculturation takes place. This is theoretically important because the social status of ethnic groups is often largely externally imposed. As a result, some ethnic minority individuals will find themselves identifying with groups that the host society values negatively relative to other groups. The importance of this broader context may be particularly salient for people with collectivistic values (Luhtanen & Crocker, 1992), such as those from Chinese culture (Bond & Hwang, 1986), because one's sense of self is intimately tied to group membership.

The specific measures that assess these five domains were factor-analysed among the current sample of Chinese Canadians prior to conducting the cluster analysis. From a methodological viewpoint, factor analyses are often performed among correlated variables prior to performing cluster analysis so that the underlying factors are equally weighted in the proximity index (Borgen & Barnett, 1987). Using an empirically validated factorial solution in cluster analyses facilitates finding a set of clusters that best characterizes the similarity that exists in a specific sample, and avoiding the drawbacks of cluster analysis research when variables have not been selected based on theoretical considerations or careful analysis of the phenomenon (Aldenderfer & Blashfield, 1984). The results of the factor analysis confirmed the theoretical model with just one exception (Chia & Costigan, 2002). Specifically, as expected, Chinese orientation included two domains, *Chinese-Internal Orientation* and *Chinese-External Orientation,* and *Ethnic Evaluation* emerged as a distinct domain. The only exception to the theoretical model was that only one domain emerged for *Canadian Orientation*; there was no evidence for separate internal and external domains. Further details regarding the results of the factor analysis are available from the first author. These four cultural orientation factors are used in the current study to classify participants into acculturation groups. Following this, the validity of the resulting acculturation groups is evaluated by examining the demographic backgrounds, language preferences, and psychological adjustment of participants in each acculturation group.

Over the last two decades, changes in immigration trends have altered the ethnic make-up of the Canadian population. An earlier picture consisting of mostly European immigrants has been replaced by a more diverse ethnic and cultural composition. Currently, Chinese people are the largest single visible minority group across Canada (Statistics Canada, 2003). The majority of these Chinese Canadians are first-generation immigrants who are confronted with the challenges of adjusting to Canadian society while also remaining connected to their culture of origin. Among Chinese Canadians, those receiving education in Canada are likely to be the most engaged with Canadian culture, in addition to their involvement with their culture of origin. Thus, Chinese Canadian university students are an appropriate sample for exploring diverse patterns of cultural orientations because they are likely to represent varying degrees of immersion into both Chinese and Canadian cultures. The following questions are addressed.

1. How many acculturation groups are evident when multiple continuous measures of ethnic and host cultural orientations are considered? Consistent with Berry's model, we expect to find four acculturation groups, representing integration, assimilation, separation, and marginalization.

2. Which acculturation group is the most and least common among the current sample? If four acculturation groups are found as hypothesized above, we expect the integration group to be the largest, and the marginalization group to be the smallest.

3. How do individuals' demographic backgrounds and language preferences relate to the acculturation groups, and which acculturation groups are associated with better adjustment? We expect foreign-born and late-arriving Chinese participants to be classified into separation and integration groups, and Canadian-born and early-arriving Chinese participants to be classified into assimilation and integration groups. Individuals in assimilated and integrated groups are expected to have a longer length of residence in Canada than those in a separated group. Individuals in an integrated group are expected to have the highest level of adjustment and individuals in a marginalized group are expected to have the lowest.

METHOD

Participants

A total of 234 university students with Chinese origins participated. All had lived in Canada for at least 2 years. There were approximately equal numbers of men (43.2%) and women (56.8%), with ages ranging from 18 to 40 years (mean age of 22.3). Of the total sample, 13.6% were born in Canada and 86.4% were foreign-born. Among foreign-born participants, the majority came to Canada after the age of 12 (76.2%), and came from either Taiwan (57%) or Hong Kong (35.3%). The mean length of residence in Canada among the foreign-born participants was 8.36 years. More than half of the participants' fathers had a college degree or more (59.5%).

The majority of the participants were recruited through Chinese student associations, fliers posted on campus, Internet list-servers, and language classes at two universities in Western Canada. Participants recruited through these means were eligible to win three prizes with a value of $30 each drawn in a lottery. The remaining participants were recruited through an undergraduate psychology course and received course bonus points for their participation.

Procedures

The current study received ethics approvals from the two universities where the participants were recruited. The consent procedure was verbally explained, and participants also signed a written consent form. All participants were given the option of completing the questionnaires in individual sessions, small-group sessions, or at home. Measures assessing ethnic and host dimensions of acculturation were alternated with one another throughout the questionnaire package. Adjustment measures were placed close to the end of the package so that participants' responses on measures of cultural orientations would not be influenced by their reactions to adjustment measures. Cultural value measures were placed last in the package so that participants would end the research experience with neutral questions versus emotion-laden adjustment questions.

Measures

A demographic background questionnaire assessed gender, age, country of origin, place of birth, length of residence, language preferences, and age at the time of immigration to Canada.

Factor 1: Chinese-Internal Orientation

Chinese-Internal Orientation was assessed with five constructs. The first two constructs were the 5-item *Ethnic Affirmation and Belonging* scale (e.g., "I feel a strong attachment towards my own ethnic group") and the 7-item *Ethnic Identity Achievement* scale (e.g., "I have a clear sense of my ethnic background and what it means for me"), both of which are subscales of the Multigroup Ethnic Identity Measure (MEIM; Phinney, 1992). Items are rated on a 4-point scale, and higher scores indicate a higher level of ethnic identity. Alpha coefficients previously reported for these two scales range from .80 to .86, and both scales demonstrate good reliability in assessing ethnic identity for Chinese university students (Eyou et al., 2000). The alpha coefficient for these two scales in the current study was .89 and .82, respectively.

The third construct was the 10-item *Ethnic Kinship and Common Fate* scale that was adapted from the Jewish Identity Scale (Zak, 1973) by replacing "Jewish" with "Chinese" (e.g., "My fate and future are bound up with that of the Chinese everywhere"). Items are rated on a 7-point scale, and higher scores indicate a higher ethnic identity. The scale demonstrates good reliability in assessing ethnic identity across ethnic groups (Der-Karabetian & Ruiz, 1997). The alpha coefficient for this scale in the current study was .77.

Fourth, *Centrality of Ethnic Group Membership* was assessed with the 4-item Identity subscale of the Collective Self-Esteem Scale (CSE; Luhtanen & Crocker, 1992). This scale was adapted to focus on individuals' "ethnic" group, rather than on their social groups (e.g., "The ethnic group I belong to is an important reflection of who I am"). Items are rated on a 7-point scale, with higher scores indicating greater centrality of ethnic identity to one's self-concept. This scale demonstrates good reliability among Chinese Canadians (Lay & Verkuyten, 1999). The alpha coefficient for this scale in the current study was .75.

The final construct, *Chinese Cultural Values,* was assessed with the 40-item Chinese Value Survey (The Chinese Culture Connection, 1987). Items are rated on a 9-point scale, with higher scores indicating a greater endorsement of traditional Chinese cultural values (e.g., filial piety). This scale demonstrates good reliability among Chinese people residing in both Chinese and Western countries (Ralston, Gustafson, Elsass, Cheung, & Terpstra, 1992). The alpha coefficient for this scale in the current study was .95.

Factor 2: Chinese-External Orientation

The external domain of Chinese Orientation was assessed with the *Ethnic Behaviours and Customs* scale. This 17-item scale was adapted from the Mexican Orientation subscale of the Acculturation Rating Scale for Mexican Americans-II (ARSMA-II; Cuéllar et al., 1995) by replacing "Mexican" with "Chinese" (e.g., "I speak Chinese"). Items are rated on a 5-point scale, and higher scores indicate greater ethnic behavioural practices. This scale shows good reliability in assessing individuals' ethnic behavioural orientation among Asian American university students (Liem et al., 2000). The alpha coefficient for this scale in the current study was .88.

Factor 3: Canadian Orientation

Canadian Orientation was assessed with four constructs. The first two constructs were the 5-item *Canadian Affirmation and Belonging* scale and the 7-item *Canadian Identity Achievement* scale. Both scales were adapted from parallel ethnic identity scales from Phinney's (1992) Multigroup Ethnic Identity Measure, by replacing "ethnic" with "Canadian" or "Canada" (e.g., "I feel a strong attachment towards Canada"; "I have a clear sense of being a Canadian and what it means for me"). Items are rated on a 4-point scale, and higher scores indicate a higher level of Canadian identity. These two scales demonstrate good reliability when adapted to assess individuals' host cultural identity (Eyou et al., 2000). The alpha coefficients for these two scales in the current study were .89 and .76, respectively.

The third construct was the 10-item *Canadian Kinship and Common Fate* scale, adapted from the American Identity Scale (Zak, 1973) by replacing "American" with "Canadian" (e.g., "My fate and future are bound up with that of the Canadian people"). Items are rated on a 7-point scale, and higher scores indicate a greater Canadian identity. The scale shows good reliability when assessing individual's host cultural identity (Der-Karabetian & Ruiz, 1997). The alpha coefficient for this scale in the current study was .86.

Finally, *Canadian Behaviours and Customs* were assessed with an adaptation of the Anglo Orientation subscale of the ARSMA-II (Cuéllar et al., 1995) by replacing "Anglo" with "Canada" (e.g., "My contact with Canada has been..."). This 5-point scale has 17 items, including the original 13 items and 4 new items added in the current study to make the items parallel to those assessing Chinese Behaviours and Customs (i.e., "I enjoy speaking English," "My father identifies himself as a Canadian," "My mother identifies herself as a Canadian," and "My family cooks Canadian foods"). The original 13-item scale demonstrates good reliability in assessing individuals' behavioural orientation toward the host culture for Asian American university students (Liem et al., 2000). The alpha coefficient for this scale in the current study was .88.

Factor 4: Ethnic Evaluation

Participants' evaluation of their ethnic group and group membership was assessed with three subscales of the Collective Self-Esteem scale (CSE; Luhtanen & Crocker, 1992). Together, these subscales include 12 items that assess private evaluations of one's group (e.g., "I feel good about the ethnic group I belong to"), public evaluations of how other people evaluate one's group (e.g., "Overall, my ethnic group is considered good by others"), and membership evaluations of how good one is as a member of one's group (e.g., "I am a cooperative participant in my ethnic group"). Items were adapted to focus on "ethnic" groups rather than social groups, and are rated on a 7-point scale. Scores are derived by reversing negative items, summing across items, and obtaining the mean. Higher scores indicate more positive feelings and higher perceived social evaluation of one's ethnic group. These scales demonstrate good reliability when adapted to assess a Chinese Canadian's perceived social evaluation of their ethnic group (Lay & Verkuyten, 1999). The alpha coefficient in the current study was .86.

Psychological adjustment

Both positive and negative aspects of psychological adjustment were assessed. *Self-esteem* was measured with Rosenberg's (1986) Self-Esteem Scale (e.g., "On the whole, I am satisfied with myself"). This 10-item scale is widely used in research and demonstrates high reliability in assessing self-esteem among Chinese Canadians (Lay & Verkuyten, 1999). Items are rated from 1 (*strongly disagree*) to 4 (*strongly agree*); scores are derived by reversing negative items, summing across items, and obtaining the mean. Higher scores indicate higher levels of self-esteem. The alpha coefficient for this scale in the current study was .90.

Depressive symptoms were assessed with the Center for Epidemiologic Studies Depression Scale (CES-D; Radloff, 1977). This 20-item scale demonstrates good reliability in assessing depressive symptoms across different ethnic minority groups, including Chinese American college students (Ying, Lee, Tsai, Yeh, & Huang, 2000). Items (e.g., "In the past week, I felt sad") are rated from 0 (*rarely or none of the time*) to 4 (*most or all of the time*). Scores are derived by reversing positive items and summing across the items. Higher scores indicate more depressive symptoms. The alpha coefficient in the current study was .90.

RESULTS

Cluster analyses: Identifying acculturation groups

Two types of clustering methods, hierarchical agglomerative and iterative partitioning, are commonly used in psychological research. The most useful solution is obtained by employing iterative partitioning clustering for the final solution based on the number of clusters derived from hierarchical agglomerative clustering methods (Borgen & Barnett, 1987). Ward's method, one of the hierarchical agglomerative methods, searches the proximity matrix and groups the two persons with the smallest distance value that is calculated based on squared Euclidean distance. Ward's method was chosen due to its good performance on a variety of data types in several Monte-Carlo type investigations (Hand & Everitt, 1987). *K*-means clustering is optimal among iterative partitioning clustering methods when the probable number of clusters can be specified in advance (Borgen & Barnett, 1987). The four cultural orientation factors were submitted to the Ward's method, followed by three strategies to determine the number of clusters that should be retained for the final clustering.

Before cluster analysis is performed, standardization within each variable is necessary to remove large effects due to arbitrary differences in the standard deviations or means of the variables (Borgen & Barnett, 1987). Because the measures used in the current study were rated on different scales, all individual scales were first standardized into *z*-scores ($M = 0$; $SD = 1$) and converted to *t*-scores ($M = 50$; $SD = 10$) before calculating factor scores. The variables that loaded on each factor were then summed and averaged to produce a total score for each of the four factors. These four cultural orientation factors were used in the subsequent cluster analysis.

Three recommended strategies to determine the optimal number of clusters were used, including visual examination of the dendrogram and fusion coefficients, and Mojena's Rule One (Milligan & Cooper, 1985). Mojena's rule, one of the most objective methods, uses the distribution of the clustering criterion (the within-group sum of squares) to determine when a significant change from one stage to the next implies a partition that should not be undertaken (Mojena, 1977). Mojena's rule suggested that the optimal number of clusters was four or five. The fusion coefficients showed a clean jump (4008.22) when five clusters were merged into four, which indicated dissimilarity in the clusters that were merged. In contrast, the jump between the merging of six clusters into five (2354.06) was relatively small. Therefore, a five-cluster solution was determined to be the most optimal. A *k*-means cluster analysis was conducted by specifying a five-cluster solution. The analyses converged in 15 iterations.

Four strategies were used to identify differences among the clusters. First, a MANOVA was performed using the four cultural orientation factor scores as dependent variables and the

TABLE 1
Means (and standard deviations) for cluster differences on the four cultural orientation factors

	Cluster 1 (*N* = 46)	*Cluster 2* (*N* = 48)	*Cluster 3* (*N* = 22)	*Cluster 4* (*N* = 33)	*Cluster 5* (*N* = 71)	*Cluster differences*
Chinese-Internal Orientation	57.67 (6.21)	51.96 (4.85)	42.61 (5.31)	50.51 (4.55)	45.89 (5.16)	1>2, 4>3, 5
Chinese-External Orientation	57.11 (5.03)	54.22 (5.16)	31.90 (7.86)	40.30 (6.89)	52.49 (6.01)	1>5, 4, 3 and 2, 5>4>3
Canadian Orientation	56.16 (5.61)	42.77 (5.12)	58.54 (7.03)	54.75 (6.98)	46.23 (6.50)	1, 3, 4>2, 5
Ethnic Evaluation	56.01 (6.40)	53.91 (4.78)	44.14 (7.67)	56.90 (4.16)	42.05 (4.47)	1, 2, 4>3, 5

Cluster 1 is the Integrated Group. Cluster 2 is the Separated Group. Cluster 3 is the Assimilated Group. Cluster 4 is the Integrated Group without Chinese Practices. Cluster 5 is the Marginalized Group with Chinese Practices.

cluster groups as independent variables to help name the clusters (see Table 1 and Figure 1). The MANOVA revealed a significant multivariate effect, $F(4, 212) = 38.42, p<.001$. This multivariate effect was accounted for by significant univariate effects on all four factor scores: Chinese-Internal Orientation, $F(4, 215) = 47.85, p<.001$, Chinese-External Orientation, $F(4, 215) = 96.35, p<.001$, Canadian Orientation, $F(4, 215) = 49.88, p<.001$, and Ethnic Evaluation, $F(4, 215) = 81.06, p<.001$. The nature of these significant univariate effects was evaluated with Scheffe's post hoc test. Second, one-sample *t*-tests evaluated whether scores on specific factors within each cluster differed significantly from the mean of 50. Third, paired *t*-tests examined whether factor scores significantly differed from each other within each cluster. Finally, univariate ANOVAs and chi-square analyses examined participants' demographic backgrounds and language preferences in relation to cluster membership. Based on these analyses, the five clusters are named and described below.

Cluster 1: Integrated Group (N = 46; 20.9% of the sample)

Participants in the first cluster scored significantly above the sample mean on all four cultural orientation factors. In addition, their scores on the four factors were among the highest across all clusters. Therefore, participants in this cluster view themselves strongly as Canadian and also as Chinese. They regard the Chinese group positively and also perceive that others share this view. They are evenly divided between males and females, and are an average age of 22.4 years. Most (91%) are foreign-born, and over 60% of these came to Canada after the age of 12, with an average of 8.71 years of residence in Canada. Members of this cluster mostly use their ethnic language at home,

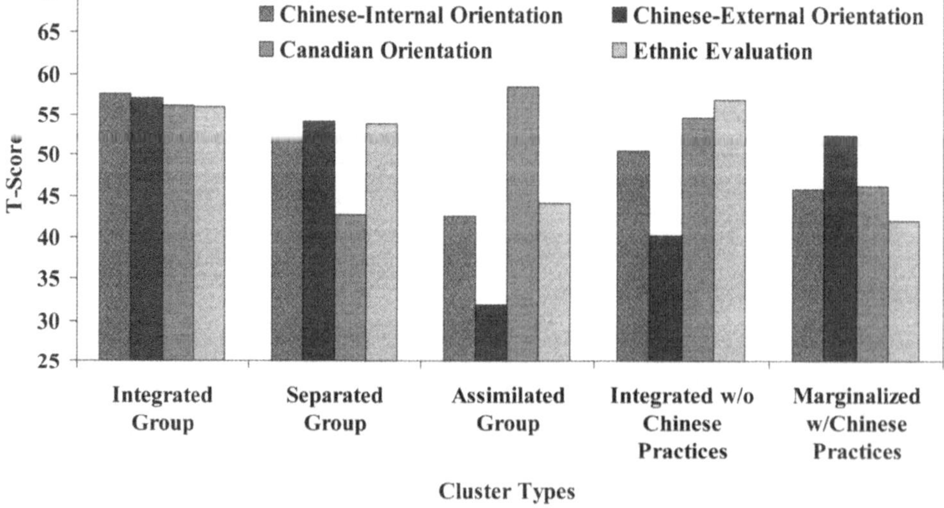

Figure 1. Five cluster solution.

and about half use their ethnic language outside the home. They report high proficiency in both their ethnic language and English.

Cluster 2: Separated Group (N = 48; 21.8% of the sample)

Participants in this cluster scored significantly above the sample mean on the three ethnic-related cultural orientation factors, and significantly below the sample mean on Canadian Orientation. What makes this cluster unique is its particularly high score on ethnic evaluation, which is one of the highest across the five clusters and is higher than the score on Chinese-Internal Orientation within this cluster. People in this cluster are an average of 22.1 years old and two thirds are female. All of the members are foreign-born, and the majority (87%) came to Canada after the age of 12 years. The average length of residence in Canada among the foreign-born participants is 6.7 years, which is the shortest among all of the clusters, and is significantly shorter than those in Cluster 4. Individuals in this cluster mostly speak an ethnic language both at home and outside the home. They report higher ethnic language proficiency and lower English proficiency than clusters characterized with a strong Canadian Orientation.

Cluster 3: Assimilated Group (N = 22; 10% of the sample)

Cluster 3 was the smallest cluster found in the current sample. Individuals in this cluster scored higher on Canadian Orientation than those in all of the other clusters. They also scored significantly below the sample mean on the three ethnic-related cultural orientation variables, especially on Chinese-External Orientation. Therefore, members of this cluster identify strongly as Canadian, and not as Chinese, and practice few Chinese behaviours and customs. They are on average 21.6 years old and three quarters are female. Approximately half are foreign-born, which is the lowest percentage of foreign-born in any cluster. Most (80%) of the foreign-born members of this cluster arrived after the age of 12 years, and have resided in Canada for an average of 8.8 years. Individuals in this cluster use an ethnic language and English roughly equally at home and the majority use English outside the home. They report lower ethnic language proficiency and higher English proficiency than groups characterized with a low Canadian Orientation.

Cluster 4: Integrated Group without Chinese Practices (N = 33; 15% of the sample)

Individuals in this cluster scored significantly above the sample mean on Canadian Orientation and Ethnic Evaluation, and significantly below the sample mean on Chinese-External Orientation. Scores on Chinese-Internal Orientation were around the mean for the sample. What separates this cluster from Cluster 1 is the low score on Chinese-External Orientation and the average score on Chinese-Internal Orientation. Therefore, individuals in this group see themselves strongly as a Canadian and evaluate the Chinese group very positively, even though they view themselves only moderately as a Chinese and they do not practise many Chinese behaviours. Members of this cluster are on average 22.9 years old, and are fairly evenly divided between males and females. Like individuals in Cluster 3, approximately half are Canadian-born. Among the foreign-born, approximately half came to Canada after the age of 12 years. Foreign-born members of this cluster have the longest length of residence in Canada of all of the clusters, significantly longer than those in Cluster 2 and 5. Similar to those in Cluster 3, individuals in this cluster use both an ethnic language and English relatively equally at home, but predominantly use English outside the home. They also report lower ethnic language proficiency and higher English proficiency than groups characterized with a low Canadian Orientation. When looking at the demographic and language profiles, participants in Cluster 3 and Cluster 4 are virtually indistinguishable. They primarily differ on the four cultural orientation factors that these two clusters are based upon.

Cluster 5: Marginalized Group with Chinese Practices (N = 71; 32.3% of the sample)

Cluster 5 was the largest of all the clusters found in the current sample. Participants in this group scored significantly below the sample mean on all cultural orientation factors, except for Chinese-External Orientation, which was significantly above the mean for the sample. That is, compared to other clusters, individuals in this cluster do not strongly identify with Chinese or Canadian culture, but practice many Chinese behaviours. They are an average of 22 years old, and are fairly evenly divided between males and females. None of these participants are Canadian-born, and the majority (84%) came to Canada after the age of 12 years. They predominantly speak their ethnic language at home, and over half use their ethnic language outside the home. In addition, they report lower English proficiency and higher ethnic language proficiency than individuals in clusters characterized with a strong Canadian Orientation.

Validation of the five-cluster solution

A cluster analysis, like most types of multivariate analyses, might result in a certain structure even when applied to a random set of data (Wångby, Bergman, & Magnusson, 1999), which speaks to the importance of validating the final cluster solution. Although multivariate tests such as MANOVA or discriminate analysis have been used to validate a clustering solution, validating against a set of external criteria that are not used to generate the cluster solution is considered a better approach (Aldenderfer & Blashfield, 1984). In the current study, the relations between acculturation groups and participants' demographic backgrounds and language preferences are examined to validate the cluster solution (e.g., Liem et al., 2000).

The relations between demographic variables and the five clusters were consistent with previous acculturation research, thus supporting the validity of the five-cluster solution. For example, the majority of foreign-born participants were found in clusters that were characterized by salient ethnic features, including Clusters 1 and 2, and particularly Cluster 5, which was comprised exclusively of foreign-born participants. Canadian-born participants were only found in the three clusters characterized by a strong Canadian Orientation (i.e., Clusters 1, 3, and 4). In addition, the foreign-born Chinese participants in Cluster 4 had resided in Canada significantly longer than those in clusters characterized by a weak Canadian Orientation (Clusters 2 and 5).

Psychological adjustment and cluster membership

Finally, cluster membership was examined in relation to participants' psychological adjustment. It was hypothesized that participants with bicultural orientations (i.e., Clusters 1 and 4) would report the best adjustment, and that participants with marginalized orientations (i.e., Cluster 5) would report the lowest levels of adjustment. Self-esteem and depressive symptoms were used to represent positive and negative aspects of adjustment, respectively. These adjustment scores were entered into a one-way (cluster membership) MANOVA (see Table 2). The results revealed a significant multivariate effect, $F(2, 213) = 4.73$, $p<.001$. This multivariate effect was accounted for by significant univariate effects for both self-esteem, $F(4, 212) = 8.34$, $p<.001$, and depressive symptoms, $F(4, 212) = 4.23$, $p<.005$.

Regarding self-esteem, as expected, participants in Cluster 5 reported significantly lower levels of self-esteem than participants in Clusters 1 and 4. They also reported significantly lower self-esteem than participants in Cluster 3. Regarding feelings of depression, also as expected, participants in Cluster 5 reported significantly higher feelings of depression than did those in Cluster 4. In addition, participants in Cluster 3 (the Assimilated Group) reported lower levels of depression than those in Cluster 5. However, contrary to expectations, participants in Cluster 1 did not report significantly lower levels of depressive feelings than participants in Cluster 5.

DISCUSSION

Cluster analysis was used to classify participants into acculturation groups by simultaneously considering continuous measures of four cultural orientation factors. This method allowed participants to have varying degrees of immersion into multiple domains of ethnic and host cultural orientations so that their distinctive and shared features were fully illustrated.

The current five cluster groups and Berry's four acculturation groups

Five distinct acculturation groups were found, rather than four acculturation strategies as hypothesized in Berry's model (1980). Three of

TABLE 2
Means (and standard deviations) for cluster differences in adjustment

	Cluster 1 (*N* = 46)	*Cluster 2* (*N* = 48)	*Cluster 3* (*N* = 22)	*Cluster 4* (*N* = 33)	*Cluster 5* (*N* = 71)	*Contrast*
Self-esteem	3.10 (0.52)	2.95 (0.44)	3.33 (0.60)	3.15 (0.50)	2.76 (0.44)	1, 3, 4>5
Depressive symptoms	0.79 (0.49)	0.84 (0.40)	0.66 (0.51)	0.69 (0.42)	1.02 (0.51)	5>3, 4

Cluster 1 is the Integrated Group. Cluster 2 is the Separated Group. Cluster 3 is the Assimilated Group. Cluster 4 is the Integrated Group without Chinese Practices. Cluster 5 is the Marginalized Group with Chinese Practices.

the groups (i.e., Clusters 1, 2, and 3) were consistent with the constellation of groups expected based on Berry's model. Individuals in Cluster 1 (20.9%) viewed themselves strongly both as a Canadian and as a Chinese. They positively regarded the Chinese as a group and believed that their group was viewed positively by other people. This cluster is similar to Berry's "integration" strategy that is characterized by high levels of both ethnic and host cultural orientations. Individuals in Cluster 2 (21.8%) were characterized by a strong ethnic cultural orientation, a weak host cultural orientation, and a very positive regard for their ethnic group. This cluster is similar to the "separated" strategy in Berry's model. Individuals in Cluster 3 (10%) were predominantly characterized by a strong host cultural orientation and weak orientations with all ethnic dimensions. This cluster is similar to Berry's "assimilated" strategy.

The other two groups (i.e., Clusters 4 and 5) presented features that only partially conformed to Berry's acculturation strategies. First, individuals in Cluster 4 (Integrated Group without Chinese Practices) were characterized by a strong Canadian Orientation and high Ethnic Evaluation, a relatively neutral Chinese-Internal Orientation, and a weak Chinese-External Orientation. They possess features similar to Berry's strategies of integration and assimilation, but no single strategy of Berry's fully describes the participants in this cluster. Second, individuals in Cluster 5 (Marginalized Group with Chinese Practices) were characterized by a low Chinese-Internal Orientation, a low Canadian Orientation, and a low Ethnic Evaluation, but a high Chinese-External Orientation. This cluster is similar to Berry's "marginalized" strategy, with the major exception of a high Chinese-External Orientation. The nature of marginalization in general is a lack of belongingness to and association with any culture. Individuals in this cluster, although not strongly identifying with either culture, practise many Chinese customs and behaviours. Thus, they still maintain an essential element of being Chinese and a connection with the Chinese culture.

Consistent with prior research, the current study found that the Assimilated Group was the least preferred by immigrants (Berry et al., 1989). Groups with integrated features (Cluster 1 and Cluster 4) together comprised 35.9% of the sample. Thus, integration was most preferred, which is also consistent with prior research (Berry et al., 1989; Coatsworth et al., 2005; Eyou et al., 2000). Overall, despite the differences between the clusters found in the current study and Berry's four acculturation strategies, the similarities between these two provide further validation of the five-cluster solution.

Several factors may account for the differences between our five clusters and Berry's four acculturation strategies. First, the construct of Ethnic Evaluation played an important role in the two clusters that differ from Berry's model (Clusters 4 and 5). That is, within the three clusters that are similar to Berry's model (Clusters 1, 2 and 3), levels of Ethnic Evaluation and Chinese-Internal Orientation were similar. However, in Clusters 4 and 5, levels of Ethnic Evaluation and Chinese-Internal Orientation diverged. Thus, for some individuals, the evaluative and psychological aspects of one's ethnic orientation are separate. Second, the division of Chinese orientation into internal and external domains also enriched the results of the clustering. Again, in the two clusters that differed from Berry's model (as well as Cluster 3), the individuals' internal sense of being Chinese was separate from their external expression of being Chinese. These nuances would not have been apparent if the domain of Ethnic Evaluation had not been assessed, if Chinese orientation had been treated as a unitary construct, or if Chinese orientation had been assessed without the external domain of Chinese behavioural practices.

A third reason for differences in the results concerns the method used to form the clusters. Previous studies adopting Berry's model have typically used a cut-off score approach to assign participants to acculturation groups. This cut-off approach can produce relatively equal numbers of people in each group and therefore facilitates further statistical analyses. However, its simplicity in categorization may be at the expense of complexity and meaningfulness in individuals' varying degrees of immersion into multiple domains. For example, members of Cluster 1, the integrated group, viewed themselves strongly as Chinese (internally and externally) and regarded the Chinese group highly. The ethnic orientations of people in Cluster 4, in contrast, were at different levels: high Ethnic Evaluation, neutral Chinese-Internal Orientation, and low Chinese-External Orientation. Similarly, members of Cluster 3, the assimilated group, were not only characterized by a strong host cultural orientation, but there were also differences in the strength with which they endorsed the various ethnic domains. In this cluster, although all of the ethnic domains were relatively weak, the Chinese-External Orientation stood out as the weakest. This variation among different aspects of ethnic orientation within one cluster would not be visible if cut-off scores had been used.

Demographic profiles and language preferences of the five clusters

Expected differences among the five acculturation groups in terms of participants' demographic backgrounds (e.g., length of residence in Canada) and language preferences supported the validity of the cluster solution. Essentially, Canadian-born Chinese were divided into two kinds: those who identify with Canadian culture only (i.e., assimilated Cluster 3) and those who identify with both cultures (i.e., Clusters 1 and 4); being born in Canada likely fosters a sense of belongingness to and identification with Canadian culture. Foreign-born individuals were distributed across the five clusters, depending on their length of residence. For example, foreign-born participants in Cluster 4, a cluster that included the Canadian-born participants, had a longer length of residence in Canada than participants in the two clusters that did not include Canadian-born participants. Thus, the results are consistent with prior research reporting that a longer length of residence in the host country is related to stronger host cultural orientations and to the classification into integrated acculturation groups (Lee et al., 2003; Liem et al., 2000; Ryder et al., 2000). This suggests that the sense of being Chinese that comes with being born in a Chinese country may slowly diminish following immigration.

Together, these results suggest a potential developmental progression in the formation of cultural orientations for foreign-born Chinese. Very recent immigrants were most likely to be separated or marginalized compared to foreign-born individuals with a longer length of residence in Canada. With a longer exposure to the Canadian context, a sense of belonging to Canada may develop. This growing sense of Canadian orientation either competes with ethnic orientation (as in assimilation, Cluster 3) or harmonizes with ethnic orientation (as in integration, Cluster 1). There may be a diverging point when people move from separation (Cluster 2) and marginalization (Cluster 5) to either assimilation (Cluster 3) or integration (Cluster 1). These two pathways may converge again when participants have resided in Canada even longer. That is, assimilated participants who reclaim their ethnic orientation over time and integrated participants who experience less external support for practicing ethnic behaviours may eventually resemble participants in Cluster 4 (integration with few Chinese practices).

Although this proposed developmental progression is solely based on cross-sectional data, it shows similarities with existing ethnic identity stage theory (e.g., Sue & Sue, 1990). On the other hand, it is evident that demographic information alone cannot fully describe the current sample. For instance, participants in some clusters (e.g., Cluster 3 and 4) were very similar in their demographic backgrounds, and were only distinguished by the four cultural orientation factors. In addition, Canadian-born participants shared similar cultural orientation profiles with more than one third of the foreign-born participants. These results raise questions about the practice of studying within-group diversity by forming subgroups based on participants' demographic backgrounds such as nativity status (e.g., Lay & Verkuyten, 1999). The current study found more heterogeneity than demographic backgrounds alone could capture. Such results are only possible when research methods allow individuals to be similar to others with different demographic backgrounds.

Another interesting phenomenon across the five clusters concerns the pervasive ethnic language use among the current sample. Participants in clusters characterized with a strong Canadian Orientation predominately used English outside the home. About half of the participants across clusters, nevertheless, reported using an ethnic language predominantly outside the home. This pervasive use of an ethnic language outside the home is meaningful given that the current sample is comprised of university students, who are assumed to have a greater immersion into Canadian culture than other groups, such as community samples. These results suggest the presence of coexisting linguistic subcultures within Canada. Some previous acculturation research has taken self-reported language use and proficiency as a sole measure of acculturation (e.g., Deyo, Diehl, Hazuda, & Stern, 1985). In a multiethnic and multilinguistic community, the validity of using language as a sole index of acculturation is questionable.

Psychological adjustment and the five clusters

Regarding the relations between cluster membership and adjustment, the findings were partially consistent with expectations. As expected, participants in Cluster 5, characterized by relatively weak

Chinese and Canadian cultural orientations, reported lower levels of adjustment in terms of both self-esteem and depression than participants in Cluster 4, one of the integrated groups, and those in Cluster 3, the assimilated group. Participants in Cluster 1, the other integrated group, also reported higher self-esteem than those in Cluster 5, as expected, but did not report lower depression as was expected. Thus, these results are largely similar to past research in which integrated acculturation strategies are associated with better adaptation among immigrants and marginalization is associated with poorer adjustment (Berry, 2003; Pawliuk et al., 1996; Sanchez & Fernandez, 1993; Ying, 1995).

Feelings of not fitting in, or not belonging to any culture, are reported by many ethnic individuals living in multicultural contexts. This sense of alienation may directly relate to the poorer adjustment reported by participants in Cluster 5. This finding is particularly striking since this cluster was the largest single cluster found in the current sample. Importantly, Cluster 5 was formulated independently from the assessment of participants' psychological adjustment, overcoming one drawback in previous acculturation research where the relations between marginalization and adjustment may be superficially inflated due to overlapping items (Rudmin, 2003). Therefore, the resulting clusters and their relations with adjustment may be applicable to Chinese groups in other settings.

It is important to note that participants in this marginalized group did not report extremely low levels of adjustment compared with those in the other four clusters; participants in Cluster 5 scored towards the mid-point on each scale of adjustment, whereas participants in the other four clusters scored around the positive end of adjustment. In fact, the lack of difference in self-esteem between participants in Cluster 2 and Cluster 5, and in depressive symptoms among participants in Clusters 1, 2, and 5, demonstrates the similarities in their levels of adjustment.

Bourhis, Moïse, Perreault, and Senécal (1997) suggested that the marginalized acculturation category should be further divided into anomie and individualism. They argue that individuals who do not identify strongly with either the ethnic culture or the host culture may prefer to identify themselves as individuals, rather than as members of specific ethnic or cultural groups. Therefore, some individuals who do not identify strongly with either culture do not feel rejected by both cultures, and they do not fail to fit into any culture. This might explain why participants in Cluster 5 did not suffer from poorer adjustment to the extent that would be expected for individuals who identify with neither culture.

Implications

The identification of two clusters (1 and 4) that are similar to the concept of "integration" highlights the need to further refine the concept of integration. For example, one view emphasizes the formation of a unitary cultural orientation that integrates ethnic and host cultural orientations. Another perspective, consistent with the idea of biculturalism, emphasizes the coexistence of multiple cultural orientations that may be independent of each other. In this view, individuals characterized by strong ethnic and host orientations may not have one unitary cultural orientation; instead, they may alternate themselves between two cultural worlds as situational demands change (LaFromboise, Coleman, & Gerton, 1993). Participants in Cluster 4 reported relatively high internal Chinese orientations and Canadian orientations, but low external Chinese orientations (few behavioural practices); these participants may represent the first perspective of integration, combining Chinese and Canadian elements into one. In contrast, because the participants in Cluster 1 report relatively high Chinese behavioural practices as well as high internal Chinese orientations and Canadian orientation, they may reflect the latter perspective of alternation—feeling and behaving as Chinese in some contexts, and as Canadian in others. It would be valuable to identify ways of distinguishing between these two meanings of integration in future research, as the social and health consequences of each may differ.

The results have implications for national policies related to acculturation. Canada has a national policy of multiculturalism that encourages ethnic minority individuals to retain their ethnic heritage. In addition, the receiving communities of the current participants are supportive of integration in that there is a large and visible population of Chinese Canadians (Statistics Canada, 2003), most of whom reside in large urban centres that offer access to the Chinese culture (e.g., Chinese TV stations, newspapers, language schools, and professional services). The multicultural policy of Canada and the composition of the receiving communities may be reflected in the nature of the five clusters found in the current study, as all but one (i.e., the smallest, Cluster 3) possessed some degree of retaining Chinese culture. This may be less likely in national contexts where assimilation is considered more desirable than integration (Phinney et al., 2001). Future research that explores the distribution of immigrants in different acculturation groups in diverse national and local contexts could help clarify the role that national policies and receiving communities play in shaping immigrants' acculturation experiences.

Despite Canada's multicultural policy, among the current sample of Chinese Canadians, the largest single cluster was unexpectedly the marginalized group in Cluster 5. This suggests a need to explore the ways in which multicultural policies are reflected in everyday experiences of immigrants, including the barriers and challenges immigrants face to full participation in both ethnic and host cultures. Some of these challenges may derive from the attitudes of members of the majority culture towards immigration and multiculturalism. The field of acculturation has devoted considerably more attention to the attitudes and behaviours of immigrating groups than to the attitudes and behaviours of members of the receiving society (see Berry & Kalin, 1995, for an exception). Research has found that majority group members who endorse multiculturalism are less likely, compared to those who endorse assimilation, to negatively evaluate ethnic minority immigrants (Verkuyten, 2005); these attitudes may be related to the health of immigrants, as members of clusters characterized by positive evaluations of the Chinese group in the current study generally reported positive adjustment. Thus, from an intervention perspective, efforts to promote positive attitudes toward immigrants among members of the majority culture may aid the acculturation and adjustment of immigrants.

Finally, participants with marginalized profiles reported the poorest adjustment. Clinical efforts should be made to identify ethnic minority individuals at risk, such as those with cultural orientation profiles similar to Cluster 5, so that effective cultural or psychological interventions can be offered. In light of the weak host cultural orientation among these prospective clients, clinicians should offer interventions in a way that does not promote assimilation as the primary goal, and instead maximizes individuals' ability to choose from multiple ways of acculturating.

Limitations and future directions

The present study is limited in a number of ways; thus several directions for future research stem from the findings. First, limitations are acknowledged with regard to the representativeness of the university student sample and the generalizability of findings to Chinese Canadians as a whole. In addition, the characteristics of the current sample (e.g., over-representation of foreign-born participants) may have contributed to the findings. It will be important to replicate the current study in community samples by employing greater effort to recruit people with Chinese origins through non-ethnic-related networks.

Second, a potential pathway for the development of cultural orientations was proposed. However, longitudinal research is needed to empirically explore the developmental trajectories of ethnic and host cultural orientations. It has been suggested that, at a global level, the patterns identified for a particular person through a pattern-centred approach are relatively stable over time (Wångby et al., 1999). Therefore, a pattern-centred approach may be a suitable methodology for understanding the relations among constructs longitudinally. Future studies could also explore critical experiences or incidences that prompt individuals to renegotiate multiple aspects of their cultural orientations.

In conclusion, the current study identified five clusters of individuals with similar patterns of cultural orientations through the use of cluster analysis. Cluster analysis allows the groups to be formed naturally through the simultaneous consideration of multiple domains of Chinese and Canadian orientations. The resultant cluster solution facilitates the examination of both common and rare cultural orientation patterns, as well as the evaluation of the relations between these patterns and important outcomes such as adjustment. Overall, the results of this study highlight the diversity that exists within a fairly homogeneous sample of Chinese Canadian immigrants (i.e., university students who are predominantly foreign-born). Policy and intervention efforts to assist individuals following immigration need to recognize multiple ways of acculturating that are associated with positive adjustment.

Manuscript received January 2005
Revised manuscript accepted August 2005

REFERENCES

Aldenderfer, M. S., & Blashfield, R. K. (1984). *Cluster analysis*. Newbury Park, CA: Sage.

Bergman, L. R., & Magnusson, D. (1997). A person-oriented approach in research on developmental psychopathology. *Development and Psychopathology*, *9*, 291–319.

Berry, J. W. (1980). Acculturation as varieties of adaptation. In A. M. Padilla (Ed.), *Acculturation:*

Theory, models and some new findings (pp. 9–25). Boulder, CO: Westview Press.

Berry, J. W. (2003). Conceptual approaches to acculturation. In K. Chum, P. Organista, & G. Marín (Eds.), *Acculturation: Advances in theory, measurement, and applied research* (pp. 17–38). Washington, DC: American Psychological Association.

Berry, J. W., & Kalin, R. (1995). Multicultural and ethnic attitudes in Canada: An overview of a 1991 national survey. *Canadian Journal of Behavioural Science, 27*, 301–320.

Berry, J. W., Kim, U., Power, S., Young, M., & Bujaki, M. (1989). Acculturation attitudes in plural societies. *Applied Psychology: An International Review, 38*, 185–206.

Birman, D., & Trickett, E. J. (2001). Cultural transitions in first-generation immigrants: Acculturation of Soviet Jewish refugee adolescents and parents. *Journal of Cross-Cultural Psychology, 32*, 456–477.

Bond, M. H., & Hwang, K. K. (1986). The social psychology of Chinese people. In M. H. Bond (Ed.), *The psychology of Chinese people* (pp. 213–266). Hong Kong: Oxford University Press.

Borgen, F. H., & Barnett, D. C. (1987). Applying cluster analysis in counseling psychology research. *Journal of Counseling Psychology, 34*, 456–468.

Bourhis, R. Y., Moïse, L. C., Perreault, R., & Senécal, S. (1997). Toward an interactive acculturation model: A social psychological approach. *International Journal of Psychology, 32*, 369–386.

Chang, T., Tracey, T., & Moore, T. (2005). The dimensional structure of Asian American acculturation: An examination of prototypes. *Self and Identity, 4*, 25–43.

Chia, A.-L., & Costigan, C. L. (2002, May). *Multidimensional and orthogonal approaches to ethnic identity and acculturation.* Poster presented at the 63rd Canadian Psychological Association annual meeting, Vancouver, Canada.

Clark, L. A., & Watson, D. (1995). Constructing validity: Issues in objective scale development. *Psychological Assessment, 7*, 309–319.

Coatsworth, J. D., Maldonado-Molina, M., Pantin, H., & Szapocznik, S. (2005). A person-centered and ecological investigation of acculturation strategies in Hispanic immigrant youth. *Journal of Community Psychology, 33*, 157–174.

Costigan, C. L., & Su, T. F. (2004). Orthogonal versus linear models of acculturation among immigrant Chinese Canadians: A comparison of mothers, fathers, and children. *International Journal of Behavioral Development, 28*, 518–527.

Cuéllar, I., Arnold, B., & Maldonado, R. (1995). Acculturation Rating Scale for Mexican Americans-II: A revision of the original ARSMA Scale. *Hispanic Journal of Behavioural Sciences, 17*, 275–304.

Der-Karabetian, A., & Ruiz, Y. (1997). Affective bicultural and global-human identity scale for Mexican-American adolescents. *Psychological Reports, 80*, 1027–1039.

Deyo, R. A., Diehl, A. K., Hazuda, H., & Stern, M. P. (1985). A simple language-based acculturation scale for Mexican Americans: Validation and application to health care research. *American Journal of Public Health, 75*, 51–55.

Eyou, M. L., Adair, V., & Dixon, R. (2000). Cultural identity and psychological adjustment of adolescent Chinese immigrants in New Zealand. *Journal of Adolescence, 23*, 531–543.

Gil, A. G., Vega, W. A., & Dimas, J. M. (1994). Acculturative stress and personal adjustment among Hispanic adolescent boys. *Journal of Community Psychology, 22*, 43–54.

Gim Chung, R. H., Kim, B. S. K., & Abreu, J. M. (2004). Asian American Multidimensional Acculturation Scale: Development, factor analysis, reliability, and validity. *Cultural Diversity and Ethnic Minority Psychology, 10*, 66–80.

Hand, S., & Everitt, B. S. (1987). A Monte Carlo study of the recovery of cluster structure in binary data by hierarchical clustering techniques. *Multivariate Behavioural Research, 22*, 235–243.

LaFromboise, T., Coleman, H. L. K., & Gerton, J. (1993). Psychological impact of biculturalism: Evidence and theory. *Psychological Bulletin, 114*, 395–412.

Lay, C., & Verkuyten, M. (1999). Ethnic identity and its relation to personal self-esteem: A comparison of Canadian-born and foreign-born Chinese adolescents. *Journal of Social Psychology, 99*, 288–300.

Lee, S., Sobal, J., & Frongillo, E. A. (2003). Comparison of models of acculturation: The case of Korean Americans. *Journal of Cross-Cultural Psychology, 34*, 282–296.

Liem, R., Lim, B. A., & Liem, J. H. (2000). Acculturation and emotion among Asian Americans. *Cultural Diversity and Ethnic Minority Psychology, 6*, 13–31.

Luhtanen, R., & Crocker, J. (1992). A collective self-esteem scale: Self evaluation of one's social identity. *Personality and Social Psychology Bulletin, 18*, 302–318.

Milligan, G. W., & Cooper, M. C. (1985). An examination of procedures for determining the number of clusters in a data set. *Psychometrika, 50*, 159–179.

Mojena, R. (1977). Hierarchical grouping methods and stopping rules: An evaluation. *Computer Journal, 20*, 359–363.

Pawliuk, N., Grizenko, N., Chan-Yip, A., Gantous, P., Mathew, J., & Nguyen, D. (1996). Acculturation style and psychological functioning in children of immigrants. *American Journal of Orthopsychiatry, 66*, 111–121.

Phinney, J. S. (1992). The Multigroup Ethnic Identity Measure: A new scale for use with diverse groups. *Journal of Adolescent Research, 7*, 156–176.

Phinney, J. S., Horenczyk, G., Liebkind, K., & Vedder, P. (2001). Ethnic identity, immigration, and well-being: An interactional perspective. *Journal of Social Issues, 57*, 493–510.

Radloff, L. (1977). The CES-D Scale: A self-report depression scale for research in the general population. *Applied Psychological Measurement, 1*, 385–401.

Ralston, D. A., Gustafson, D. J., Elsass, P. M., Cheung, F., & Terpstra, R. H. (1992). Eastern values: A comparison of managers in the United States, Hong Kong, and the People's Republic of China. *Journal of Applied Psychology, 77*, 664–671.

Richman, J. A., Gaviria, M., Flaherty, J. A., Birz, S., & Wintrob, R. M. (1987). The process of acculturation: Theoretical perspectives and an empirical investigation in Peru. *Social Science and Medicine, 25*, 839–847.

Rosenberg, M. (1986). *Conceiving the self.* Melbourne, Australia: Krieger.

Rudmin, F. W. (2003). Critical history of the acculturation psychology of assimilation, separation, integration, and marginalization. *Review of General Psychology*, *7*, 3–37.

Ryder, A. G., Alden, L. E., & Paulhus, D. L. (2000). Is acculturation unidimensional or bidimensional? A head-to-head comparison in the prediction of personality, self-identity, and adjustment. *Journal of Personality and Social Psychology*, *79*, 49–65.

Sanchez, J. I., & Fernandez, D. M. (1993). Acculturative stress among Hispanics: A bi-dimensional model of ethnic identification. *Journal of Applied Social Psychology*, *23*, 654–668.

Statistics Canada (2003). *Visible minority population.* (data products: 2001 census of population), Ottawa, ON: Statistics Canada.

Sue, D. W., & Sue, D. (1990). *Counseling the culturally different: Theory and practice* (2nd ed.), New York: John Wiley.

The Chinese Culture Connection (1987). Chinese values and the search for culture-free dimensions of culture. *Journal of Cross-Cultural Psychology*, *18*, 143–164.

Torres, V. (1999). Validation of a bicultural orientation model for Hispanic college students. *Journal of College Student Development*, *40*, 285–298.

Tropp, L. R., Erkut, S., Coll, C. G., Alarcon, O., & Garcia, H. A. V. (1999). Psychological acculturation: Development of a new measure for Puerto Ricans on the US mainland. *Educational and Psychological Measurement*, *59*, 351–367.

Van de Vijver, F. J. R., & Phalet, K. (2004). Assessment in multicultural groups: The role of acculturation. *Applied Psychology: An International Review*, *53*, 215–236.

Verkuyten, M. (2005). Ethnic group identification and group evaluation among minority and majority groups: Testing the multiculturalism hypothesis. *Journal of Personality and Social Psychology*, *88*, 121–138.

Wångby, M., Bergman, L. R., & Magnusson, D. (1999). Development of adjustment problems in girls: What syndromes emerge? *Child Development*, *70*, 678–699.

Ying, Y. (1995). Cultural orientation and psychological well-being in Chinese Americans. *American Journal of Community Psychology*, *23*, 893–911.

Ying, Y.-W., Lee, P. A., Tsai, J. L., Yeh, Y.-Y., & Huang, J. S. (2000). The conception of depression in Chinese American college students. *Cultural Diversity and Ethnic Minority Psychology*, *6*, 183–195.

Zak, I. (1973). Dimensions of Jewish-American identity. *Psychological Reports*, *33*, 891–900.

INTERNATIONAL JOURNAL OF PSYCHOLOGY, 2006, 41 (5), 413–422

The MMPI-2 Gender-Masculine and Gender-Feminine scales: Gender roles as predictors of psychological health in clinical patients

Matthew Woo and Tian P. S. Oei

University of Queensland, Brisbane, Australia

Previous research measuring various biosocial factors such as age, sex, and marital status has found them to be essentially unrelated to measures of psychological health. Recent empirical studies have revealed that personality constructs may be more significant than demographic variables in the prediction of psychological well-being. The present study assessed the personality constructs of masculinity and femininity and hypothesized that the Gender-Masculine (GM) scale of the MMPI-2 would be more effective than the Gender-Feminine (GF) scale in predicting psychological well-being. This hypothesis stems from previous research that has indicated the dominance of the masculinity model. It is suggested that previous research supporting androgyny as a primary indicator of well-being was influenced by the masculinity component of this gender orientation. One hundred and seventy-seven psychiatric patients from Australia (N = 107) and Singapore (N = 70) completed the MMPI-2. Hierarchical multiple regression revealed significantly stronger masculinity effects, with significance achieved on measures of ego strength and low self-esteem. No significant relationship between psychological well-being and the GF variable was found. Similarly, androgyny did not add any further variance to the model when masculinity was controlled for. Overall, the results are consistent with an interpretation that GM is a better correlate of psychological well-being as compared to the GF scale.

Les études antérieures mesurant divers facteurs biosociaux tels que l'âge, le sexe et le statut conjugal ont révélé que ces facteurs sont essentiellement non reliés aux mesures de santé psychologique. Des études empiriques récentes ont montré que les construits de personnalité peuvent être plus significatifs que les variables démographiques dans la prédiction du bien-être psychologique. La présente étude a évalué les construits de personnalité de masculinité et de féminité en posant l'hypothèse que l'échelle de genre masculin (GM) du MMPI-2 allait être plus efficace que l'échelle de genre féminin (GF) pour la prédiction du bien-être psychologique. Cette hypothèse est basée sur une recherche antérieure qui a indiqué une dominance du modèle de Masculinité. Il est suggéré qu'une recherche antérieure qui soutient l'Androgynéité comme indicateur premier de bien-être était influencée par la composante de masculinité de cette orientation de genre. Cent soixante-dix-sept patients psychiatriques d'Australie (N = 107) et de Singapour (N = 70) ont complété le MMPI-2. Une régression hiérarchique multiple a révélé des effets de la masculinité significativement supérieurs en regard des mesures de Force de l'ego et de Faiblesse de l'estime de soi. Aucune relation significative ne fut trouvée entre le bien-être psychologique et la variable GF. De façon similaire, l'Androgynéité n'a pas ajouté de variance au modèle lorsque la masculinité était contrôlée. En somme, les résultats soutiennent l'interprétation que le GM est davantage associé au bien-être psychologique que le GF.

La investigación antecedente que mide diversos factores biosociales como la edad, el sexo, y el estatus marital ha encontrado que esencialmente no se relacionan con medidas de salud psicológica. Algunos estudios empíricos recientes han revelado que los constructos de personalidad parecen predecir de manera más importante el bienestar psicológico que las variables demográficas. El presente estudio evaluó los constructos de personalidad masculinidad y femineidad y plantea como hipótesis que la escala (GM) Género Masculino del MMPI-2 predice con mayor efectividad el bienestar psicológico que la escala (GF) Género Femenino. Esta hipótesis surge de la investigación previa que ha señalado la dominancia del modelo Masculino. Se sugiere que el

Correspondence should be addressed to Professor Tian Oei, School of Psychology, University of Queensland, Brisbane, Queensland 4072, Australia (E-mail: oei@psy.uq.edu.au).

Matthew Woo is now at the Department of Psychology, Institute of Mental Health, Singapore. Professor Oei is also Director, CBT Unit, Toowong Private Hospital.

 DOI: 10.1080/00207590500412185

componente de masculinidad de esta orientación de género influyó sobre la investigación antecedente que apoya la androginia como indicador primario de bienestar. Ciento setenta y siete pacientes psiquiátricos de Australia (N = 107) y Singapur (N = 70) respondieron al MMPI-2. Una regresión múltiple jerárquica reveló que los efectos de la masculinidad significativos más fuertes se observaron con las medidas de la Fuerza del Ego y Autoestima Baja. No se encontró que hubiese relación significativa entre el bienestar psicológico y la variable GF. De manera similar, la androginia, al controlarse la masculinidad, no añadió varianza al modelo. En general, los resultados coinciden con la interpretación de que la escala GM, en comparación con la GF, es un mejor correlato del bienestar psicológico.

Many biological and social factors, such as age, sex, and marital status have been found to be essentially unrelated to measures of well-being (De Neve & Cooper, 1998). In a meta-analysis conducted by De Neve and Cooper, it was revealed that basic demographic factors often accounted for less than 6% of the variance in measures of well-being, whereas personality traits accounted for more than 20%. Taken together, these findings suggest that personality may be more influential than demographic variables in the prediction of psychological health. However, the personality constructs of masculinity and femininity have recently gained more attention as measures of psychological well-being (Bassoff & Glass, 1982; Taylor & Hall, 1982; Whitley, 1983, 1985). Traditionally, researchers have viewed gender as a continuum, with masculinity and femininity located at opposite endpoints, and therefore logical reversals of each other (Constantinople, 1973). These bipolar scales typically characterize masculinity as instrumental or goal-directed behaviour, which includes self-confidence, independence, leadership, and assertiveness, whereas femininity is viewed as a constellation of nurturing personality features such as empathy, gentleness, tactfulness, and communication (Castlebury & Durham, 1997; Lawrance, Taylor, & Byers, 1996; Stake, 2000; Ward, 2000). However, in recent decades, this bipolarity assumption has been challenged. Constantinople's (1973) landmark review suggested locating masculinity-femininity traits on two separate unidimensional scales. Specifically, this indicates that an individual can have a combination of both masculine and feminine traits, irrespective of their sex.

Following Constantinople's lead, Bem (1974) developed the Bem Sex Role Inventory (BSRI) to measure masculine and feminine gender roles separately. Baucom (1976) also used his two California Psychological Inventory (CPI) scales, Masculinity (MSC) and Femininity (FMN), to define four groups: stereotyped masculine (high masculinity, low femininity), stereotyped feminine (low masculinity, high femininity), androgynous (high masculinity, high femininity), and undifferentiated (low masculinity, low femininity). Further, Ricciardelli and Williams (1995) suggest that a four-factor model including both positive and negative aspects of gender-linked traits is essentially an improvement over a two-factor model reflecting just masculinity and femininity. As such, the two unidimensional scales have the capacity to distinguish between undifferentiated and androgynous individuals, whereas bipolar scales are unable to discriminate between these individuals because both groups will tend to score somewhat in the middle.

The mid-1970s and early 1980s saw a rush of literature depicting androgyny as an ideal psychological state and androgynous individuals as exemplars of psychological health (Bem, 1974; Kaplan & Bean, 1976; Rawlings & Carter, 1977; Spence & Helmreich, 1981). Bem (1981) expressed the then bullish sentiment among advocates of the androgynous position as, "A concept whose time had come ... that appeared to provide a liberated and more humane alternative to the traditional, sex-biased standards of mental health" (p. 362). Despite this enthusiasm, there was not a single study at the time that substantiated the construct validity of androgyny (Lubinski, Tellegen, & Butcher, 1983).

From the mid-1980s, and particularly in the past decade, there has been a spate of studies calling for a contextual understanding and examination of androgyny (Stake, 2000). The idea that gender roles differentially interact with psychological well-being in different contexts is endorsed by androgyny theorists. For example, Steenbarger and Greenberg (1990) revealed that the relationship between masculinity and favourable adjustment was applicable in the context of achievement stress, whereas femininity contributed to adjustment in the context of interpersonal stress. Similar research has also investigated this theory of gender orientation and context in areas including social expectations (Miller, Moen, & Dempster-McClain, 1991; Stake, 1997), coping strategies (Holland & Andre, 1994; Stake, 2000), decision making (Baril, Elbert,

Mahar-Potter, & Reavy, 1989; Kirchmeyer, 1996), perception of physical health (Baffi, Redican, Sefchick, & Impara, 1991; Shifren & Bauserman, 1996), parenting strategies (Uleman & Weston, 1986), and sexual behaviour (Lawrance et al., 1996). Overall, recent research suggests that self-perceptions of gender roles are fluid and are influenced by circumstances.

In contrast, the masculinity model suggests that a high masculine orientation is associated with improved psychological well-being, with more feminine traits being less influential (Castlebury & Durham, 1997). Apart from Lubinski et al.'s (1983) critical article debunking androgyny as a valid statistical construct, there are numerous other studies that have supported the masculinity model as correlating highly with measures of adjustment, higher self-esteem, and psychological well-being (Antill & Cunningham, 1979; Castlebury & Durham, 1997; Feather, 1985; Lau, 1989; Payne, 1987; Zeldew, Clark, & Daughterty, 1985). Critical reviews that apply meta-analyses have similarly upheld this masculinity model (Bassoff & Glass, 1982; Taylor & Hall, 1982; Whitley, 1983, 1985). It is suggested, therefore, that empirical findings showing a positive relationship between androgyny and psychological well-being could primarily be attributed to the masculinity component. That is, psychological well-being may be chiefly determined by the individual's level of masculine attributes, regardless of their actual gender.

Most of the knowledge in the literature pertaining to the well-documented masculinity effect has been uncovered with the use of the BSRI (Baldwin, Critelli, Stevens, & Russell, 1986). However, it has been suggested that the Male and Female scales of the BSRI identify only positive or desirable traits,[1] and in this regard, Baldwin et al. point out that it is misleading to artificially create socially desirable sex role scales in order to demonstrate positive effects of masculinity and femininity. Baldwin et al. further claim that a true test of the hypothesis that a combination of masculine and feminine traits results in a healthy individual will require that the BSRI Male and Female scales representatively sample both positive and negative components of gender.

[1]In the BSRI, respondents were instructed: "We would like you to indicate how desirable it is in American society for a man/woman to possess each of these characteristics. We are not interested in your personal opinion of how desirable each of these characteristics is. Rather, we want your judgment of how our society evaluates each of these characteristics in a man/woman" (Bem, 1981, p.17).

As such, the MMPI-2 Gender-Masculine (GM) and Gender-Feminine (GF) scales, which constitute a four-factor model, represent more validity, since they take into consideration a broader array of gender types (Peterson & Dahlstrom, 1992). The GM and GF scales add a different dimension because these scales have a significant advantage over the BSRI. The MMPI-2 GM and GF scales therefore provide the balance that is missing in the BSRI, and contribute to the already robust findings surrounding the Masculinity model by including negative trait items. Recent research by Castlebury and Durham (1997) has used the GM and GF scales of the MMPI-2 to measure differences in psychological well-being for each of the masculine, feminine, androgynous and undifferentiated groups. However, rather than these groups existing as separate categories, it is suggested that gender traits occurring along a continuum can predict psychological health.

The present study aims to investigate empirical support for the masculinity model. It is hypothesized that the Gender-Masculine (GM) scale of the MMPI-2 will be more effective than the Gender-Feminine (GF) scale in predicting psychological well-being. It is further predicted that when controlling for the effect of masculinity, androgyny will not add any further variance to the overall model. Finally, it is predicted that individuals with more masculine (high GM-low GF) traits will have a higher psychological well-being score than persons with androgynous (high GM-high GF), feminine (low GM-high GF), or undifferentiated (low GM-low GF) traits.

METHOD

Participants in this research were from Australia and Singapore, two countries with strong multi-ethnic or multicultural influences. The diverse ethnic groups present the problem of within-groups heterogeneity. There is a considerable amount of research demonstrating methodologies to address this within-groups heterogeneity, and the findings are summarized in five reviews (Graham, 2000b; Greene, 1987; Hall, Bansal, & Lopez, 1999; Pritchard & Rosenblatt, 1980; Valasquez, Ayala, & Mendoza, 1998). Following the cue of researchers as reviewed by Hall et al., the present study has statistically controlled the demographic variables of age, gender, and education. It is not possible to match the two samples, as the two groups of participants are of different sample sizes. Since the sample spans a variety of clinical disorders, the present study has also controlled for the influence for psychiatric diagnoses.

Participants

One hundred and seventy-seven participants, consisting of 52 male and 18 female Singaporeans (Mean age = 34.60; *SD* = 11.02) and 39 male and 68 female Australians (Mean age = 32.56; *SD* = 8.12), who experienced a wide range of clinical disorders (schizophrenia, adjustment problems, mood disorders, OCD, sexual disorders, substance abuse, and personality disorders) as classified according to DSM-IV (American Psychiatric Association, 1994) criteria, were recruited for this study. The participants were representative of the clientele or patient population of the three centres from which the chief investigator collected the MMPI-2 data, although no particular clinical disorder was being investigated exclusively. The respective diagnoses of the Australian and Singaporean participants are summarized in Table 1.

The majority of participants were high school graduates with 12 years of education. The mean number of years of education for Singaporean and Australian participants were very similar: 11.87 (*SD* = 1.74) and 11.86 (*SD* = 2.52), respectively. Participants had at least 9 years of formal education, fulfilling Hathaway and McKinley's (1989) guideline of having at least an eighth grade reading level for the comprehension of the content of all the MMPI-2 items and to respond to them appropriately.

Measures

Minnesota Multiphasic Personality Inventory-2 (MMPI-2; Butcher, Dahlstrom, Graham, Tellegen, & Kaemmer, 1989). The MMPI-2 consists of 567 items that can be combined to yield a number of scales, which are grouped together to form four clusters: validity, clinical, supplementary, and content. MMPI-2 scale scores are calculated by totalling the number of items per specified subset, and are reported as T-scores. Each cluster measures different aspects of psychopathology, with elevations on these scales beyond the T = 60 cut-off indicating the presence of psychopathology. Concurrent as well as construct validity has been reported for the MMPI-2 (Butcher et al., 1989; Graham, Barthlow, Stein, Ben-Porath, & McNulty, 2002).

Ego Strength and Low Self-Esteem scales. Ego Strength (ES) from the Supplementary scales and Low Self-Esteem (LSE) from the Content scales were used to measure psychological well-being. The Ego Strength scale was originally developed to predict individual psychotherapy outcome, with higher scores on this scale indicating a higher level of adjustment and lower scores indicating a higher level of maladjustment. Subsequent research has also revealed that the ES scale is related to the presence of psychological resources needed for day-to-day functioning (e.g., Archer, Elkins, Aiduk, & Griffin, 1997; Schuldberg, 1992). Further, Graham (2000a) has cited research data showing that the ES indicates overall psychological adjustment, as assessed concurrently by other MMPI-2 indexes and extra criteria.

The Low Self-Esteem scale assesses characteristics such as poor self-concept, anticipation of failure, sensitivity to criticism, passivity in relationships, difficulty in decision making, and excessive worrying (Brems & Lloyd, 2000; Englert, Weed, & Watson, 2000). High scores on LSE items indicate higher levels of pathology (i.e., less self-confidence, more fault finding, and negative evaluation; Butcher, Graham, Williams, & Ben-Porath, 1990), with individuals reporting low self-opinion, low popularity with peers, and unattractiveness (Englert et al., 2000).

TABLE 1
Diagnostic disorders (as classified according to DSM-IV criteria) for the Singaporean and Australian samples

	Australian (A) (N = 107)		*Singaporean (S) (N = 70)*		*Total (T) (N = 177)*	
	Freq	*% of S sample*	*Freq*	*% of A sample*	*Freq*	*% of T sample*
Schizophrenia	21	19.6	14	20.0	35	19.8
Adjustment problem or disorder	29	27.1	19	27.1	48	27.1
Mood disorder	27	25.2	17	24.3	44	24.9
Obsessive Compulsive disorder	1	0.9	3	4.3	4	2.3
Sexual disorder	0	0.0	2	2.9	2	1.1
Substance abuse	18	16.8	7	10.0	25	14.1
Personality disorder	11	10.3	8	11.4	19	10.7

Overall, higher *t* scores on Ego Strength infer psychological health, whereas higher *t* scores on the Low Self-Esteem Content scale reflect a reduced sense of psychological well-being and the greater likelihood of pathology (Castlebury & Durham, 1997; Graham et al., 2002). Numerous studies have revealed relationships between these two constructs and psychological health, and have demonstrated that they are more than adequate in their independent measurement of psychological well-being. As such, psychological well-being or health as described in the present study is therefore defined by scores obtained on the ES and LSE scales.

Gender-Masculine (GM) and Gender-Feminine (GF) scales. The MMPI-2 GM and GF scales were used in the present study as measures of masculine and feminine traits. Butcher et al. (1989) reported the test–retest reliability of the GM scale to be .73 for men and .89 for women, with internal consistency α = .67 and α = .75 for men and women, respectively. The GF scale test–retest reliability was .86 for men and .78 for women, whereas internal consistency was the same for both sexes, α = .57.

Procedure

The study consisted of two phases, with the first phase being undertaken in Singapore between March 1996 and July 1998. The data collection for the second phase was carried out in Queensland, Australia between December 1999 and December 2000. In phase 1, the treating psychiatrist first made specific referrals for MMPI-2 personality assessment to the Department of Psychology. Participants made their responses on an Optical Mark Reader (OMR) form. After scanning the forms, the MMPI-2 profiles were generated by a computer program written by the author for the specific purpose of translating the data into meaningful interpretable sets. The procedure undertaken for the second phase was different insofar as there was no scanning and generation of profiles with an Optical Mark Reader. Instead, the profiles were hand scored. After interpreting profiles, verbal feedback was given to each participant. All other aspects of the procedure, as per phase 1, were repeated in phase 2. These aspects included the general instructions for administration. In addition to completing the MMPI booklet, all participants in both phases completed a biographical information form that included self-reports of ethnic origin, gender, age, marital status, and years of education. All participants completed the MMPI-2 in English and reported no difficulty in completing the MMPI-2.

RESULTS

From the original sample of 233, 56 participants were excluded from the sample because their MMPI-2 profiles failed to meet Graham's (1990) recommended criteria for interpretability. Specifically, using the same exclusion criteria as Castlebury and Durham (1997), participants were not included in the sample if they omitted answers to any of the items, or if they produced F-scale *t* scores greater than 100. Graham (1990) argues that validity scale scores in excess of 100 suggest the likelihood that individuals may have responded randomly, or all true or false to the MMPI-2 items, or may have been faking bad responses when taking the test.

Prior to analysis, a median split was done to group participants by gender type. For the Singaporean participants, the GM median score was 28.5 for males and 32.0 for females, whereas the GF median score was 29.5 for males and 34.5 for females. For the Australian participants, the GM median score was 31.0 and 25.0 for males and females, respectively, and the GF median score was 28.0 for males and 37.0 for females.

In investigating empirical support for the masculinity model, the hypothesis was an attempt to determine if the possession of masculine traits would favourably influence an individual's psychological well-being. As shown in Table 2, it was revealed that individuals classified as stereotyped masculine or androgynous had scores indicating improved psychological well-being, compared to those classified as stereotyped feminine and undifferentiated. That is, those participants with high GM traits were more likely to present with higher ego strength and higher self-esteem than those with predominantly GF traits.

The partial correlations of the ES and LSE scales with masculine and feminine traits are shown in Table 3. Both LSE and ES scales demonstrated significant main effects for GM, but not for GF. Further, the coefficients for GM were in the expected direction and showed a positive relationship with ES as well as a negative relationship between masculine traits and LSE. These correlations suggest that the GM scale has the capacity to predict psychological well-being, and that the relationship is stronger than the relationship between well-being and the GF scale.

TABLE 2
Means and standard error (SE) of *t*-scores on measures of psychological well-being for each category of gender type

Scales	*Gender types*	*Australian participants*		*Singaporean participants*		*Total participants*	
		M	*SE*	*M*	*SE*	*M*	*SE*
Ego Strength	Undifferentiated	31.07	1.98	24.01	2.66	29.15	1.77
	Stereotyped feminine	32.75	1.97	19.57	3.01	25.76	1.77
	Stereotyped masculine	42.30	1.90	47.49	3.17	42.66	1.75
	Androgynous	42.49	1.70	43.63	2.51	43.83	1.53
Low Self-Esteem	Undifferentiated	64.85	2.05	65.74	3.00	65.71	1.75
	Stereotyped feminine	66.18	2.04	72.06	3.39	68.87	1.75
	Stereotyped masculine	56.53	1.96	59.52	3.57	57.07	1.73
	Androgynous	49.80	1.76	54.93	2.83	51.76	1.51

TABLE 3
Partial correlations of Ego Strength and Low Self-Esteem scales with Gender-Masculine and Gender-Feminine scales

Scale	*ES*	*LSE*	*GM*	*GF*
ES	1.00			
LSE	−.57***	1.00		
GM	.72***	−.61***	1.00	
FM	−.02	−.11	−.08	1.00

*** $p<.001$.

Hierarchical multiple regression was conducted to investigate the extent to which masculine, feminine and androgynous traits contribute to psychological health. The basic approach in hierarchical multiple regression is to include the main effects (i.e., GM and GF) with the interaction terms (i.e., GM × GF). The proposed regression equation is as follows:

$$\hat{Y} = b_1 G_F + b_2 G_M + b_3 G_M G_F + a$$

It contains the terms that will enable the investigation of the construct validity of masculine $(G_M)^2$ and feminine (G_F) traits as linear predictors of psychopathology, and the validity of the androgyny concept as interactive ($G_M G_F$). The results were obtained by first entering the three main effects (Femininity–G_F; Masculinity–G_M; and the interaction term–$G_M G_F$) in an incremental stepwise fashion. To avoid the problem of mulitcollinearity arising from androgyny being a composite of masculinity and femininity scores, the predictors were entered in separate steps with the interactive term ($G_M G_F$) being entered last (cf. Kirchmeyer, 1996; Korabik, 1982; Motowidlo, 1982). Tables 4 and 5 present the stepwise entry results for hierarchical regression analysis for ES and LSE scales, respectively.

For both the LSE and ES scales and across the three categories of participants (Australian, Singaporean, pooled), G_M was significant in contributing to variance increase on inclusion in the regression model. The range of variance increase, evident from ΔR^2, was from 40% to 64%, all significant at the $p<.001$ level. The results of these analyses for both LSE and ES scales are therefore similar, demonstrating significant main effects for GM but not for GF. Also consistent with prediction, G_F, and the interaction variable G_F G_M, did not increase R^2 significantly or contribute significantly to the final regression model for either scale or across data representing Australian, Singaporean and pooled participants.

DISCUSSION

The theory that androgynous individuals are psychologically healthier than gender-typed individuals is attractive and probably more politically correct. However, the results of the present study do not appear to support this proposition. The current study treated the GM and GF scale scores as continuous variables in the regression model, which revealed the superiority of masculine influences over feminine and androgyny effects in measures of ego strength and self-esteem.

This finding lends further supports to earlier literature suggesting the superiority of the masculinity model in predicting psychological health (Antill & Cunningham, 1979; Bassoff & Glass, 1982; Castlebury & Durham, 1997; Feather, 1985; Lau, 1989; Payne, 1987; Whitley, 1983, 1985). Specifically, the findings of the present study are consistent with previous research demonstrating that individuals with more masculine traits have better psychological adjustment than their feminine and undifferentiated counterparts. Compared to stereotyped feminine individuals, stereotyped

[2] G_M and G_F are used instead of the usual GM and GF to avoid confusion with interaction terms.

TABLE 4
Hierarchical regression analysis for Ego Strength scale

	Step	*Independent variable*	*T*	*B*	*SE*	*ΔR*^{2}
Australian participants	*1*	(constant)	8.53***	36.48	4.28	.00
		G_F	0.14	0.01	0.09	
	2	(constant)	0.70	3.12	4.47	.51***
		G_F	0.21	0.01	0.06	
		G_M	10.11***	0.78	0.08	
	3	(constant)	−0.08	−1.18	14.77	.00
		G_F	0.34	0.10	0.30	
		G_M	2.67**	0.87	0.33	
		G_F x G_M	−0.31	0.00	0.01	
Singaporean participants	*1*	(constant)	5.09***	44.70	8.78	.02
		G_F	−1.31	−0.23	0.18	
	2	(constant)	−1.17	−8.17	6.96	.64***
		G_F	1.46	0.16	0.11	
		G_M	11.34***	0.94	0.08	
	3	(constant)	−0.79	−11.75	14.89	.00
		G_F	0.84	0.23	0.27	
		G_M	3.14**	1.02	0.33	
		G_F x G_M	−0.27	0.00	0.01	
All participants	*1*	(constant)	9.26***	40.31	4.35	.01
		G_F	−1.11	−0.10	0.09	
	2	(constant)	−0.39	−1.48	3.80	.60***
		G_F	1.13	0.06	0.06	
		G_M	15.99***	0.85	0.05	
	3	(constant)	−0.64	−6.37	9.89	.00
		G_F	0.86	0.16	0.19	
		G_M	4.38***	0.96	0.22	
		G_F x G_M	−0.54	0.00	0.00	

* $p<.05$; ** $p<.01$; *** $p<.001$.

masculine individuals who possessed high masculine qualities revealed significant relationships with both measures of psychological well-being as defined by measures of low self-esteem and ego strength. The matrix of partial correlations between the various scales of interest also appeared to bear out this relationship, as indicated by the strong associations between masculine traits and measures of ES and LSE, and nonsignificant relationships in the same comparisons for feminine traits. In other words, associations between the two gender roles and the well-being measures revealed that individuals with higher masculine traits were more likely to have higher levels of ego strength and self-esteem, whereas these factors were not found in those individuals with more feminine traits.

It was further suggested that previous research supporting the androgyny model as an indicator of psychological health was influenced by the high masculinity component found in these individuals. The hypothesis that when controlling for masculinity, androgyny would not add any further variance to measures of psychological well-being, was supported. In fact, the effect size of GM exceeded GF in terms of the contribution to variance increase (ΔR^2) by a minimum of 20 times and a maximum of 60 times across data representing Australian, Singaporean, and pooled participants.

A major strength of the current study was the use of psychiatric patients from diverse ethnic groups. The findings of masculinity effects were demonstrated in clinical populations from both Australia and Singapore. Extending the investigation of masculine–feminine attributes and gender types to two different nations has therefore served theoretical purposes. It essentially highlights the feasibility of applying the MMPI-2 in deriving gender types, much akin to the way in which the BSRI has furnished the empirical foundations for the theoretical models of androgyny. These cross cultural data have also supported theories surrounding the dominance of the masculinity effect in explaining psychological well-being. Demonstrating that the masculine effect holds across different cultures therefore lends generalizability to a model that is already entrenched in androgyny research.

A weakness of the present study is the small sample size. Hence, the results may not necessarily generalize to both countries' clinical populations.

TABLE 5
Hierarchical regression analysis for Low Self-Esteem scale

	Step	*Independent variable*	*t*	*B*	*SE.*	*ΔR²*
Australian participants	*1*	(constant)	14.20***	64.68	4.56	.02
		G_F	−1.46	−0.14	0.10	
	2	(constant)	18.48***	96.52	5.22	.40***
		G_F	−1.89	−0.14	0.07	
		G_M	−8.26***	−0.74	0.09	
	3	(constant)	4.52***	77.52	17.14	.01
		G_F	0.74	0.26	0.35	
		G_M	−0.82	−0.31	0.38	
		G_F x G_M	−1.16	−0.01	0.01	
Singaporean participants	*1*	(constant)	8.40***	62.53	7.44	.00
		G_F	0.00	0.00	0.15	
	2	(constant)	12.41***	97.35	7.85	.40***
		G_F	−2.08*	−0.26	0.12	
		G_M	−6.63***	−0.62	0.09	
	3	(constant)	6.37***	106.60	16.74	.00
		G_F	−1.41	−0.43	0.31	
		G_M	−2.29*	−0.84	0.37	
		G_F x G_M	0.63	0.00	0.01	
All participants	*1*	(constant)	15.52***	63.10	4.07	.00
		G_F	−0.79	−0.07	0.08	
	2	(constant)	22.16***	95.44	4.31	.41
		G_F	−2.96**	−0.19	0.07	
		G_M	−10.91***	−0.66	0.06	
	3	(constant)	8.80***	98.74	11.22	.00
		G_F	−1.21	−0.26	0.21	
		G_M	−2.94**	−0.73	0.25	
		G_F x G_M	0.32	0.00	0.00	

* $p<.05$;. ** $p<.01$; *** $p<.001$.

Nonetheless, it is still heartening to achieve significant relationships with small sample sizes. Larger effect sizes are usually possible with more participants (Anatasi, 1988). This necessarily means that the masculinity effect is strong to begin with. It should also be noted that the current study utilized participants from a psychiatric population. It could be argued that their separate diagnoses may impact the overall findings. As such, the results should be viewed with caution when generalizing to a broader, nonpsychiatric group. It is further suggested that future research should consider the use of a general population sample when assessing these factors.

The findings of the current study supporting the masculinity model may be explained by the higher value that society (especially Western society) places on these traits (Castlebury & Durham, 1997). That is, masculine attributes that are characterized by goal-directed behaviour, control over environment, self-confidence, leadership, and assertiveness are more esteemed than the nurturing or expressive feminine traits, which are less direct or underplayed. However, it is argued that the terms "masculinity" and "femininity" are not entirely descriptive of the diverse constellation of gender traits, and many researchers have suggested the use of "instrumentality" and "expressiveness" to respectively connote these two gender roles.

Manuscript received May 2005
Revised manuscript accepted September 2005

REFERENCES

American Psychiatric Association. (1994). *Diagnostic and statistical manual of mental disorders (DSM-IV)*. Washington, DC: Author.

Anatasi, A. (1988). *Psychological testing* (6th ed.). New York. MacMillan.

Antill, J., & Cunningham, J. D. (1979). Self-esteem as a function of masculinity in both sexes. *Journal of Consulting and Clinical Psychology*, *47*, 783–785.

Archer, R. P., Elkins, D. E., Aiduk, R., & Griffin, R. (1997). The incremental validity of MMPI–2 supplementary scales. *Assessment*, *4*, 193–205.

Baffi, C. R., Redican, K. J., Sefchick, M. K., & Impara, J. C. (1991). Gender role identity, gender role stress, and health behaviors: An exploratory study of selected college males. *Health Values, Health Behavior, Education and Promotion*, *15*, 9–18.

Baldwin, A. C., Critelli, J. W., Stevens, L. C., & Russell, S. (1986). Androgyny and sex role measurement: A personal construct approach. *Journal of Personality and Social Psychology*, *51*, 1081–1088.

Baril, G. L., Elbert, N., Mahar-Potter, S., & Reavy, G. C. (1989). Are androgynous managers really more effective? *Group and Organization Studies*, *14*, 234–249.

Bassoff, E. S., & Glass, G. V. (1982). The relationship between gender roles and mental health: A meta-analysis of twenty-six studies. *Counseling Psychologist*, *10*, 105–112.

Baucom, D. H. (1976). Independent masculinity and femininity scales on the California Psychological Inventory. *Journal of Consulting and Clinical Psychology*, *44*, 876.

Bem, S. L. (1974). The measurement of psychological androgyny. *Journal of Consulting and Clinical Psychology*, *42*, 155–162.

Bem, S. L. (1981). Gender schema theory: A cognitive account of sex typing. *Psychological Review*, *88*, 354–364.

Brems, C., & Lloyd, P. (2000). Validation of the MMPI-2 Low Self-Esteem Content scale. In J. N. Butcher (Ed.), *Basic sources on the MMPI-2* (pp. 369–374). Minneapolis, MN: University of Minnesota Press.

Butcher, J. N., Dahlstrom, W. G., Graham, J. R., Tellegen, A., & Kaemmer, B. (1989). *Manual for administration and scoring: MMPI-2*. Minneapolis, MN: University of Minnesota Press.

Butcher, J. N., Graham, J. R., Williams, C. L., & Ben-Porath, Y. S. (1990). *Development and use of the MMPI-2 content scales*. Minneapolis, MN: University of Minnesota Press.

Castlebury, F. D., & Durham, T. W. (1997). The MMPI-2 GM and GF scales as measures of psychological well-being. *Journal of Clinical Psychology*, *53*, 879–893.

Constantinople, A. (1973). Masculinity–femininity: An exception to a famous dictum? *Psychological Bulletin*, *80*, 389–407.

De Neve, K. M., & Cooper, H. (1998). The happy personality: A meta-analysis of 137 personality traits and subjective well-being. *Psychological Bulletin*, *124*, 197–229.

Englert, D. R., Weed, N. C., & Watson, G. S. (2000). Convergent, discriminant, and internal properties of the Minnesota Multiphasic Personality Inventory (2nd ed.) Low self-esteem content scale. *Measurement and Evaluation in Counseling and Development*, *33*, 42–49.

Feather, N. T. (1985). Masculinity, femininity, self-esteem, and subclinical depression. *Sex Roles*, *12*, 491–500.

Graham, J. R. (1990). *MMPI-2: Assessing personality and psychopathology*. New York: Oxford University Press.

Graham, J. R. (2000a). Supplementary scales. In J. R. Graham (Ed.), *MMPI-2: Assessing personality and psychopathology* (pp. 146–187). New York. Oxford University Press.

Graham, J. R. (2000b). Use with special groups. In J. R. Graham (Ed.), *MMPI-2: Assessing personality and psychopathology* (pp. 215–244). New York: Oxford University Press.

Graham, J. R., Barthlow, D. L., Stein, L. A. R., Ben-Porath, Y. S., & McNulty, J. L. (2002). Assessing general maladjustment with the MMPI-2. *Journal of Personality Assessment*, *78*, 334–347.

Greene, R. L. (1987). Ethnicity and MMPI performance: A review. *Journal of Consulting and Clinical Psychology*, *55*, 497–512.

Hall, G. C. N., Bansal, A., & Lopez, I. R. (1999). Ethnicity and psychopathology: A meta-analytic review of 31 years of comparative MMPI or MMPI-2 research. *Psychological Assessment*, *11*, 186–197.

Hathaway, S. R., & McKinley, J. C. (1989). *MMPI-2: Manual for administration and scoring*. Minneapolis: University of Minnesota Press.

Holland, A., & Andre, T. (1994). The relationship of self-esteem to selected personal and environmental resources of adolescents. *Adolescence*, *29*, 345–360.

Kaplan, A. G., & Bean, J. P. (1976). *Beyond sex-role stereotypes: Readings toward a psychology of androgyny*. Oxford, UK: Little & Brown.

Kirchmeyer, C. (1996). Gender roles and decision-making in demographically diverse groups: A case for reviving androgyny. *Gender roles: A Journal of Research*, *34*, 649–663.

Korabik, K. (1982). Gender role orientation and leadership style. *International Journal of Women's Studies*, *5*, 329–337.

Lau, S. (1989). Sex role orientation and domains of self-esteem. *Sex Roles*, *2*, 415–422.

Lawrance, K. A., Taylor, D., & Byers, E. S. (1996). Differences in men's and women's global, sexual, and ideal-sexual expressiveness and instrumentality. *Sex Roles*, *34*, 337–357.

Lubinski, D., Tellegen, A., & Butcher, J. N. (1983). Masculinity, femininity, and androgyny viewed and assessed as distinct concepts. *Journal of Personality and Social Psychology*, *44*, 428–439.

Miller, M. L., Moen, O., & Dempster-McClain, D. (1991). Motherhood, multiple roles, and maternal well-being: Women of the 1950s. *Gender and Society*, *5*, 565–582.

Motowidlo, S. J. (1982). Sex role orientation and behaviour in a work setting. *Journal of Personality and Social Psychology*, *42*, 935–945.

Payne, F. D. (1987). Masculinity, femininity, and the complex construct of adjustment. *Sex Roles*, *17*, 359–374.

Peterson, C. D., & Dahlstrom, W. G. (1992). The derivation of gender-role scales GM and GF for MMPI-2 and their relationship to Scale 5 (MF). *Journal of Personality Assessment*, *59*, 486–499.

Pritchard, D. A., & Rosenblatt, A. (1980). Racial bias in the MMPI: A methodological review. *Journal of Consulting and Clinical Psychology*, *48*, 263–267.

Rawlings, E. I., & Carter, D. K. (1977). *Psychotherapy for women: Treatment toward equality*. Oxford, UK: Charles C. Thomas.

Ricciardelli, L. A., & Williams, R. J. (1995). Desirable and undesirable traits in three behavioural domains. *Gender Roles: A Journal of Research*, *33*, 637 655.

Schuldberg, D. (1992). Ego strength revised: A comparison f the MMPI-2 and MMPI-1 version of the Barron Ego-Strength scale. *Journal of Clinical Psychology*, *48*, 500–505.

Shifren, K., & Bauserman, R. L. (1996). The relationship between instrumental and expressive traits, health behaviors, and perceived physical health. *Gender Roles: A Journal of Research*, *34*, 841–864.

Spence, J. T., & Helmreich, R. L. (1981). Androgyny versus gender schema: A comment on Bem's gender schema theory. *Psychological Review*, *88*, 365–368.

Stake, J. E. (1997). Integrating expressiveness and instrumentality in real-life settings: A new perspective on the benefits of androgyny. *Sex Roles*, *37*, 541–564.

Stake, J. E. (2000). When situations call for instrumentality and expressiveness: Resource appraisal, coping strategy choice, and adjustment. *Sex Roles*, *42*, 865–885.

Steenbarger, B. N., & Greenberg, R. P. (1990). Sex roles, stress, and distress: A study of person by situation contingency. *Sex Roles*, *22*, 59–68.

Taylor, M. C., & Hall, J. A. (1982). Psychological androgyny: Theories, methods and conclusions. *Psychological Bulletin*, *92*, 347–366.

Uleman, J. S., & Weston, M. (1986). Does the BSRI inventory sex roles? *Sex Roles*, *15*, 43–62.

Valasquez, R. J., Ayala, G. X., & Mendoza, S. A. (1998). *Psychodiagnostic assessment of US Latinos: MMPI, MMPI-2, and MMPI-A results*. East Lansing, MI: Julian Samora Institute.

Ward, C. A. (2000). Models and measurements of psychological androgyny: A cross-cultural extension of theory and research. *Sex Roles*, *43*, 529–552.

Whitley, B. E., Jr. (1983). Gender-role orientation and self-esteem: A critical meta-analytic review. *Journal of Personality and Social Psychology*, *44*, 765–778.

Whitley, B. E., Jr. (1985). Gender-role orientation and psychological well-being: Two meta-analyses. *Gender Roles*, *12*, 207–225.

Zeldew, P. B., Clark, D., & Daugherty, S. R. (1985). Masculinity, femininity, Type A behavior, and psychosocial adjustment in medical students. *Journal of Personality and Social Psychology*, *48*, 481–492.

INTERNATIONAL JOURNAL OF PSYCHOLOGY, 2006, 41 (5), 423–429

INTERNATIONAL PLATFORM FOR PSYCHOLOGISTS

Report from the Asian Applied Psychology International-Regional Conference, Bangkok, Thailand

M. C. Knowles

Monash University, Melbourne, Australia

The Asian Applied Psychology International-Regional Conference (AAPI-RC) was held in Bangkok from 14–16th November 2005 under the auspices of the International Association of Applied Psychology (IAAP), the International Union of Psychological Science (IUPsyS), and the International Association for Cross-Cultural Psychology (IACCP). The Conference was organized by Thammasat University and the Thai Psychological Association under the Conference Presidency of Ubolwanna Pavakanun. The Conference attracted a large number of Thai psychologists and students as well as a wide range of participants from 24 other countries, most from Thailand's near and far neighbours but others also from Europe and North America. Apart from the merits of its Scientific Program, the Conference had two important outcomes. One was to pave the way for the formation of a National Committee that will enable Thailand to become a member of the International Union of Psychological Science. The other was to facilitate the first Convention of the newly formed Asian Psychological Association in August 2006.

Le Congrès asiatique régional-international de psychologie appliquée s'est tenu à Bangkok du 14 au 16 novembre 2005 sous les auspices de l'Association internationale de psychologie appliquée (AIPA), de l'Union internationale de psychologie scientifique (UIPsyS) et de l'Association internationale de psychologie interculturelle (AIPI). Le congrès a été organisé conjointement par l'Université Thammasat et par l'Association thaïlandaise de psychologie, et il était présidé par la professeure Ubolwanna Pavakanun. Le congrès a attiré un grand nombre de psychologues thaïlandais et d'étudiants, ainsi qu'une très grande variété de délégués en provenance de 24 pays, dont la plupart étaient des pays limitrophes ou voisins de la Thaïlande mais comprenant également des pays européens et nord-américains. Mis à part les mérites évidents de son programme scientifique, ce congrès a livré deux résultats additionnels. Le premier a été de jeter les bases de la constitution d'un Comité national devant permettre à la Thaïlande de devenir membre de l'Union internationale de psychologie scientifique ; le second, de faciliter la tenue en août 2006 de la première rencontre de la toute nouvelle Association asiatique de psychologie.

La Conferencia Asiática Internacional-Regional de Psicología Aplicada ha tenido lugar en Bangkok, del 14 al 16 de Noviembre de 2005, bajo los auspicios de la Asociación Internacional de Psicología Aplicada (IAAP), la Unión Internacional de Psicología Científica (IUPsyS) y la Asociación Internacional de Psicología Transcultural. Organizó la conferencia la Universidad Thammasat y la Thai Asociación de Psicología, bajo la presidencia de Ubolwanna Pacakanum. La Conferencia reunió un gran número de psicólogos Thai y de estudiantes, así como numerosos delegados de otros 24 países, muchos del entorno próximo o más lejano de Tailandia, pero también otros procedentes de Europa y de Norteamérica. Dejando a un lado los valores propios de su programa científico, la conferencia tuvo además, dos importantes resultados. Uno ha sido el permitir la formación de un Comité Nacional, que permitirá a Tailandia integrarse como miembro en la IUPsyS. El otro ha sido hacer posible la reunión , en agosto de 2006, de la primera Convención de la Asociación de Psicología Asiática recientemente establecida.

 DOI: 10.1080/00207590600891999

The Asian Applied Psychology International-Regional Conference (AAPI-RC) held in Bangkok from 14–16th November 2005 was the sixth regional conference of psychology, all of which have been jointly sponsored ventures of the International Association of Applied Psychology (IAAP), the International Union of Psychological Science (IUPsyS), and the International Association of Cross-Cultural Psychology (IACCP). The general idea of these cooperative undertakings is to foster the development of psychology in selected regions of the world. Previous conferences along these lines have been every second year, starting with Guangzhou in 1995, followed by Mexico City (1997), Durban (1999), Mumbai (2001), Dubai (2003), and now Bangkok (Barnes & Knowles, 2004; Knowles, 1995, 1998; Sabourin & Knowles, 2005).

The current Conference was organized by Thammasat University and the Thai Psychological Association, and was coordinated under the conference Presidency of Ubolwanna Pavakanun (Department of Psychology, Thammasat University). Wide personal and institutional support was achieved through a collective conference Vice-Presidency consisting of Wiladlak Chuawanlee (Behavioural Science Research Institute, Srinakharinwirot University), Siriwat Srikreudong (Buddhist Psychology Department, Mahachulalongkornradchawitdhayalai University), Mookda Sriyong (Psychology Department, Ramkhamhang University) and Surin Rannakiert (Thai Psychological Association). In addition to these officers the Organizing Committee consisted of dual Secretaries in Sarun Gorsana (Hua Chiew Chalermprakiet University) and Paneenuch Pussadeesopon (Chaophaya Hospital), and dual Treasurers in Tipawadee Emavardhana (Thammasat University) and Sarintorn Chiewsothorn (Royal Thai Army Nursing College), and was supported by an Active Staff Team and a Translation Team.

PARTICIPANTS

The Conference attracted over 400 participants. About three quarters were from Thailand, including around 100 Thai students, and the remaining participants came from a range of near and far neighbouring countries including South Africa, Pakistan, India, Sri Lanka, Bangladesh, Cambodia, Laos, South Korea, China, Hong Kong, Taiwan, The Philippines, Malaysia, Singapore, Indonesia, Australia, and New Zealand. Other countries also represented at the Conference from further afield included the United Arab Emirates and Israel from the Middle East, Greece, Germany, The Netherlands, and Belgium from Europe, and Canada and the United States from North America.

OPENING CEREMONY

The Opening Ceremony was chaired by Ubolwanna Pavakanun who introduced in turn Michael Frese, Bruce Overmier, and Shalom Schwartz, the Presidents of IAAP, IUPsyS, and IACCP, respectively, each of whom welcomed all delegates and briefly described the roles and principal activities of their respective international organizations. The Conference was then formally opened by the founder of psychology in Thailand, Prasop Ratanakorn, who set the tone of the meeting by citing the quotations that "all we know is that we must be good, be just, and be happy" and always, as far as practicable, "aim to do the best we can." These statements, he emphasized, embody values that form the basis of a healthy society in which psychology contributes in its special way as a neuroscience, a behavioural science, and a health science, taking into account both cultural and religious values. Among other things, he said, an indicator of a healthy society is the way it treats its elderly, where the intent should be "to add life to years rather than years to life." The declaration opening the Conference was followed by artistic performances by students from Srinakharinwirot University, including a colourful and elegant display of traditional Thai dancing, an accomplished performance of classical Thai music, and a lively routine of regional dancing originating from north-eastern Thailand.

SCIENTIFIC PROGRAM

The Scientific Program was organized mainly into three but sometimes four or more groups of parallel sessions, each including Invited Addresses, Invited Symposia, Paper Presentations, and Poster Presentations. One of the leading Invited Addresses was helpful in setting the context of the Conference by painting the "big picture" of the basic science of applied psychology, starting with Kurt Lewin's famous dictum that "there is nothing as practical as a good theory." Numerous examples were cited of the contributions that psychology has made to making people's lives safer, saner, and more psychologically healthy across a range of areas such as education, health, work, and advancing age, as well as helping to combat pervasive societal problems such as violence and drug abuse. A model was presented describing how psychology is also contributing by conducting basic research grouped under themes such as mind/brain behaviour, growing up and development, social groups, and education, training, and performance. While a major challenge facing psychology is that politicians are oriented towards immediate applications and cures, the fact remains that, if policy makers are interested in changing behaviour, they need the social sciences. This is because behavioural change is seldom likely to be achieved the first time around, and if it is to occur then it is best approached through the application of a psychosocial technology.

From this basis the rest of the Scientific Program unfolded, and given that Thailand hosted the Conference and thus the majority of the presentations were by Thai psychologists, what emerged was a very positive picture of the vigour of Thai psychology as well as the similarities and differences between it and psychology in the rest of the world. This is illustrated by reviewing the Scientific Program under topic headings, including educational psychology and psychological assessment, clinical psychology and behavioural health psychology, organizational psychology, morality and spirituality, psychological rebuilding in the tsunami aftermath, cross-cultural psychology, and the profession of psychology.

Educational psychology and psychological assessment

Because psychology in Thailand developed partly out of educational psychology and vocational guidance, this has remained an active subdiscipline and has led to a considerable amount of work being done on the assessment and evaluation of personality, attitudes, values, and intelligence. Specific areas of research included such topics as the social referencing of infants, numerical ability in 3- to 4-year-old children, enhancing preschool children's life skills, and the effect of watching beneficial television programs on the development of psychosocial factors. Since language-based intelligence tests have often been criticized for their dependence on school learning and command of the dominant language in which the test is administered, one study reported on the development of a nonverbal test in The Netherlands to assess the cognitive development of children, a test that currently is widely used in European countries.

Given the collectivist nature of Asian cultures it was interesting to discover that emotional intelligence was a popular area of research, including, among other things, the Emotional Intelligence Screening Test developed by the Department of Mental Health within the Thai Ministry of Public Health. Programs to enhance the growth of emotional intelligence in Thai youths were also described, as was an especially constructed Oriental-based program in which emphasis was placed upon the development of both body and mind through physical exercise, crisis management, and meditation. Other allied lines of research in Thailand have produced the Emotional Dissonance Scale, the Adult Meta-Emotion Inventory, and the Behaviour-Temperament Inventory, while in Taiwan the Chinese Emotional Intelligence Inventory has also been constructed.

Clinical psychology and behavioural health psychology

The other cornerstone in the early development of psychology in Thailand was clinical psychology, although as time has progressed, this has led to burgeoning growth in the area of behavioural health psychology. One keynote address relating to the latter outlined the issue in Western societies as follows. While it is generally recognized that we should all follow general health guidelines (no-one should smoke tobacco, males should not consume more than four or women more than two standard alcoholic drinks per day, saturated fat should be limited to no more than 10% of total energy intake, we should consume at least 300g of vegetables and 300g of fruit per day, and we should engage in at least 30 minutes of moderate-intensity physical activity), we also know that between 10 and 50% of the population do not meet any of these guidelines and practically no one meets all of them. Thus the challenge for psychologists working in this field is to develop ways of facilitating behavioural change. In this keynote address a model integrating a number of these approaches was outlined.

In Thailand the three issues most actively researched, especially among adolescents, are smoking, sexual behaviour, and drug use. The most vulnerable groups for smoking are those from families with high incomes who have low future orientations, and who have favourable attitudes towards smoking, which are influenced by their peer groups. This research is helping to identify those factors upon which remedial programs should concentrate, such as future orientation, locus of control, and attitude towards smoking. In the area of sexual behaviour the major problems are inappropriate sexual relationships, unwanted pregnancy, and unsafe abortion, and research in this field is focusing upon the role that teachers can play in counselling their students. This is being broadened by increasing the teachers' awareness and understanding of sexual health as well as improving their counselling skills. For drug use, risk factors include the individual's personal condition, the situation with respect to their families and friends, exposure to liquor and cigarettes, and community attitudes to drug use. Programs to combat drug use involved parents, teachers and community members.

One section of the Scientific Program dealt with particular therapeutic methods that are being used to treat specific psychological conditions. These include Group Reality Therapy to improve academic achievement, Group Rational Emotive Behaviour Therapy to increase students' self-acceptance and deepen their understanding of emotions, Vision Therapy to enhance self-esteem among overt male adolescent gays, Reality Therapy to treat sexually abusive delinquent juveniles, and Satir psychotherapy to treat mass hysteria in teenage girls. All these methods reflect a change in thinking about psychotherapeutic interventions—away from the more negative, deficit, pathological approach to a more optimistic, solution-oriented, and problem-solving approach, which is being adopted not only in Thailand but also in Europe, Australia, and North America.

Organizational psychology

Building upon the early establishment in Thailand of educational psychology, vocational guidance, and clinical psychology, a more recent growth area has been organizational psychology, where leadership is an important topic of research. One study examined the importance of entrepreneurial orientation, planning strategy, and the development of human capital in the success of small business entrepreneurs, while another major study involving over 1000 middle managers found that the most important factors affecting effective leadership were power distance, future orientation, and organizational culture. Since a good number of Thai publicly listed companies are controlled by majority shareholders and their families, another study into corporate governance found that the performance of these companies was highly correlated with authoritative capability and control power, which, in turn, were moderated by cultural consensus consisting of trust, cultural values, social norms, social beliefs, and ethics.

Two invited addresses dealt with training and development in the workplace. One of these was in the area of action learning and action research, and summarized a broad line of research concerned with strengthening the relationship between knowledge and practice. One of its important findings is the emerging realization of just how useful the making of errors is in learning. The second invited address also summarized a major research project into decision making, where participants manage virtual employees in a furniture factory. Contrary to the conventional wisdom espoused in a number of textbooks on organizational behaviour, which argue for the efficacy of specifically directed feedback, in this continuing line of inquiry it has been repeatedly found that while this benefits performance and satisfaction in the short term, on a longer timescale less structured and less supportive feedback fosters the development of unsystematic exploration and initiative, which, in turn, lead to high performance and satisfaction.

Other papers reported on studies into the leader competence model and factors affecting safe working practices, both in Thailand; learning about emotions in the workplace in Malaysia; and team emotional intelligence and team effectiveness in Taiwan.

Morality and spirituality

Given the centrality of Buddhist traditions in Thai society, and as may have been judged from the remarks of Prasop Ratanakorn in the Opening Ceremony, morality and spirituality are central values to many people in Thailand, and this was reflected also in the Scientific Program. One paper described how the methods of participant observation, interview, and documentation were used over a 5-month period in a preschool for young children to study how the Buddhist concept was taught emphasizing concentration, firmness, humility, sensitivity, gratitude, and the ability to handle difficulties. What was also noted was that the teachers themselves developed techniques for calming and controlling their deepest emotions in order to cope with the stresses of teaching. Another study into the applicability of the Buddhist concept in psychological research described a healthy organization as one in which employees did not experience irritation to the six

Ayatana perceptions of sight, sound, smell, taste, touch, and thought, and it developed a six-item physical environment scale to measure employee perceptions of lighting, noises, dust or fumes, temperature, and physical and mental stress in the workplace.

In the public sector arena, one case study described how a subcommittee was established to improve the values of civil servants and the culture of the Civil Service. The set of new creative values to be promoted among officials included moral courage, integrity, transparency and accountability, nondiscrimination, and results orientation. Out of a sample of over 2000 officials, 15 were identified as possessing the highest ratings; these officers were further interviewed about their work and their lives.

The role of religion was also examined in Indonesia in a study of spirituality as a critical success factor among Muslim women entrepreneurs.

Psychological rebuilding in the tsunami aftermath

Following the devastation caused by the tsunami in South East Asia in 2004, a workshop was organized by IUPsyS in May 2005, attended by sponsored participants from Sri Lanka, Indonesia, India, and Thailand. Financial support for the workshop came from IUPsyS, the American Psychological Association, the Australian Psychological Society, the International Society for the Study of Behavioral Development (ISSBD), and the Chinese Association for Science and Technology (CAST). At the workshop, participants from the affected areas described the physical and psychological impact of the tsunami in their respective countries, and engaged in interactive training and discussion on how best to proceed with psychological rebuilding in the traumatized communities.

The follow-up symposium in Thailand, 6 months after the initial workshop, was funded by IAAP and jointly organized by IAAP and IUPsyS. It focused on conditions since the tsunami and what had been achieved by the psychological rebuilding programs undertaken in various countries. The aftermath of the tsunami brought massive immediate problems including loss of life, loss of homes, and loss of occupations, as well as a host of subsequent problems including child abuse, substance abuse, trafficking, and privacy issues for women, all accompanied by persistent heat and rain. The symposium described the serious psychological problems remaining, including grief and loss, frustration and anger, a sense of helplessness and dependency, fear of the sea and another tsunami, and post-traumatic stress disorder (PTSD). Participants noted that these problems were compounded by the development of anger and distrust due to the fact that very little of the considerable funds collected worldwide in the name of humanitarian aid has actually been received by those at the front line of the tsunami disaster zone.

What was clear from the presentations was that there were many different ways of providing psychological support and therapy. There were two common themes. One was the remarkable degree of resilience shown by many; the other involved the cultural and community methods of coping that were used in the different areas affected by the tsunami. It was also clear that so-called help provided by merely enthusiastic people who were untrained in psychology and who lacked cultural sensitivity was counterproductive and could actually cause more harm than good, by increasing PTSD as well as delaying the process of psychological recovery. Another important lesson was recognition of the need for psychologists to work in cooperation with other nongovernment organizations (NGOs) and local and national government organizations (GOs). One example presented was the Mobile Mental Health Team, consisting of 2–3 psychologists, 1 social worker, 1 psychiatrist, 2 nurses, 1 pharmacist, and 1 driver. Such a team would provide physical first aid, psychological and psychiatric assessment, counselling, mental health care for children, and psychoeducation.

Cross-cultural psychology

Although the presentations in the Scientific Program covered a wide range of topics, there were cross-cutting themes that served as models of describing culture. Two invited addresses provided examples. One dealt with basic values that characterize people as individuals. Ten such values have been identified— benevolence or kindness, tradition, conformity, security, power, achievement, hedonism, stimulation, self-direction or autonomy, and universalism or concern for all others. As may be seen from the above discussion of the Scientific Program, a number of these values such as kindness, tradition, and conformity surfaced time and time again. A second theme was examining culture from a national perspective, in which cultures across the world can be mapped with respect to three dimensions—autonomy vs embeddedness, egalitarianism vs hierarchy, and harmony vs mastery. One of the notable findings of this map is the clustering of countries from the Asian region. For example, the cultures of Indonesia, Malaysia, and Singapore are very high on embeddedness and also relatively high on hierarchy, and located close to them are the cultures of Thailand, India, and China, which are very high on hierarchy and relatively high on embeddedness. As such this map provided a useful and fruitful way of understanding the basis of a lot of the research interests of the presenters in the Scientific Program.

Other topics in this section of the program included acculturation and cultural adaptation, childlessness among highly educated women in Germany and the Philippines, a cross-cultural study of self-presentation in Korea and the USA, an international study demonstrating little or no difference in various types of intelligence among children from different cultures, the assessment of credibility in a multiethnic environment, and an examination of how to sample individuals and societies in ways that permit reliable comparative research.

The profession of psychology

An invited address that presented a global view of events dealt with the development of professional psychology around the world. As was pointed out, the great philosophers of Europe and Asia were concerned with human behaviour and ways of changing it, mostly through instruction, reward, and punishment, and this laid the foundation for the development of psychology's scientific basis. It was the second half of the 20th century, however, that witnessed the expansion and rapid growth of psychology, especially as a profession, so that today it is firmly established in Europe, North America, Australia, and Latin America. In fact, Brazil has the largest psychological society or association of any country, with a membership of some 140,000. Looking to the future, psychology is growing and, indeed, booming in South East Asia, which some day should become the largest region of psychology in the world.

In the meantime, a number of challenges face psychology in the developing and majority world. At one end of the spectrum is Bangladesh, where there is an overwhelming problem of scarcity and inadequacy in the training of psychologists and lack of awareness of the relevance of psychology in both the general public and the national leadership. Thailand represents the situation some way down the road, where academic training and the professional practice of psychology are firmly established, and licensure of psychologists in clinical practice was recently mandated by the government. What lies ahead is the development and maintenance of curriculum standards and, as reported in another paper, the balance in the curriculum that is achieved between laying the scientific basis of psychology and catering to the vocational interests of students. Other issues include setting licensure standards, the establishment and dissemination of ethical guidelines, and provision for continuing professional education.

While the overall picture for international psychology and regional psychology is positive, there are some cases such as South Africa, where the status of psychology has retreated because of a lack of sustained contact with the country's principal decision makers, especially in governmental circles. This is a good reminder that psychology does not have the same financial resources as some other professions, which means that psychology has to "punch above its weight," as it were, to maintain and develop its role.

FAREWELL OCCASION

A Farewell Dinner involving the Conference Organizing Committee and representatives from the three international bodies (IAAP, IUPsyS, and IACCP) was held to celebrate the conclusion of the Conference and congratulate the Organizing Committee on its widely acclaimed success. The restaurant was pleasantly situated on the banks of the Chao Phraya River, the main river upon which Bangkok is located. As dinner progressed convivially and those gathered tasted a delicious range of traditional Thai dishes, brightly coloured ferries plied up and down the river in between the busy barges that were still working into the night. The dinner coincided with the Festival of Light (Loy Krathong), a local tradition in which thanks are given to the river for the bounteous gifts it bestows upon those who depend upon it for their livelihood. On leaving the restaurant by ferry each person entered into this custom by placing on the water a basket of flowers with a lighted candle, which floated away on the swiftly flowing river.

IMPACT OF THE CONFERENCE

An important meeting held towards the end of the Conference focused on what action could be taken to foster the future development of psychology in Thailand. This meeting brought together representatives from the Thai Association of

Psychology and the three international bodies of IUPsyS, IAAP, and IACCP. At the present moment the International Union of Psychological Science (IUPsyS) membership of approximately 70 national societies or associations of psychology does not include representation from Thailand. Among other things this is because there are multiple psychological associations, including the Thai Association of Psychology and the Thai Clinical Psychology Association, and a large number of psychologically trained professionals also belong to the Association of Vocational Guidance. Discussion focused on the need for the three Thai associations to form a single committee that would speak with one voice for Thai psychologists and represent them at the Union's General Assembly. In this way Thailand could become a member of the Union and join its network of international psychological associations, and could have access to the Union's experience and the wide range of services that it offers.

Another outcome of the Conference arose from networking by members of the newly formed Asian Association of Psychology in planning its first Convention in Bali, Indonesia, from August 18–20, 2006. The Convention President is Salito Sarwono and the event will be supported by the Indonesian Association of Psychologists, the Faculty of Psychology of the University of Indonesia, and the Faculty of Psychology of the University of Tarumanugara. Information about the Convention can be obtained from its website at www.apsya.org

In addition to these organizational outcomes, the Conference had a strong effect on its participants, especially those who were international visitors to Thailand. What struck everyone was the kindness and hospitality shown by every Thai person, from the members of the Organizing Committee to the willing band of Thai students whose interest and enthusiasm was invaluable in enabling the Conference to run smoothly. Thoughtfulness and attention to detail was shown in many ways on many occasions, right down to the gift presented to every Invited Speaker—a ceramic vase artistically hand-painted in traditional Thai patterns and colours. For those fortunate enough to attend the Conference, it was a richly rewarding experience.

REFERENCES

Barnes, B., & Knowles, M. C. (2004). The Southeast Asian Regional Congress on Scientific and Applied Psychology. *International Journal of Psychology*, *38*, 119–124.

Knowles, M. C. (1995). Asia-Pacific Conference of Psychology, Guangzho. *Newsletter of the International Association of Applied Psychology*, *7*, 3–4.

Knowles, M. C. (1998). Regional Congress of Psychology for Professionals in the Americas. *International Journal of Psychology*, *33*, 363–366.

Sabourin, M., & Knowles, M. C. (2005). Middle East and North Africa Regional Conference of Psychology, Dubai, United Arab Emirates. *International Journal of Psychology*, *39*, 145–152.

Congresses and scientific meetings

October 11 - 13, 2006
4th World Conference on the Promotion of Mental Health and Prevention of Mental and Behavioral Disorders: "Developing Resilience and Strength Across the Life Span"
Oslo, NORWAY
URL: www.worldconference2006.no

October 16 - 20, 2006
Human Factors & Ergonomics Society (HFES) Annual Meeting
San Francisco, California, USA
URL: www.hfes.org/web/HFESMeetings/meetings.html

October 18 - 22, 2006
29th National Conference of the Australian Association for Cognitive and Behavioural Therapy
Sydney, AUSTRALIA
URL: www.aacbt.org.au/Conference/index.htm

October 19 - 21, 2006
14th International Conference on Eating Disorders
Alpbach, Tyrol, AUSTRIA
URL: www.netzwerk-essstoerungen.at

October 25 - 29, 2006
Society for Physiology Research, 46th Annual Meeting
Vancouver, BC, CANADA
URL: www.sprweb.org/meeting/index.html

October 27 - 28, 2006
2nd International Conference "Cortical Dementias - Cognitive Deficits in Alzheimer's Disease"
Freiburg, GERMANY
URL: www.neurolabor.de

November 4 - 7, 2006
International Society for Traumatic Stress Studies 22nd Annual Meeting
Hollywood, California, USA
URL: www.istss.org/meetings/index.htm

November 20 - 21, 2006
Third International Conference on Enactive Interfaces
Montpellier, FRANCE
URL: www.enactive2006.org

November 16 - 19, 2006
Psychonomic Society Annual Meeting
Houston, Texas, USA
URL: www.psychonomic.org/meet.htm

November 16 - 19, 2006
Association for the Advancement of Behavior Therapy (AABT) Annual Convention
Chicago, Illinois, USA
URL: www.aabt.org/Future%20Conventions.html

November 18 - 20, 2006
Annual Meeting Society for Judgment and Decision Making
nbsp;Houston, Texas, USA
URL: http://sql.sjdm.org

2007

February 7 - 10, 2007
International Neuropsychological Society (INS) Annual Conference
Portland, Oregon, USA
URL: www.the-ins.org/meetings

March 15 - 18, 2007
First Symposium of Pedagogy and Psychology PhD Students
Wroclaw, POLAND
URL: http://www.conference.dawid.uni.wroc.pl

March 24 - 31, 2007
3rd European Spring Conference on Social Psychology
St.Moritz, SWITZERLAND
URL: http://132.187.160.5/download/StMoritz07.pdf

March 29 - April 1, 2007
Society for Research in Child Development Biennial Meeting
Boston, Massachusetts, USA
URL: www.srcd.org/biennial.html

April 17 - 21, 2007
2nd International Congress or the World Federation of Societies of Biological Psychiatry
Santiago, CHILE
URL: www.wfsbp.org

April 18 - 21, 2007
Society for Behavioral Medicine Annual Meeting
Miami Beach, Florida, USA
ULR: www.sbm.org

May 9 - 12, 2007
European Congress of Work and Organizational Psychology
Stockholm, SWEDEN
URL: www.eawop2007.org

May 9 - 13, 2007
5th Biennial Conference of the International Academy for Intercultural Research
URL: http://www.interculturalacademy.org

Summer 2007
International Association for Research in Economic Psychology (IAREP) Annual Conference
Ljubljana, SLOVENIA
URL: http://www.iarep.org/conferences.htm

* Please send details of forthcoming events as far in advance as is possible to Dr Merry Bullock, Deputy Secretary-General, International Union of Psychological Science and Associate Editor of the *International Journal of Psychology*, Science Directorate, APA, 750 First Street NE, Washington DC 20002, USA; E-mail: mbullock@apa.org; URL: http://www.iupsys.org

DOI: 10.1080/00207590600960620

July 1 - 5, 2007
31st Interamerican Congress of Psychology: Integrating the Americas
Mexico City, MEXICO
URL: www.sipmexico2007.org.mx

July 3 - 8, 2007
Xth European Congress of Psychology
Prague, CZECH REPUBLIC
URL: www.ecp2007.com/intro.htm

July 3 - 8, 2007
3rd International Congress of Psychology and Law
Adelaide, South Australia, AUSTRALIA
URL: http://www.sapmea.asn.au

August 16 - 19, 2007
112th Annual Convention of the American Psychological Association (APA)
Location: San Francisco, California, USA
URL: www.apa.org/convention

August 23 - 26, 2007
2007 World Conference of Stress
Budapest, HUNGARY
URL: www.stress07.com

October 17 - 21, 2007
Society for Physiology Research, 47th Annual Meeting
Savannah, Georgia, USA URL: http://www.sprweb.org

November 15 -18, 2007
48th Psychonomic Society Annual Meeting
Long Beach, California, USA
URL: http://www.psychonomic.org/meet.htm

2008 AND BEYOND

February 6 - 9, 2008
International Neuropsychological Society (INS) Annual Conference
Waikoloa, Hawaii, USA
URL: http://www.the-ins.org/meetings

July, 14 - 16, 2008
6th International Conference, International Test Commission: The Public Face of Testing
Liverpool, UK
URL: www.intestcom.org

July 20 - 25, 2008
XXIX International Congress of Psychology
Berlin, GERMANY
URL: http://www.icp2008.de

August 14 - 17, 2008
116th Annual Convention of the American Psychological Association
Boston, Massachusetts, USA
URL: www.apa.org/convention

November 20 - 24, 2008
49th Psychonomic Society Annual Meeting
Chicago, Illinois, USA
URL: http://www.psychonomic.org/meet.htm

February 11 - 14, 2009
International Neuropsychological Society (INS) Annual Conference
Atlanta, Georgia, USA
URL: http://www.the-ins.org/meetings

April 1 - 5, 2009
Society for Research in Child Development Biennial Meeting
Denver, Colorado, USA
URL: http://www.srcd.org/biennial.html

Summer, 2009

August 13 - 16, 2009
117th Annual Convention of the American Psychological Association
Toronto, Ontario, CANADA
URL: www.apa.org/convention

Summer, 2010
International Congress of Applied Psychology
Melbourne, AUSTRALIA

Summer, 2012
International Congress of Psychology
Cape Town, SOUTH AFRICA

Manuscripts are invited for submission. All submissions should be made online, in a standard document format type such as Word or Rich Text Format, at the *International Journal of Psychology*'s **Manuscript Central site (http://mc.manuscriptcentral.com/pijp)**. New users should first create an account. Once a user is logged onto the site submissions should be made via the Author Centre. If any assistance is needed with this, please feel free to e-mail on ijp@uni-halle.de

If for any reasons, surface mail submission is preferred please send one copy of the manuscript AND a disk version to: **Prof. Dr. Claudia Dalbert**, Martin Luther University, Institute of Education, D-06099 Halle, Germany.

All manuscripts should be submitted in American Psychological Association (APA) format following the latest edition of Publication Manual of the APA (currently 5th edition). All manuscripts must include a 300-word abstract in English. Submission of empirical papers must be accompanied by the author's confirmation to have access to the original data on which the manuscript reports.

Manuscripts should be presented double spaced. Please leave wide margins. Instructions on preparing tables, figures, references, metrics, and abstracts all appear in the *APA Publication Manual* (5th edition). Any manuscript which does not conform to these guidelines may be returned for necessary revision before reviewing. The Editor retains the right to reject manuscripts that do not meet established scientific or ethical standards.

In case of rejection, manuscripts cannot be returned.

Reviews are conducted in a single-blind fashion, thus the reviewers remain anonymous. Every effort is made to have the initial review process completed less than three months after submission, but there are occasional delays due to circumstances beyond our control. Most accepted manuscripts require some revision; suggestions to facilitate the preparation of the revision will be communicated to the author(s) in the editorial decision letter. Accepted papers written in incorrect English may be returned to the author for language correction, in that case, the authors are advised to contact a native speaker.

When first submitting a manuscript, send only copies of the figures, not original figures. With the final revision of an accepted manuscript, send glossy prints of figures, writing lightly on the back of each figure the name of the author and the number of the figure.

Manuscripts should not be submitted for concurrent consideration in other journals. Duplicate publication—that is, the publication of a manuscript that has already been published wholly (in the same or another language) or in substantial part in another journal—is also prohibited. It is the responsibility of the author to ensure that the paper contains nothing that is libellous or infringes copyright.

Any change of address after submission must be sent promptly to the Editor's or an Associate Editor's office. If available, e-mail and fax numbers should be included in the covering letter.

Page proofs in the form of a pdf file will be sent to the corresponding author (unless otherwise indicated). Corrections, other than typesetter's errors, may be charged to the author(s). Offprints are available, at a cost, and must be ordered when returning the proofs.

International Platform Section

Manuscripts for publication in the *International Platform* should be sent to either of the Associate Editors: **Pierre L.-J. Ritchie**, School of Psychology, University of Ottawa, 145 Jean-Jacques Lussier St., PO Box 450, Stn A, Ottawa, K1N 6N5, Canada, or **Merry Bullock**, Science Directorate, APA 750 First Street NE, Washington DC 20002, USA

Back Issues: Taylor & Francis retains a three-year back issue stock of journals. Older volumes are held by our official stockists: Periodicals Service Company, 11 Main Street, Germantown, NY 12526, USA to whom all orders and enquiries should be addressed. Tel: +1 518 537 4700; Fax: +1 518 537 5899; Email: psc@periodicals.com; URL: http://www.periodicals.com/tandf.html

For Product Safety Concerns and Information please contact our EU representative GPSR@taylorandfrancis.com Taylor & Francis Verlag GmbH, Kaufingerstraße 24, 80331 München, Germany

Batch number: 10732718

Printed by Printforce, the Netherlands